The Devil's Workshop

*A Memoir of the Nazi
Counterfeiting Operation*

Adolf Burger

FRONTLINE BOOKS, LONDON

Adolf Burger, prisoner number 64401, arrested on 11 August 1942 in Bratislava.
Forced to work in the forgery squad in KZ Sachsenhausen forging banknotes, stamps
and documents. Sketch by Salamon Smolianoff – KZ Sachsenhausen, 1944

The Reason I Am Still Alive

My fourteen friends from the Czech Republic, who worked with me in the forgery workshop are no longer alive.

My Austrian comrades are dead too.

Only one of my fifteen German friends is still alive in Berlin.

Abraham Jacobson from the Netherlands, who was my foreman then, is no longer alive.

I, the Slovakian, Adolf Burger, am the only one alive today.

For two years I stared death in the face day in and day out in Auschwitz and Birkenau. I survived the typhus experiments of I.G. Farben, for eighteen months. I was stationed in the special *Kommando* on the ramp at Auschwitz and had to watch thousands of women, children and men over forty being driven in lorries to the gas chambers every day.

I survived the selection by the SS doctors such as Mengele, Klaubert, Fürst, Fischer – I do not know all their names. When they pointed their finger at a prisoner that meant the death sentence.

When we had to step forward for selection, I only weighed 35 kilos, and then I prayed to God that the SS doctor would not point to me, and I survived.

I survived the worst news I ever heard: my wife Gisela, only twenty-two years of age, and other friends were sent to be gassed at a selection by SS doctors a week before Christmas 1942.

So I have often wondered why I survived all these terrible years.

Today at the age of eighty-nine, I know why I survived. As one of the surviving witnesses, it is to tell younger generations about the countless crimes perpetrated, so that nothing like this will ever happen again. I warn people about the ideology of murder and cruelty that today is being repeated in one form or another in some parts of the world.

That is my responsibility, that is why I am still alive.

Adolf Burger
September 2006

FRONTLINE BOOKS, LONDON

The Devil's Workshop: A Memoir of the Nazi Counterfeiting Operation

This edition published in 2009 by Frontline Books,
an imprint of Pen & Sword Books Ltd, 47 Church Street, Barnsley, S. Yorkshire, S70 2AS
www.frontline-books.com

ISBN: 978-1-84832-523-4

Original title: *Des Teufels Werkstatt* published by arrangement with
Elisabeth Sandmann Verlag GmbH, Munich, Germany
www.esverlag.de

Publisher's Note

In accordance with the wishes of the author, *The Devil's Workshop* has been published in
the same format as the previous German and Czech language editions of the book. The
author, who worked as a typographer before the war, was also responsible for the design of
the previous editions of the book and this edition remains as true to that original design as
possible.

The jacket has been designed by Helmut Henkensiefken
and has been approved by Adolf Burger.

CIP data records for this title are available from the British Library and the Library of Congress

For more information on our books, please visit
www.frontline-books.com, email info@frontline-books.com
or write to us at the above address.

Typeset by JCS Publishing Services Ltd, www.jcs-publishing.co.uk
Printed in the UK by the MPG Books Group

Contents

III. KZ MAUTHAUSEN – KZ 'SCHLIER' – REDL-ZIPF – KZ EBENSEE – TOPLITZSEE

IV. APPENDICES

Hardly reachable, you!
Buried in the concentration camps
cut off from every human word
subject to the abuses
Clubbed to the ground, but
Not refuted!

Vanished, but
not forgotten!

Bertold Brecht

Dedicated to my wife Gisela Burger, born 30 May 1920.
In December 1942 she was sent to the gas chambers during a selection
at the flick of the fingers of an SS doctor

**This book was written
so that what happened
will never be forgotten.**

Part I

Slovakia –
Auschwitz –
Birkenau

Childhood and Youth in Slovakia

MY CHILDHOOD WAS SPENT IN Velká Lomnica, in the district of Kežmarok, in Slovakia. I was born here in 1917 into a Jewish family. I had a brother and two sisters. My father was a master brewer and worked in a distillery. We also owned a small farm.

This was during the First World War. I am sure my father was glad that his son was not aware of the horror. The war only reached our little mountain village in the foothills of the High Tatra in the form of death notices or reports of family members wounded or missing. When my father died in 1921, my mother could not run the farm on her own, so we moved into the little town of Poprad. After leaving school I was trained as a printer. When my apprenticeship finished I was called up for military service in the Czechoslovakian army in the officers' training corps of the 3rd Mountain Infantry regiment.

The dominant, politically conservative, force in Slovakia was the Catholic Slovakian People's Party (Volkspartei), founded in 1905 in what was then Hungary by Andrej Hlinka, a priest. After his death on 16 August 1938, Monsignor Josef Tiso was elected as his successor.

The Munich Diktat of 29 September 1938 brought about a fateful turn of events. The followers of the Slovakian People's Party availed themselves of the political climate of the time and the weakness of the state. They increasingly demanded autonomy, in order to introduce measures to curb left-wing organisations. On 6 October Josef Tiso formed an autonomous Slovakian government, then the Communist Party was declared illegal and its members persecuted.

The Hlinka-Garde (HG) militia was founded on the model of the armed party groupings in Nazi Germany. This black-uniformed SS-style militia had the task of spreading the clerical–fascist ideology of the regime and of eliminating its political opponents.

On 13 March 1939 there was a decisive development in this stormy and confused period in Slovakia. Tiso announced at the HG annual conference that he had been invited by Hitler to bring about the withdrawal of Slovakia from the Bohemian territories, under the threat of occupation by Hungary.

Tiso rose to Hitler's challenge. On 14 March the Slovakian parliament decided to form the State of Slovakia. Immediately afterwards, on the night of 14/15 March, Hitler summoned Emil Hacha, president of the Czechoslovak Republic, to Berlin, to the Chancellery (Reichskanzlei), where he was informed by the Führer that German troops would occupy the remaining Bohemian territories,

13 March 1939: Monsignor Josef Tiso, president of the Slovakian State,
pictured with Hitler

which were incorporated into the Reich as the 'Protectorate of Bohemia and
Moravia'.

After Slovakia had been transformed into a German protectorate Monsignor
Josef Tiso became president and head of state (Führer). Vojtech Tuka became
prime minister. Between them they turned Slovakia into a National Socialist
state. Tuka promised that 'Slovakian National Socialism will be based on the
principles of German National Socialism.' They both kept their word. The
position of Slovakian Jews became more and more critical every day.

On 9 September 1941 the Nuremberg Laws were introduced into Slovakia in
the form of the Jewish Code, Slovakian State Law, Art. No. 198 of 9 September
1941. The Slovakian anti-Jewish laws surpassed even the German laws in their
small print. For example, Jews were forbidden not only to own a car, but also to
drive one. Just before this, at the beginning of September, the German imperial
minister for home affairs, Frick, and secretaries of state Stuckart and Globke,
who drew up the Nuremberg Racial Laws, had been in Bratislava for the second
time (Globke's first visit as German government representative had taken place
in January 1941).

On 18 September 1941 the rule came into effect that every Jew over the age
of six had to wear the yellow Star of David in public. Thus began the tragedy
of the Slovakian Jews – in a state that prided itself on being Christian and

Monsignor Josef Tiso, president,
murderer of Slovakian Jews

Black Hinka-Garde militia on parade. An organisation modelled on the SS, which
provided reliable support for German Nazi criminals

Slovakian parliament in session: the government are in the front row, in the background is President Josef Tiso

According to the decree of 18 September 1941, Jews over six years of age were obliged to wear the yellow Star of David in public

SS-OSF Adolf Eichmann, who organised the deportation of Jews

whose president was a priest. It was a state that proclaimed to the world that it was founded on the principle of love your neighbour, respect for the Ten Commandments and the equality of all men before their creator.

On 23 March 1942 the first deportation left Poprad. It consisted of 1,000 Jewish girls, aged sixteen to twenty-five: final destination, Auschwitz. One transport after another followed; entire families were deported to Auschwitz and Treblinka, Lublin or Majdanek.

In total 109,153 Slovakian Jews were victims of this extermination policy. Only a tiny number of them survived. The Christian Slovakian government paid the SS 54.5 million Reichsmarks (RM) for them.

This hyper-Catholic, 'strictly Catholic', state drew up an agreement in 1942 with SS-Obersturmbannführer (OSF) Eichmann to pay the imperial government 500 RM and three weeks' provisions for the 'Final Solution' for every Jew who was deported. The imperial government guaranteed in a 'Verbal Note' (from the German Embassy in Pressburg, 29 April 1944) that the deported Jews would never be brought back to Slovakia. The Reich left the property of these Slovakian Jews to Slovakia.

The deportations from Slovakia were run exactly like the other deportations organised by Eichmann from all over Germany, the countries it occupied and its allies.

First there was fierce anti-Jewish propaganda, then came the laws: Aryanisation of Jewish shops and businesses, employment bans, confiscation of property and finally the deportations. All in the name of the Christian State of Slovakia.

According to the Jewish code, I was demoted, expelled from the army and sent to a work camp in Lavoča for six months. After that I worked in a printing works in Bratislava.

I was friendly with Edith Beck. She was twenty-two years old and lived in Bratislava, at 7 Mariánska Street. She was of medium height, had dark hair and beautiful brown eyes. We had known each other well for five years. When we first met, in 1934, she was attending commercial college. In the holidays we were both leaders in a left-wing Jewish socialist organisation, called Haschomer Hazair, which organised three-week trips for nine-year-olds to the mountains near Krompachy. It was a wonderful time. I will never forget the evenings round the campfire. How could we ever have imagined the war and the persecution of the Jews?

Once, when I was visiting Edith at home in 1939, she told me about her illegal work for the Communist Party and asked me if I wanted to get involved as well. Her reasons and the nature of the work convinced me and I said yes. This decision would change my whole life.

I joined a party cell consisting of four members. We were all very young. For security reasons only small cells were formed.

German Embassy
Pol 4 Nr 2/Nr
2565

Re: Cost of accommodation of Jews moved
        from Slovakia into Reich territory

1 copy

V e r b a l   N o t e .

Addressed to the Slovakian Foreign Ministry:
Jews who have been deported and future deportees
will be trained and sent to work in occupied eastern
territories.

The estimated cost of 500 RM per person for accommodation, clothing and training, including family
members, cannot be covered immediately by the ear-
nings of the Jews, as training will take a few weeks
and not all are fit for work.

The Slovakian government is hereby requested to
pay this amount for each Jew to the government of the
Reich.

The Ministry is requested to comply with this di-
rective immediately.

Pressburg 29th April 1944.

Document from German Embassy, Pressburg, 29 April 1944, Pol 4 Nr 2/Nr.2565

27 April 1942: Alexander Mach,
minister for home affairs and chief
commander of the HG militia,
announces in an address to its
officers: 'Our highest orders:
the deportation of all Jews from
Slovakia'

HG militia members ill-treating a Slovakian Jew

The tragedy of Slovakian Jews, drawing by Leo Haas

Jews are Marked

Minister of the Interior publicised the proclamation concerning the identification of Jews on 18 September, which stated:

Jews are obliged to wear a visible Jewish emblem on the left breast, the Star of David, made of yellow material, such as linen or similar material, measuring six centimetres across and with a half-centimetre lighter border.

After 20 October 1941 Jews may only wear this uniform badge, which they can obtain from the Jewish Centre.

Jews who need not wear the badge include: Jews under the age of six, Jewish men and women in mixed marriages and their children, provided they are not of the Jewish faith, those who are still employed in general state services, concerns, foundations and facilities, likewise Jewish men and children who hold an employment permit from the Central Ministry of Economic Affairs, Jews who belong to a recognised Christian denomination provided they were baptised before 10 September 1941.

Jews who are not obliged to wear the Jewish badge will receive an exemption certificate from their District Police Station.

This proclamation comes into effect on 22 September.

Highest Orders of the HG Militia: All Jews Out!

Proceedings of meeting of HG district inspectors, commanders and HG raiding parties

Štôla 27 April (1942)

The meeting of representatives from all parts of Slovakia began on Saturday afternoon. After the HG flag was raised discussion of the Jewish question began. The discussion was chaired by HG staff officer Kuballa, who explained all the recommendations and answered all questions arising. All problems surrounding the evacuation from Slovakia were thoroughly analysed. It was decided that the programme would be carried out exactly, but particular care would be taken that the welfare, economy and interests of Slovakia would not be affected. Measures have been prepared to place our people on all abandoned farms. They would guarantee to run the farms, so that maximum yield would be maintained. These measures would be mainly preventive.

Many interesting and important recommendations were made during the debate. The HG district commanders gave examples of how best to go about the management of the evacuation of the Jews, based on their recent experience. Jews are only hidden occasionally as the Slovakian public is behind the fastest possible evacuation of the Jews. Since we began to deport entire Jewish families, there has not been as much resistance on the part of the Jews as before. The discussion continued until midnight.

On Sunday morning there was early morning sport and the deacon, Fr Haitar, led prayers. At nine o'clock the highest-ranking officer of the HG militia, Mach, came to Štôla, accompanied by Mila Urban, the editor-in-chief of the 'Gardist'.

Dr Mečiar, HG officer in charge of cultural propaganda, SA OSF Gmelin, HG senior press officer, Kovar and adjutant Höfer. After the parade and inspection of the HG district commanders these high-ranking HG officials carried out military training exercises with the raiding parties. Later Rabina, commander of the HG raiding parties held a talk about the military badge and Košovský, a member of a raiding party, held a talk on national-socialist political education.

After a meal, to which the deacon, Fr. Haitar welcomed everyone, the activities continued. HG Führer, Mach, gave a long speech in which he covered all current events in our land and answered all the questions, which had been tabled. He emphasised how the HG militia had achieved the establishment of the Slovakian state on 14 March 1939, and how it was aware of its responsibility to the nation and its history and would do all in its power to secure the state for future generations.

Mach stated that in a few generations there would be no more disagreements, such as were still continuing, but they would remember 25 March 1942, the day of the expulsion of all Jews from Slovakia. The highest order is: get all Jews out.

After the speech, which was greeted with loud applause by all present, Führer Mach left Štôla. The HG commander Málek gave a talk about the 'Gardist' – the HG militia newspaper. Otomar Koballa made the closing speech and proceedings ended with the HG anthem and the flag was lowered.

They Organised the Murder of 71,000 Slovakian Jews

Ludin,
German consul

Sidor,
commander of the HG militia

Dieter Wisliczeny,
specialist liquidator of Jews,
war criminal

Dr Anton Vašek,
director of Interior
Ministry

Imrich Vašina,
commander in Sered camp

Komissar Švitler

HG militiaman Gindl

HG militiaman Vachálek

HG militiaman Brežni

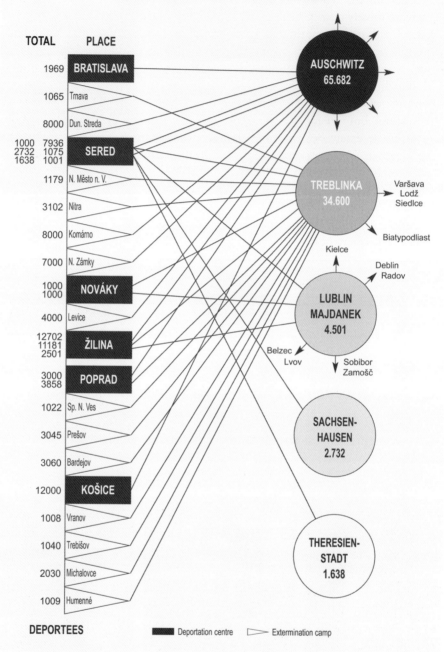

DEPORTATION OF JEWS FROM SLOVAKIA

TOTAL	PLACE
1969	**BRATISLAVA**
1065	Trnava
8000	Dun. Streda
1000 2732 1638	7936 1075 1001 **SERED**
1179	N. Město n. V.
3102	Nitra
8000	Komárno
7000	N. Zámky
1000 1000	**NOVÁKY**
4000	Levice
12702 11181 2501	**ŽILINA**
3000 3858	**POPRAD**
1022	Sp. N. Ves
3045	Prešov
3060	Bardejov
12000	**KOŠICE**
1008	Vranov
1040	Trebišov
2030	Michalovce
1009	Humenné

AUSCHWITZ 65.682

TREBLINKA 34.600 → Varšava / Lodž / Siedlce

→ Biatypodliast

Kielce

Deblin Radov

LUBLIN MAJDANEK 4.501

Belzec / Lvov

Sobibor Zamošč

SACHSEN-HAUSEN 2.732

THERESIEN-STADT 1.638

DEPORTEES

■ Deportation centre   ▷ Extermination camp

109,153 Slovakian Jews perished in the concentration camps, very few survived

First I was entrusted with apparently simple yet dangerous tasks. I was to have forged documents signed by a public notary, who of course suspected nothing. They were mostly citizenship papers. Then I had to take them to Nitra.

Later I had other assignments. Edith would give me printing plates. I did not know where they came from. At the printers I would produce various documents, among them baptismal certificates. For three years I did underground work like this.

On my trips to Nitra I met Gisela, who later became my wife. We shared the same outlook but our feelings brought us even closer. So we decided to marry; in spite of the dangerous times, we felt we could better face the hard times to come together. We were so young, so full of life and hope for a better future. At the weekends we used to go hiking in the high Tatra Mountains. In those days we thought of nothing but ourselves and lived for each other.

We were firmly convinced that our illegal activity was in a good cause. So many of the documents I forged or had authenticated by a notary saved the lives of people who were being persecuted by the official machinery of the Slovakian state.

Arrest

At the end of June 1942 I came to the attention of the Slovakian Gestapo. I did not know how it came about. The Slovakian HG militia and Gestapo raided my flat and searched it. They were most interested in my books and confiscated ten books by left-wing authors. That was only the beginning of a much worse disaster. It happened on 11 August 1942, one day before my twenty-fifth birthday, and hit me like a bolt out of the blue.

I was in the printing shop, working as usual at a machine. It was 9.30 by the clock on the wall. Suddenly a policeman and two HG militiamen entered the room. They asked which of us was Adolf Burger. A colleague turned to me and pointed to my bench. The militiamen came straight over to me. Without a word they grabbed me and led me out of the room. The police officer nodded, satisfied. My request to wash my hands was refused. The militiamen kept me between them and brought me home to the flat first.

Actually my wife should have been at home but she must have gone out on an errand, or so I thought. I could not think of anything else. There was no time. The HG thugs ordered me to pack a few things – only necessities. I had only started when one of them shouted, 'That's enough, quick, hurry!'

Then they led me away. After we left the house they kept really close to me. I noticed that the policeman sealed our front door. I was taken straight to the police station and brought before an inspector for questioning. As I entered the interview room, I saw my confiscated books on his desk and then came the first question.

'Whose are these books?'

'Mine,' I answered hesitantly, not yet realising how the interview would end.

Already the next question came, 'Were you ever a member of an illegal political party?'

'No,' I answered, a bit more sure of myself now.

Evidently the police inspector knew more than I thought. He pressed on, 'Name the people who worked with you in your cell.' From that moment on I knew I had to keep silent. The inspector asked again, this time much more forcefully, about my contacts. I looked him straight in the eye and said, 'I know no one.'

'It doesn't matter,' said the inspector casually as if they only wanted to try me out. 'We know who they all are anyway.' That was the end of the interview.

Finally I was brought to the old munitions factory by uniformed Slovaks. The HG militia had turned it into a collection point for political detainees. I was held there with other detainees. Meanwhile the militia had arrested members of the resistance and Jews in their homes and workplaces, and brought them here. On 21 August 1942, the prisoners were assembled for deportation to Žilina. We were herded into wagons that were waiting at the station.

I had not seen my wife, Gisela, since my arrest. I was very concerned. I did not know what had happened to her and was worried about her.

When the train reached Žilina, I suddenly saw her at the station. I thought my heart would stop, I was so excited. Then I realised that she had arrived on the same train in a different wagon. I couldn't wave to her because she was too far away. It was only when we were in Žilina concentration camp that we had an opportunity to talk in peace. She too had been taken from our flat by HG militiamen without being given any reason. She had been interviewed and then dragged off the same way as I was to the old munitions factory.

We were obsessed with one thought: escape. How could we escape from here? We soon abandoned the idea, because a rumour was going around the camp that we were to be taken to Germany to work. Then we considered that we might endanger our families: as well as the risk of trying to escape, Hlinka's followers had arrested entire families in Slovakia, following the German model.

After twenty-four days the militia had assembled 1,000 detainees/prisoners – the number necessary for deportation. The Žilina concentration camp, a former barracks was now called 'Concentration Centre for prisoners in the suburb of Žilina, Rajecka cesta'. The HG commanders in this camp were Vojtech Zavodský,

Slovakian Jews in Žilina concentration camp lining up for deportation: 1. Kraus, 2. Ruth Neubauer from Bratislava, 3. Ruth Neubauer's mother, 4. Laco Morgenbesser

Laco Mutnanský and Marecek. These fascists ill-treated the prisoners with sly cruelty.

On 17 September we had to line up and the HG leader told us we were going to Germany to work. 'Everything is arranged. You are to leave all belongings here. You are only allowed one suitcase each.'

We had to line up under close guard and march in columns five abreast from Žilina camp to the station. On our right and left stood militiamen giving each other military commands. Then came the order: 'March.' Men, women and children were driven through a phalanx of Slovakian HG militiamen. These humiliated people were carrying their few remaining possessions.

The uniformed men drove the thousand women, children and men to the goods yard and straight into cattle trucks. The screams had only just died down into silent sobbing when the wagon doors were slid shut and locked. Everywhere there were armed guards with rifles and machine guns cocked. The train moved off slowly. None of us knew where to.

During the long journey it was relatively quiet. Everyone was exhausted, sitting thinking and talking quietly to relatives. The uncertainty was torture for all of us. It made us weak as our courage faded. We had to submit to armed superior power and we were defencelessly delivered to our unknown fate.

After all we had experienced, no one believed that we were going to Germany to work. Did the HG leader not say we would be able to return home after a certain length of time?

Much later we found out how we had been deceived so that the HG militia could get the transport to its destination without any resistance from the prisoners. Thus our wagons rolled on into the unknown. None of us had any idea of what lay ahead.

The condemned at the start of their painful journey

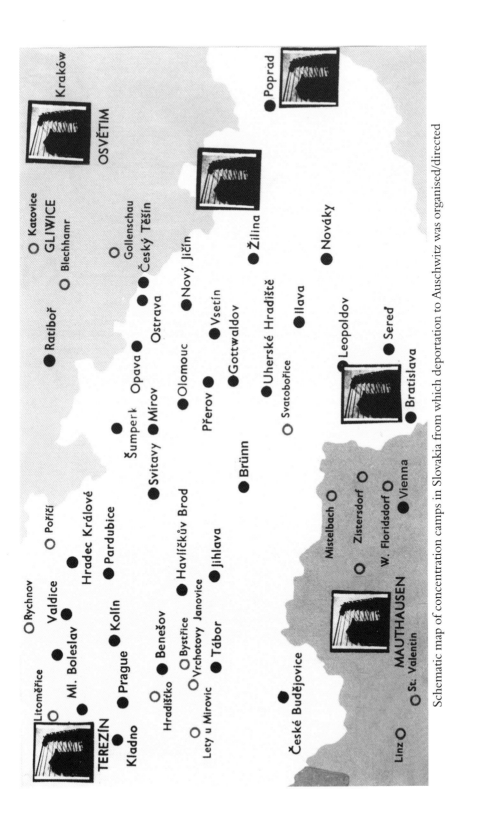

Schematic map of concentration camps in Slovakia from which deportation to Auschwitz was organised/directed

While the president of the Slovakian puppet state, Josef Tiso, pinned
distinctions on Wehrmacht and SS men, he despatched Slovakian Jews
to extermination camps and paid the SS for them

Transport to the Ramp at Auschwitz

OUR TRAIN REACHED THE GERMAN border during the night of 17 September 1942. When it stopped, the doors were slid open and we had to get out. For the first time we saw SS men in uniform. From this point on, they guarded our every step. Here they were giving orders: 'Line up in fives.' Then came the roll call by numbers. An SS officer checked that the number of prisoners corresponded to the number on his list. Then he ordered us to hand over all preserves and tinned food. To give weight to this order the sentries pointed their guns at us. After we had been robbed a second time, we had to climb into the cattle trucks again and the train moved off. Still no one knew our destination.

The train did not stop for two days until early in the morning of 19 September. The wagon doors were pulled open. Still a bit dazzled in the dawn, we saw a broad plain. The first rays of the sun shone right into the stinking dirty wagons. But there was no warmth in the autumn glow.

Right in front of us was a group of SS guards and menacing gun barrels: the sight that greeted millions of Jews from all over Europe. We only learnt later where we were: on the infamous ramp of the concentration camp at Auschwitz.

While we were climbing out, limbs stiff from the long time crouching, sitting or standing on the journey, the SS men shouted, 'All luggage out of the wagons.' Then more orders: 'Put the luggage on the ramp.' It would be sent on later, so we were told. Then followed the worst shock: saying goodbye to our wives and children. Families were cruelly separated. The children started screaming; they were not the only ones. To this day I can still see those heart-rending scenes on the ramp, they are burned into my memory. They took place under the eyes of the SS guards, who were most of them fathers themselves. At first the children were allowed to stay with their mothers. But that was the last time they saw their fathers. The extermination began here on the ramp at Auschwitz.

My wife, who had managed to travel with me in the same wagon this far, was just able to whisper to me to think of her every evening at eight o'clock. That way we would at least be together in our thoughts.

Men and women were next lined up in marching columns, again five abreast. An SS doctor and two assistant SS men scrutinised the men's column. Each prisoner was asked three questions by the doctor. Age? Occupation? State of health? The answers determined life or death.

The SS and the business that profited to an extraordinary degree from the slave labour of the concentration camp (Konzentrationslager – KZ) prisoners

The ramp at KZ Auschwitz, final destination for millions of Jews.
For most of them the ramp led directly to the gas chambers

On the ramp SS doctor Mengele or eight other SS doctors decided on life or death by
jerking a thumb. Men and women had to line up in separate marching columns

Your age? Forty-eight! Step to the left! That meant death in the gas chamber

had set an upper age limit for the labour force of forty. Anyone older or who reported sick had to step to the left. Mothers and children and women over forty were also ordered to the left.

Then a convoy of lorries covered with tarpaulins drew up. Those over forty, the sick and women with children had to get in. The convoy moved off. An ambulance followed behind.

Two hundred and six men and seventy-one women were left behind. I breathed a sigh of relief. Almost everyone believed that the old, weak and the children would be looked after. Of the Jews on our train, 732 were men and women over forty, sick, or women with children.

Only much later we found out what was being transported in the ambulance with the red cross on it: it was 'Zyklon B' – the poisonous gas produced by I.G. Farben. It represented big business for the shareholders of the chemical giant.

Finally, we who had been classified as fit for work were ordered to march off. The marching columns, which were separated from each other by armed SS men, set off in opposite directions. The men were taken one and a half kilometres from the ramp to Auschwitz concentration camp and the women were taken three kilometres away to Birkenau. We could only look at each other to say goodbye.

I will never in my life forget our first encounter on the march to the camp: a column of female prisoners came towards us marching to work. They were completely exhausted, their heads shaven, dressed in the most unbelievably filthy men's clothes, stripped of all dignity. They dragged themselves along, laboriously as if on their last legs, in silent apathy. Alsatian dogs held on the leash by SS men and women threatened the terrified girls and women. Was this to be the fate of our women too?

A few minutes later we passed a marching column of men coming towards us. The prisoners who dragged themselves past us were mere shadows of their former selves. We could now sense what fate awaited us in Auschwitz.

The concentration camp at Auschwitz was set up on the orders of the
SS Commander-in-Chief (Reichsführer) in an existing barracks.
The first transport of political prisoners from Poland arrived on 14 June 1940.
SS-Sturmbannführer Rudolf Höss was camp commander 1940–3

Arrival in Auschwitz Concentration Camp

Entrance to the main camp at Auschwitz

OVER THE ENTRANCE THE CYNICAL slogan '*Arbeit macht frei*' (work liberates) greeted us. Then we passed through the gate and the 1,000-volt electrified barbed-wire fence. It surrounded the entire camp and was secured by high wooden watchtowers from which machine guns guarded the camp perimeter.

We stopped and were counted again. Then SS men came with prisoners who had to gather our last belongings into sacks, the things we had managed to hold onto after two searches: money, cigarettes, valuables, groceries. All the SS thugs we had encountered had robbed us, but always left something for the next one. It was a well-worked system.

Then came the order: 'Get ready to wash!' We had to strip naked and place items of clothing in a pile. Now we had lost our last personal possessions. We only had our memories and our bare bodies. We were herded to the showers. Before showering, our heads were shaved bald in the corridor. Then we had a short, cold shower and left the room by another door.

We had to line up again in the yard. On that cold, autumn day we had to wait for an hour, wet and naked – this was the lot of all new arrivals in the concentration camp, in all weather.

At last an SS man and two prisoners appeared and told us to line up in alphabetical order. Then we were tattooed. Each new prisoner had his number tattooed with a sharp needle, dipped in dye, on the lower left forearm. We lost our names – we became numbers, from 64396 to 64602. I became number 64401.

After this procedure each prisoner received a shirt, a pair of underpants, prison clothes and a cap. We lined up again and stood in silence for an hour. Then SS personnel led us into an office, where a file card was filled out with all our personal details.

Finally our personal number and the corresponding triangular badge were sewn on. This classified each prisoner: political prisoners got a red triangle; Bible scholars a purple one; 'antisocial elements' wore black triangles; and murderers

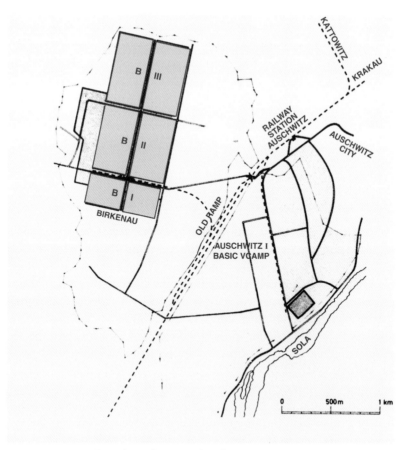

Location plan of Auschwitz and Birkenau concentration camps

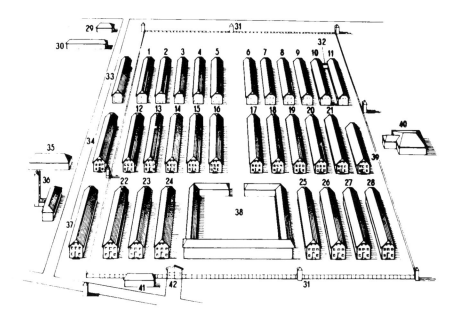

Ground plan of Auschwitz main camp

1–8	Accommodation	
12–16	Accommodation	
22–23	Accommodation	
25–27	Accommodation	
9	Prisoners' sick bay	
10	Experiments block	
11	Bunker Block	
19	Prisoners' sick bay	
20	Quarantine block	
21	Prisoners' sick bay	
24	Office	
28	Out-patients	
29	Camp commander's residence	
30	Chief sentry	
31	Watchtower	
32	'Black wall'	
33	Command HQ	
34	Administration	
35	Political department	
36	Old crematorium	
37	SS patrol doctor	
38	Camp kitchen	
39	Building (annexe)	
40	'Theatre'	
41	Block-leader's office	
42	Main gate	

and thieves a green one. Jews were recognised by the Star of David. The SS determined who got which badge. With us thus identified, the supervisor led us to the block that was to be our 'home' in Auschwitz

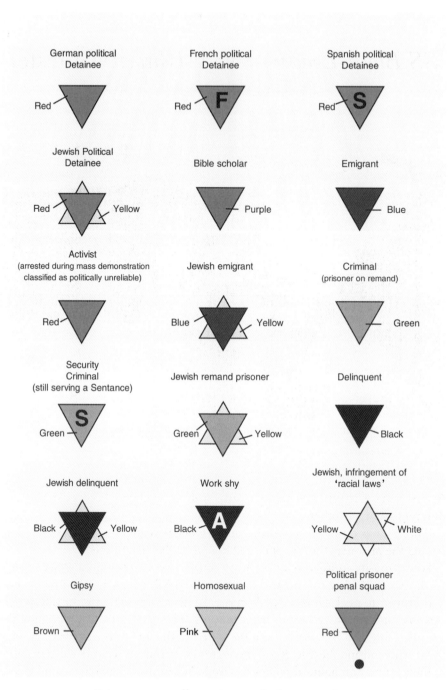

German political Detainee — Red

French political Detainee — Red, F

Spanish political Detainee — Red, S

Jewish Political Detainee — Red, Yellow

Bible scholar — Purple

Emigrant — Blue

Activist
(arrested during mass demonstration classified as politically unreliable) — Red

Jewish emigrant — Blue, Yellow

Criminal
(prisoner on remand) — Green

Security Criminal
(still serving a Sentance) — Green, S

Jewish remand prisoner — Green, Yellow

Delinquent — Black

Jewish delinquent — Black, Yellow

Work shy — Black, A

Jewish, infringement of 'racial laws' — Yellow, White

Gipsy — Brown

Homosexual — Pink

Political prisoner penal squad — Red

Prisoners were allocated to particular categories

SS *Block-Leader* – *Block-Wardens (*Älteste*)* – Kapos

A double 1,000-volt electrified barbed-wire fence surrounded
Auschwitz concentration camp

ABOUT TWELVE HUNDRED HUMAN BEINGS were cooped up in a barracks block no different from any other.

The real master of life and death in the block was an SS 'block-leader'. From among the prisoners the SS appointed the job of 'block-warden'.

It was mostly murderers or other criminals – prisoners with a green triangle – who were block-wardens in the autumn of 1942. Here they had every legal opportunity to steal and murder. A criminal with a truncheon was the hut orderly (*Stubendienst*) for every twenty-five prisoners. The leader of the work gangs, the so-called foreman (*Vorarbeiter*), and the leader of the foremen were distinguished by an armband and the title '*Kapo*' and were also criminals. They decided whether in their estimation political prisoners should live or die. If the block-warden said to someone, 'Tomorrow you are for the wire', the prisoner was forced to go up to the high-tension wire fence. But before the victim reached it he had usually been used by the sentries in the watchtowers as a live target and was shot by a burst of machine-gun fire.

His way out – a prisoner who could no longer bear being tortured by the
SS chose death on the 1,000-volt electrified fence

Prisoners often threw themselves against this fence in despair. They could no longer bear the physical and mental torture and ended their lives themselves.

The barrels of cold water that stood between the blocks were also used for murder. A prisoner had to get into the barrel, and the block-warden would hold his head under water until his victim was dead.

Kapos and block-wardens were particularly interested in prisoners who had gold teeth. They had to die: at the first opportunity they were killed and the gold teeth broken off. These murderers exchanged the teeth for alcohol and food. And if they were not killing someone, they were beating people constantly, from morning till night.

Our block-warden was a German criminal sentenced to life for murder and he was given full scope to serve out his sentence by the SS. He greeted us with the words, 'There were thousands here. They are dead and gone. If you behave yourselves, you will live. If you don't behave properly, you will die!' He did not specify what 'proper behaviour' was. No one asked; his threats worked.

Then came the lower functionaries: the block-registrar and the hut orderly. The registrar was often a criminal too. Every day he checked the state of the prisoners in the block, the number of living and the number who had just died.

If he made a mistake in his totals and noted a lower number he did not correct his entry but changed the number of the living instead. He killed one prisoner after another until the number of prisoners matched the number on the sheet again. The registrars, block-wardens and *Kapos* profited from these 'mistakes' in that they got the food rations of the dead.

As we crowded into the rooms allocated to us, we met the hut orderly. He was in charge of individual cells, was supposed to keep order in the hut and to distribute food. He used his poisition to beat prisoners at every opportunity.

At that time the rooms in Auschwitz were kept clean. I would like to emphasise this in particular, because I had to suffer the exact opposite later. On each bunk in the three-tiered wooden platforms lay a sack of straw. Each prisoner had a blanket to cover himself in relative comfort compared to the concentration camp at Birkenau.

I was woken in Auschwitz at half-past four in the morning by the roars of the orderly. The 'bed' had to be made as quickly as possible. Then everyone tried to get a free place at the water taps, to freshen up at least. A little later the catering service, to which ten prisoners had been assigned the evening before, brought our 'breakfast': containers of ersatz coffee. The orderly roared, 'Line up for breakfast.' We were given the ersatz coffee but no slice of bread. Then they shouted, 'Everybody out.' It was five o clock. Only the orderlies, *Kapos* and criminals remained in the warm block. It was a mystery to everyone why we

Roll call. Resistance – Despair – Hope

were sent out so early, because we had to wait for two hours in the roll call square for the head count. During this uncertain time we huddled close together to warm each other's bodies.

Many of us who were already weakened became ill with fever from this daily harassment and began to cough up blood. Many comrades were overcome by fainting fits. They fell on the ground and fellow prisoners dragged them to the back row and laid them on the ground there. After roll call the block-warden or the *Kapos* whipped the weakened prisoners into an upright position. Anyone who could not stand up lay there and from that moment on was condemned to death.

The head count in the evening was the same, after ten hours' hard work. Everything had to be done very quickly although we then had to wait, standing lined up five abreast, for the block-warden. The *Kapos* beat us again while straightening up the lines, because many of these thugs thought there had to be blood, or the block-warden would not be satisfied. When he finally arrived, the order 'Caps off!' resounded and the prisoners stood bareheaded in front of the warden – a criminal from Berlin and a murderer. He reported the total from the list to the block-leader. Then the *Kapos* drove us back into our accommodation, where the orderly distributed the daily ration: 300 grams of bread and a little jam or margarine. After that, we could finally move about in the camp free of *Kapos* and foremen.

'Sport' in Auschwitz

It was September 1942, our first Sunday in Auschwitz. The early roll call was over, and we were waiting for the command 'Move it!' On the top step of the block stood a block-registrar, a criminal. From here he could see every corner of the yard, and his commanders roared, 'Stand still. Caps on. Move it!' When 'Caps off!' sounded for the hundredth time we tore the flat caps off our shaven heads and slapped them on our right thigh. It had to sound like the crack of a whip otherwise it was repeated until the commander was satisfied. This apparently harmless harassment gave the clerk the excuse to pick out victims for punishment exercises. He would pounce on a prisoner, drag him across the yard to the next block and put him with his face to the wall. Another man had clicked his heels a second too late. Everyone was waiting for it to end but he let us drill on. Two weren't enough for him. He pulled more out of the rows, for no reason. A long nose, thick glasses, a crooked cap – anything he did not like gave him a reason to drag one after the other out of the rows, until there were twenty standing at the wall. The clerk and the orderly ordered them to line up in fives. Then began the Auschwitz 'drill'.

'Run! March! Lie down! Get up! March, march! Lie down! Crawl! Get up! March, march! Hop! Run! March, march! Turn! March, march!' The pitiful prisoners were harried and chased as if in a drag hunt. They threw themselves on the ground, wriggling, panting and shoving each other, to get away from the blows, which constantly rained down on them. Their faces were flushed with exertion, sweat streamed down their foreheads and necks and mingled with the blood from their wounds. Just don't lie down. Anyone who did not keep moving was lost. A blow with a club; if necessary, a few more. Many had already given up. More than half lay motionless on the ground, although only thirty minutes had passed. 'Run! March, march! Lie down! Crawl!' One command followed another – the remainder tried with their last strength to carry out these orders. But it was not long until the last lay there motionless in their zebra-striped outfits, exhausted, and were then beaten to death. Meanwhile, the dead were piled up as if nothing had happened.

A new series of commands: 'Stand still! Caps on! Caps off! Move it!' The hour-long drill was finished for that Sunday. The criminal *Kapos* and their power were an essential part of the concentration camp system. 'My God, where are we, what is going on here? Prisoners are killing other prisoners, while the SS officer in charge gives the impression that this murderous activity has nothing to do with him.' These were my baffled thoughts.

The evening roll call brought more blows. The inhabitants of the block were driven into the yard, everything had to be done quickly, even though we waited for two hours or more for the block-warden, standing in rows of five. The *Kapos* laid about them as they straightened the rows. The rows were exactly as before, but the *Kapo* was not satisfied unless there was blood. After roll call the *Kapos* drove us back into our huts under a hail of blows and kicks.

The first night in the camp sleep was long in coming. What I had seen and experienced exceeded my worst fears. I had thought they were going to take us to Germany to work. Now we realised the pitiless, brutal reality of the fascist concentration camp. None of us could ever have imagined this. Now we knew what sort of hell we faced. This hell was far crueller than that described

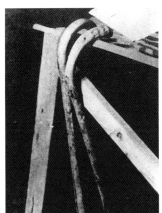

The most important 'tool' of the criminal *Kapos*, block-wardens and orderlies – these were the cudgels used to hit the prisoners

in the Bible, worse than Dante's medieval Inferno, because the new hell of the concentration camps – thought up by the brains of the Nazis and their leaders – was designed so that the scum of humanity tortured and killed innocent people. This was the horror of those years. Here the Nazis, along with their open and secret followers, showed their true colours.

'Death! Our death or theirs!' Such were my thoughts as I finally fell into a deep sleep.

On 21 June 1944 Reichsführer-SS Heinrich Himmler Addressed High-Ranking SS Officers:

Heinrich Himmler, Reichsführer-SS

The address outlines the hierarchy of administration in camps accommodating 40–50,000 people. One person in charge could be dangerous. We have nominated supervisors to oppress the sub-species . . . One is the overseer. Supervisors are as follows: room orderly in charge of 30 prisoners, foreman in charge of 100, *Kapo* in charge of 200. Block-warden is in charge of a block of 600 prisoners. The block-registrar is subordinate to him. One SS-Reichsführer is adequate to control 600. When a *Kapo* is appointed, he has to sleep somewhere else. His responsibilities are: to reach work targets, prevent sabotage, ensure cleanliness in the huts and that the beds are made. It must be as tidy as a barracks. He has to be a leader to his men. If he is not satisfactory he is sent back to sleep with the men, and he may be killed by them. The *Kapo* has some privileges.

It is not my job . . . to design a welfare system.

SS-Obersturmbannführer Rudolf Höss, Commandant of Auschwitz (Oswiecim) extermination camp 1940–3. At the Nuremberg trial he admitted that one and a half million people were killed in KZ Auschwitz–Birkenau. He was condemned to death by a tribunal court in Warsaw and executed on 2 April 1947 in Auschwitz

SS-Obersturmbannführer Rudolf Höss explains details of the construction and organisation of the extermination camp to SS officers

6

Hard Labour in a Kommando

THE CAMP ADMINISTRATION DIVIDED THE prisoners into different labour gangs, called 'Kommandos'. Skills or former occupations were not taken into account. For instance, in KZ Auschwitz there was the building Kommando, clear-up gang, bodies gang, road-building gang, the Kommando for Deutsche Ausrustungs-Werke (DAW), the German armaments factory and many others. I had to work in the road-building gang. The working conditions were indescribable. The foremen beat us constantly, even though the work consisted of carrying stones.

I still remember those cold October days of 1942. An icy wind was blowing. For ten hours at a stretch we had to carry paving stones a kilometre and lay them. A week later we were forced to carry the same stones back to the place we had taken them from – completely pointless work. This way the prisoners would be physically and mentally broken.

The SS men who guarded us always found new reasons to beat and kill us. They made sure that their Kommando brought wheelbarrows full of dead and injured bodies back to the camp in the evening. A Kommando hardly ever came back without some dead.

One day I nearly ended up coming back on the barrow myself. The two SS guards had the habit of calling a prisoner over to them a few times a day for no reason other than because they were bored. The prisoner had to stand to attention and say: 'Prisoner number . . . reporting for duty.' Then the guards would give various orders to torture him with drill exercises. Sometimes the SS men would shout, 'Run, run!' and then shoot the prisoner from behind. We lived in constant fear.

I was carrying paving stones. The freezing wind blew. Suddenly the SS guard shouted 'Come here,' and pointed to me. I ran over, stood to attention and said, 'Prisoner number 64401 reporting, sir.' The SS man screamed, 'Name?' Hesitantly I said, 'Burger, Adolf', although it was strictly forbidden to give one's name. The SS man hit me in the face with his rifle butt, knocking out four of my top front teeth. Then he shouted, 'Clear off!' He could have hit me on the forehead – if he had I would have been taken back to the camp on the cart.

I realised very quickly that staying in the road-building Kommando meant certain death. So I tried everything I could to get into another Kommando, even though I was not one of the biggest or strongest prisoners.

In some of the Kommandos, which were considered more important by the Nazis, the steady turnover of workers due to the high death rate led to the work being of uneven quality. As a result these gangs got an extra ration of bread and sausage, and sometimes margarine and jam too. This food was the only good nourishment that the prisoners would have. It was absolutely essential, in order to keep the workforce alive.

After two weeks, with the help of a friend from Slovakia who had been deported to Auschwitz before me, I succeeded in being moved to the DAW *Kommando*. We considered it one of the better squads.

Fifteen hundred prisoners laboured away. They had to make wooden crates for grenades in a section of the nearby munitions factory. The conditions were harsh there too, but some things made camp life more bearable. I came to an agreement with a foreman who looked after the electrical installations in the factory. He took me into his squad on condition that I left him all the extra rations that I got as a member of the squad. In return I was allowed to hammer cable ducts for electrical wiring into the walls. That meant I had to stand on a ladder all day long, where no *Kapo* could reach me, or so I thought. This seemed to offer me a slight chance of surviving.

I soon found out how wrong I was. The prisoners' rations in Auschwitz in 1942 certainly did not contain the minimum daily requirements of vitamins and calories. First thing there was ersatz coffee made from roast wheat and chicory; at midday we were given a litre of watery soup; in the evening we had 300 grams of bread and more ersatz coffee. No prisoner could keep up his strength and work in such harsh conditions on such a meagre diet. Our reserves of strength were quickly used up. Life expectancy sank rapidly. From day to day we noticed more signs of deterioration.

A prisoner's daily rations: 1,300 to 1,700 calories for a
ten-hour day of heavy labour. SS doctors confirmed that
75 per cent of the prisoners were starving

When I had negotiated my food 'contract' in good faith, I did not know the laws of the camp jungle. I had not been there long enough to know what was going on. I did not know that I could not work for ten hours on 300 grams of bread. At first the most important thing for me was to get away from constant beatings by the *Kapos*. Later I would pay dearly for my optimistic estimate of my stamina.

It was a Thursday. I was standing on a ladder. Suddenly I got dizzy. I was only able to keep my balance with enormous effort. My legs nearly gave under me. Everything was swimming in a fog. The next day I felt worse. I had completely overestimated my strength. Was I going to die like this? Around that time DAW munitions production stopped because of lack of materials. Prisoners were no longer needed for this work, and I was one of the five hundred who were let go. My health was deteriorating due to malnourishment.

Statement of KZ Commander Kaindl at the Sachsenhausen Trial, 1947

The Department of Economic affairs SS-WVHA, calculated the following estimated costs of concentration camp prisoners who were hired as labour to the various industries. These were mostly munitions factories.

Estimates:

	Income	Outgoings
Day's pay for hire of prisoner	RM6.00	
Maintenance		RM0.60
Hire/of clothing deposit		RM0.10
Total	RM6.00	RM0.70

The SS aimed to make a clear profit of RM5.30 from each prisoner.

Average life expectancy of a prisoner was 9 months, i.e. 270 days 270 days @ RM5.30	RM1431.00
Gains from stripping bodies of usable materials: gold teeth, clothing, valuables, money	RM200.00
Net income over 9 months	RM1631.00
Cost of cremation of body	– RM2.00
Total profit from a prisoner over 9 months	RM1629.00

The SS estimated the life expectancy of a prisoner to be nine months!

7

Victims (Muselmänner)

I FOUGHT TO SURVIVE WITH every ounce of willpower. I volunteered for work in the wood-yard *Kommando*. The prisoners who worked there had already come to terms with the fact that death would be a release, and their remaining strength was dissipated in total exhaustion. These skeletons, creatures disfigured by sickness and hunger, drifted about in a pathetic state and were called '*Muselmänner*'. They dragged themselves around breathing heavily and using their last strength working. They hovered between life and death. They did not react to commands nor to anything that happened round them. This was probably the reason why the wood-yard prisoners were not beaten by the *Kapos* or the foremen. The *Kommando* was usually short-lived. Every time the workforce gave out it was completely liquidated.

As we were marching to work on 14 December 1942 we were stopped by the order: 'Wood-yard *Kommando*, halt!' and then, 'Wood-yard *Kommando*, about turn!' In a flash we were surrounded by SS men. They led us to the washrooms. We had just arrived when an SS officer gave the order, '*Kapos* and foremen, leave!' Was this it? Everyone had heard of this moment and expected it to come. We had volunteered for the wood-yard *Kommando* because we could no longer take the strain of daily ill-treatment. The only thing left for us was death. Yet we clung to life nevertheless. The feeling of human dignity surfaced from our deepest subconscious. The condemned workers, university professors, teachers, clerks and doctors surged forward, fired with the courage of despair, and attacked their guards. But the SS rifle butts were stronger than the last efforts of the tortured prisoners. They were pushed into the showers to await their transport to the gas chambers of Birkenau. The doors were closed on two hundred men condemned to be murdered.

When I realised fully what was happening before my eyes, I took advantage of the confusion and jumped through the ranks of *Kapos* and foremen and hid behind them. It was an act of desperation. However, I did not have an armband, which would have distinguished me as a *Kapo* or foreman. These were the only ones not sent to the gas chambers, so I had to ensure that I was not discovered standing among them.

At a favourable moment I fled behind the nearest block. Then I ran along between a few others and reached a group of prisoners who were shovelling snow onto a wagon between two buildings. Without hesitating I grabbed a shovel that was lying against a cart and began shovelling.

I knew the prisoners would not object to my presence out of solidarity. It was the actions of the foreman that would decide my survival. If he had already written his list of workers he would definitely hand me over or report me. But when he appeared, he had paper and pencil in his hand and was taking down the prisoners' numbers. Anyone who had not been allocated to other work outside the camp could work in this *Kommando* in the yard.

The foreman had barely completed his list when an SS man and a *Kapo* turned up looking for someone who had escaped. They looked at the prisoners shovelling snow and saw me, one of the *Muselmänner*. I must have looked suspicious to them, but luckily they could not remember what the escapee looked like. It seemed to irritate them that so many of the prisoners looked wretched. The SS man called the foreman over and he showed him his list. My number 64401 was on it. When the SS man nodded to the *Kapo* I heaved a sigh of relief. After another quick look at me they went off and disappeared round the nearest corner. That was how I was saved.

Thanks to those prisoners and the list containing my name, my life was saved, for the time being. My survival would not have meant anything if I had been killed a few days later. What actually decided it was which *Kommando* I was allocated to. My current situation was not very hopeful. At first glance I was among the doomed: a man of medium height, I weighed at most forty kilos.

Prisoners from KZ Birkenau after six weeks of slave labour.
They lingered between life and death

8

Sick

IN THE CAMP WE CONTINUED working in the most horrific conditions. We had to work outside from early morning to late evening in all weathers. In winter, in sharp frost and snow we worked without socks, scarves, gloves or other warm clothing. I got frostbite in the big toe of my left foot. Any sort of work seemed impossible for me. I should have reported sick, but to do so was tantamount to suicide and I would have ended up in the crematorium. In spite of the nearly intolerable pain I did not go to the sick bay. A friend from Poprad, Dr Peter Bartoš, whom I had known as a political activist and had met up with again in the camp, helped me. My chilblains were in a critical condition, so he suggested operating without medical instruments or anaesthetic or any medicines. He had no surgical instruments other than a simple kitchen knife. I had no choice. If I wanted to survive I had to give in.

In the evening Bartoš operated on me. He disinfected the knife over a flame. Then he shortened the toe without any anaesthetic. I gritted my teeth and dug my nails into the straw mattress so that I would not cry out in pain. Comrades whispered encouragement. They kept saying, 'Stick it out! Hold on there. Don't give up.' Finally he wrapped a paper bandage round my toe and I tried to sleep.

We were not out of danger yet. The next day we had to stand for two hours in severe frost for roll call until the head count was over. The stabbing pains from the fresh wound were torturing me. I could not scream because the *Kapos* and warden were not supposed to notice anything unusual.

There was only one sick bay for the entire camp, for ten thousand prisoners. If a prisoner reported sick he had to stand for roll call in front of the sick bay block. Only five sick prisoners at a time were allowed into the building. Whoever was at the end of the queue had to wait his turn for a few hours, in hail, rain or snow, even if he was injured or running a temperature. Examination was quick and superficial; wounds were only dressed with paper bandages. The next morning the prisoner had to march to work. Only those who could not get up remained in the sick bay. Then an SS doctor would come on his 'rounds', and on his directions an orderly would kill the patient with an injection of carbolic acid (*Karbolsaure*). Only sick *Kapos* and prisoners who were needed by the SS because of their qualifications were not murdered.

I knew what went on in the sick bay. A few days previously I had tried in vain to talk a twenty-six-year-old comrade out of reporting sick. He had been a strong, healthy lad a short while before he went into the sick bay. There his strength deteriorated and we never saw him again.

There were only a few of us still alive who had come from Žilina. But I wanted to survive. I wanted to be a human being again, not just a mere number.

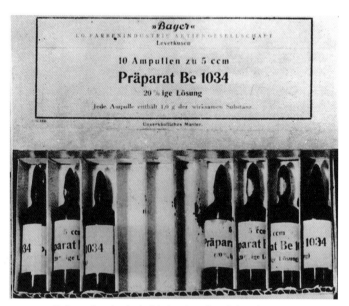

Poison for the lethal injection for sick prisoners

9

Clear-Up Kommando 'Canada'

IN AUSCHWITZ THERE WAS WORK consisting of 'processing' the luggage of new arrivals. On this detail there was not only plenty of dry bread but food that was otherwise unobtainable for 'normal prisoners'. Everyone had to leave their cases, bags and all the last belongings they had brought with them on the ramp. The prisoners had to remove this baggage from the ramp, sort it and load it onto wagons for transport to Germany. This paradise on earth was the 'clear-up' *Kommando*, where prisoners could eat their fill.

I intended to disappear into this *Kommando*, which was easier said than done. To achieve my purpose I had to try a simple old trick. I decided to be persistent. One morning as the prisoners were setting off to work I stepped in with them, joined their ranks. Of course I was spotted by the *Kapo*. He gave me a beating and sent me back to my *Kommando*.

I had reckoned with that and did not let it put me off. The next morning I joined them again. Most prisoners would have loved to work in the *Kommando*. Of course I was discovered again and beaten. I tried this 'little game' twice more. On the fifth day my plan worked.

Six prisoners, yoked like horses, were beaten and forced to pull the heavy cart

Two more people were needed in the wagon *Kommando* because two had fallen sick. The *Kapos* had to order two new prisoners into the squad. I happened to cross their path. They took a note of my number. So from that day on I, number 64401, was in the wagon *Kommando* – for the time being at least, this saved me from death by starvation.

The wagon *Kommando* worked day and night shifts, according to when the trains full of deportees arrived. About one hundred prisoners were allocated to it. While six prisoners pulled the cart the others loaded it with suitcases, bags, packages and all the things the new arrivals had had to leave behind on the ramp. The clear-up *Kommando* was called 'Canada' after a country where there was plenty of food. It consisted of three hundred prisoners and two hundred women. The numbers of workers were increased according to the numbers of deportees arriving. However, luggage was only sorted during the day.

As soon as the arrival of a trainload of deportees was announced, the wagon *Kommando* moved towards the ramp. In spite of the vigilance of the supervisors it was always possible to remove some items of food. Prisoners would try to smuggle them into the camp, hidden in various places: on their bodies, under their clothes or under their caps. This was dangerous because the SS punished all efforts to 'improve' on the rations with a beating, or sometimes with death. But hunger forced us to run the risk. On the first day I dared to hide a piece of dry bread under my clothes and smuggle it into the accommodation block for the clear-up and wagon *Kommandos*. Both were accommodated in a separate block. When it got dark I intended to feast on dry bread for the first time since my arrival in Auschwitz. I was lying on my bunk and noticed that everyone around me had plenty to eat so I did not have to hide my food from my comrades. This was not because the rations were better or more plentiful for this *Kommando* but because everyone from Canada helped themselves to food. There was plenty to eat in the rucksacks and suitcases that the newly arrived deportees had had to leave on the ramp.

Word got round the camp about the name of the *Kommando*, Canada. Soon not only the *Kommando* was called Canada, but also the entire area, into which a driveway led to a loading platform. The wagons were lined up here, into which the sorted stolen goods were loaded. The SS had the booty transported to the German Reich. Canada was a kind of yard consisting of five wooden huts, two brick buildings and a wooden shed called 'Albert's shed' after a prisoner, Albert Davidovič from Spišská Nová Ves – a Slovakian Jew who was the foreman here and looked after us, his subordinates, as best he could.

The men and women who worked there did a rough sorting first. Then the goods were sorted into groups such as textiles, shoes, toiletries, kitchen utensils, and so on, according to their quality. Finally skirts, blouses and trousers were sent for disinfection. In 'Albert's shed' shaving things were sorted. We packed razor blades, cut-throat razors, shavers, shaving soap and such like separately in suitcases. Other toiletries such as skin cream and toothpaste were taken out. We had to slice open the tubes to check for hidden valuables. If we found gold, for example, we had to put it in a slit in a particular box.

All valuables, even paintings and antiques, were meticulously listed in an inventory. The SS had these sent from the 'store' with an accompanying docket to Germany. Trains full of booty left Canada every day. If you remember that one and a half million people were murdered in Auschwitz, you can only imagine what vast quantities of valuables and objects were stolen in this camp alone.

This is what it was like on the ramp: hundreds of suitcases and packets.
This plundered booty was sorted and transported to Nazi Germany under the supervision of the SS (see delivery dockets)

Prisoners in the clear-up *Kommando* Canada loading the luggage onto lorries

A u f s t e l l u n g

über die von den Lagern Lublin und Auschwits auf Anordnung des ₮-Wirt-
schafts-Verwaltungshauptamt abgelieferten Mengen an Textil-Altmaterial:

1. **Reichswirtschaftsministerium**

Männer-Altbekleidung ohne Wäsche	97 000	Garnituren
Frauen-Altbekleidung ohne Wäsche	76 000	Garnituren
Frauen-Seidenwäsche	89 000	Garnituren
	insgesamt:	34 Waggons

Lumpen	400 Waggons	2 700 000 kg
Bettfedern	130 Waggons	270 000 kg
Frauenhaare	1 Waggon	3 000 kg
Altmaterial	5 Waggons	19 000 kg
	insgesamt:	2 992 000 kg

insgesamt: 536 Waggons

570 Waggons

2. **Volksdeutsche Mittelstelle**

Männerbekleidung:

Mäntel	99 000	Stck.
Röcke	57 000	"
Westen	27 000	"
Hosen	62 000	"
Unterhosen	38 000	"
Hemden	132 000	"
Pullover	9 000	"
Schals	2 000	"
Pyjamas	6 000	"
Kragen	10 000	"
Handschuhe	2 000	Paar
Strümpfe	10 000	"
Schuhe	31 000	"

Frauenbekleidung:

Mäntel	155 000	Stck.
Kleider	119 000	"
Jacken	26 000	"
Röcke	30 000	"
Hemden	125 000	"
Blusen	30 000	"
Pullover	60 000	"
Unterhosen	49 000	"
Schlüpfer	60 000	"
Pyjamas	27 000	"
Schürzen	36 000	"
Büstenhalter	25 000	"
Unterkleider	22 000	"
Kopftücher	85 000	"
Schuhe	111 000	Paar

Kinderbekleidung:

Mäntel	15 000	Stck.
Knabenröcke	11 000	"
Knabenhosen	3 000	"
Hemden	3 000	"
Schals	4 000	"
Pullover	1 000	"
Unterhosen	1 000	"
Mädchenkleider	9 000	"
Mädchenhemden	5 000	"
Schürzen	2 000	"
Schlüpfer	5 000	"
Strümpfe	10 000	Paar
Schuhe	22 000	"

Wäsche usw.:

Bettbezüge	37 000	Stck.
Bettlaken	46 000	"
Kopfkissen- bezüge	75 000	"
Geschirrtücher	27 000	"
Taschentücher	135 000	"
Handtücher	100 000	"
Tischdecken	11 000	"
Servietten	8 000	"
Wolltücher	6 000	"
Krawatten	25 000	"
Gummischuhe und Stiefel	24 000	Paar
Mützen	9 000	Stck.

insgesamt: 211 Waggons

Delivery docket from KZ Auschwitz

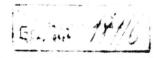

3. **Reichsjugendführung - Landdienst**

Männer-Altbekleidung	4 000	Garnituren
Männer-Mäntel	4 000	Stück
Männer-Schuhe	3 000	Paar
Frauen-Altbekleidung	4 000	Garnituren
Frauen-Mäntel	4 000	Stück
Frauen-Unterwäsche	3 000	Garnituren
Frauen-Pullover	20 000	Stück
Frauen-Schürzen	5 000	Stück
Schals versch. Art	6 000	Stück
Frauen-Schuhe	3 000	Paar

4. **Unternehmen "HEINRICH"**

Männer-Altbekleidung	2 700	Garnituren

5. **I.G.Farbenindustrie Auschwitz**

Männer-Altbekleidung	4 000	Garnituren

6. **Organisation "TODT" - Riga**

Männer-Altbekleidung	1 500	Garnituren

7. **Generalinspektor des Führers für das Kraftfahrwesen**

Männer-Altbekleidung	1 000	Garnituren
Männer-Unterwäsche	1 000	"
Männer-Schuhe	1 000	"
Männer-Mantel	1 000	Stück

8. **Konzentrationsläger**

Männer-Jacken	28 000	Stück
Männer-Hosen	25 000	"
Männer-Westen	7 000	"
Männer-Hemden	44 000	"
Männer-Unterhosen	34 000	"
Männer-Pullover	1 000	"
Männer-Mäntel	6 000	"
Frauen-Mäntel	25 000	"
Männer-Schuhe	100 000	Paar

insgesamt:	44 Waggons
	============

zusammen:	825 Waggons
	==========================

F.d.R.d.R.:

Rusten

SS-Hauptsturmführer

Delivery docket for 825 wagon loads of booty. Thousands of wagons full of deported Jews from all over Europe arrived at the ramp in Auschwitz.
On the return journey the same wagons carried the possessions of those who had by then already been killed, to Nazi Germany

C o p y
List

Delivery docket for consignments of clothes and other material from the camps of Auschwitz and Lublin, by order of Central administration office. Reich Ministry of the Economy

1. Reich Ministry of the Economy

Old clothes – men's	97,000 sets
no underwear	
Old clothes – women's	
no underwear	76,000 sets
Women's silk underwear	89,000 sets
Total:	34 wagons

Rags	400 wagons	2 700 000	kg
Feathers (bedding)	130 wagons	270 000	kg
Women's hair	1 wagon	3 000	kg
Old material	5 wagons	19 000	kg
	Total	2 992 000	kg
	Total	536 wagons	
		570 wagons	

2. Ethnic German Distribution Centre

Men's Clothing			Children's clothing		
Overcoats	99,000	pcs.	Overcoats	15,000	pcs.
Jackets	57,000	pcs.	Boys' jackets	11,000	pcs.
Waistcoats	27,000	pcs.	Boys' trousers	3,000	pcs.
Trousers	62,000	pcs.	Shirts	3,000	pcs.
Underpants	38,000	pcs.	Scarves	4,000	pcs.
Shirts	132,000	pcs.	Pullovers	1,000	pcs.
Pullovers	9,000	pcs.	Underpants	1,000	pcs.
Scarves	2,000	pcs.	Girls' dresses	9,000	pcs.
Pyjamas	6,000	pcs.	Girls' blouses	5,000	pcs.
Collars	10,000	pcs.	Aprons	2,000	pcs.
Pairs gloves	2,000	pcs.	Knickers	5,000	pcs.
Pairs Socks	10,000	pcs.	Pairs stockings	10,000	pcs.
Pairs Shoes	31,000	pcs.	Pairs shoes	22,000	pcs.

Women's clothing			Household linens etc.		
Overcoats	155,000	pcs.	Bed linen	37,000	pcs.
Dresses	119,000	pcs.	Sheets	46,000	pcs.
Jackets	26,000	pcs.	Pillowslips	75,000	pcs.
Skirts	30,000	pcs.	Tea towels	27,000	pcs.
Shirts	125,000	pcs.	Hand towels	100,000	pcs.
Blouses	30,000	pcs.	Tablecloths	11,000	pcs.
Pullovers	60,000	pcs.	Serviettes	8,000	pcs.
Knickers	49,000	pcs.	Woollen cloths	6,000	pcs.
Pyjamas	27,000	pcs.	Ties	25,000	pcs.
Aprons	36,000	pcs.	Pairs wellingtons		
Brassieres	25,000	pcs.	& galoshes	24,000	pcs.
Underclothes	22,000	pcs.	Caps	9,000	pcs.
Headscarves	85,000	pcs.			
Pairs shoes	111,000	pcs.			

total: 211 wagons

3. Youth Service or Reich-Land labour

Men's old clothing	4,000	outfits
Men's overcoats	4,000	pcs.
Men's shoes	3,000	pairs
Women's old clothing	4,000	outfits
Women's overcoats	4,000	pcs.
Women's underclothes	3,000	sets
Women's pullovers	20,000	pcs.
Various scarves	6,000	pcs.
Women's shoes	3,000	pairs

4. Operation 'Heinrich'

Men's old clothing	2,700	outfits

5. I.G. Farben industry Auschwitz

Men's old clothing	4,000	outfits

6. Organisation 'Death' - Riga

Men's old clothing	1,500	outfits

7. General Inspector of Transport

Men's old clothing	1,000	outfits
Men's underwear	1,000	outfits
Men's shoes	1,000	pairs
Men's overcoats	1,000	pcs.

8. Concentration camps

Men's jackets	28,000	pcs.
Men's trousers	25,000	pcs.
Men's waistcoats	7,000	pcs.
Men's shirts	44,000	pcs.
Men's underpants	34,000	pcs.
Men's pullovers	1,000	pcs.
Men's overcoats	6,000	pcs.
Women's overcoats	25,000	pcs.
Men's shoes	100,000	pairs

Total **44 wagons**

Grand total **825 wagons**

Hauptsturmfuhrer (Captain)

· 10 ·

Guards

THE SS MEN CALLED THE shots in Canada, of course. They 'did business' with the prisoners too, which was strictly forbidden. If an SS man was found dealing on the black market he was sent to the front. That happened to Scharführer (SF) Wiegleb, the commanding officer of the Canada guard. He ended up on the front, where he was killed in action for 'Führer, people and Fatherland', due to his unbelievable avarice.

The SS men had power of life and death over us. Their ruthlessness knew no bounds. To this day there are some of them I will never forget. Wiegleb's commander was typical of the attitude of the SS. He did not come to Canada often, but when he did he brought his seven-year-old son along and trained him to torture us with his dog. SS-Unterscharführer (USF) Heinz Kühnemann[1] was also a member of the guard. He used to be an opera singer in Vienna so he considered everything in Auschwitz to be a drama in which he played a part. He declaimed orders and curses. Although he was the most intelligent of the SS men, he was just as terrible as the rest. If he found a piece of bread during a search, ten or twenty truncheon blows would rain down on the prisoner.

SS-USF Wünsch was firmly convinced that the Nazi ideology was right. They all treated the prisoners accordingly; brute force seemed justified and they beat prisoners at every opportunity.

Another man who was renowned for his extraordinary cruelty was an ethnic German SS-USF from Yugoslavia, once a butcher by trade. Because he had only a limited vocabulary in German he stuck to a few obscenities, which he used on us prisoners. Whenever he was ill-treating us he strutted round like peacock in his highly polished jackboots.

On the ramp SS-OSF Schillinger was in charge. Whenever he turned up on his motorbike everyone was horrified by his sadistic cruelty.

We had to protect ourselves in particular from Fritz, a German criminal, the *Kapo* of the night shifts. He had come from Mauthausen camp, where he had made common cause with the SS for years. He died in 1944, supposedly from typhus, but the rumour went around that he had been despatched to the next life by the prisoners he had tortured.

---

1 *After the war Heinz Kühnemann went back home to Essen and became an opera singer. He was arrested in 1990 and went on trial in Duisburg in 1991–3. I (the author) gave evidence as a witness at the trial. In October 1993 the trial was suspended on the grounds that Kühnemann was taken ill with a heart condition.*

11

Arrival in Birkenau

On 15 January 1943 the order came to move the clear-up *Kommando* to Birkenau. There was a general flight from the *Kommando* at this news. At first no one wanted to go to Birkenau, not even at the price of having plenty to eat. Even experienced Auschwitz inmates were frightened of the place. On the other hand the work in the clear-up *Kommando* had saved me from death by starvation. Furthermore, somewhere in Birkenau, in a camp only three and a half kilometres away, my wife Gisela was still alive, or so I hoped. So I decided to go to Birkenau.

It lay in an unhealthy marshy area, near the village of Rajsko. Before the SS had the camp built, they evacuated the population of the villages of Zasola, Babice, Klucznikowce, Rajsko, Brzeszce, Bor and Berezinka. Thus the concentration camp with its crematoria would remain sealed off from the outside world, with no witnesses who could tell the world about the crimes of the SS. Apart from the SS men and women who were actively involved in the killings, the majority of the German population heard nothing about the bestiality and killing of one and a half million people that the SS carried out in KZ Auschwitz–Birkenau.

On 15 January 1943 the prisoners in the clear-up *Kommando* left Auschwitz. After marching for an hour we reached Birkenau. We had expected a terrifying place, but what we encountered exceeded our worst expectations. The prisoners' accommodation was not in buildings as in Auschwitz. Here there were only rough wooden huts, built like stables for horses. Daylight only seeped in through narrow windows in the roof. The side walls had no windows. A barbed-wire fence separated the men's camp from the women's.

When we reached the men's camp we saw through the barbed-wire fence a line of naked creatures in a pitiful state in the yard of the women's camp. They did not react to us being so near. It seemed as if all human dignity had died long ago. They were waiting apathetically for their next orders.

Our *Kommando* was led into Block 16, a stable. In the dormitory there were three-storey bunks made of planks where five prisoners lay beside one another. From now on we would vegetate here. There were no sanitary facilities in the huts. There were only washing facilities at points between the blocks, where thousands of emaciated, barely human-looking figures pushed and thronged. In the mornings they all rushed for the few drops of water to 'wash'. There was indescribable filth everywhere. In Auschwitz we had been used to being painfully clean, which helped us to preserve our self-respect. And we were subjected to the strict discipline of forced labour. In Birkenau there was no such thing.

There were between 450 and 600 prisoners in each hut. The conditions in Auschwitz were incomparably better than in Birkenau.

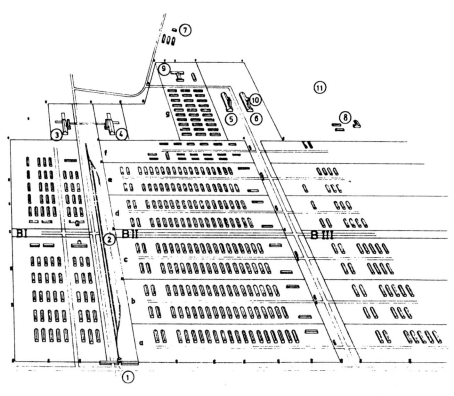

1	Main gate	B.I	Women's camp
2	Ramp	B.II.a	Quarantine camp
3	Crematorium II	B.II.b	Family camp
4	Crematorium III	B.II.c	Women's camp
5	Crematorium IV	B.II.d	Men's camp
6	Crematorium V	B.II.e	Gypsy camp
7	Bunker 2 (later Bunker 5)	B.II.f	Prisoners' sick bay
	with 3 changing huts	B.II.g	'Canada' belongings store
8	Bunker 1 with 2 changing huts	B.III	'Mexico'
9	'Saunas'		
10	Cremation trenches 1944		
11	Mass graves 1941/42		

Birkenau extermination camp

The 'cemetery without graves' in Birkenau covered 175 hectares, was sixteen kilometres long and surrounded by a 1,000-volt electrified barbed-wire fence.
One and a half million men, women and children were murdered in this part of KZ Auschwitz

Block 16, one of the 250 stable-blocks in KZ Birkenau. There were no windows or running water. At night 600 prisoners were squashed in on three-tier wooden bunks

12

Typhoid Fever

THE MOST DISTINCTIVE ASPECT OF Birkenau camp was the dirt, a fertile breeding ground for germs of all kinds of illnesses. Cases of spotted and gastric typhus were a daily occurrence. There was no protection against them. It was a great stroke of luck not to be struck down. There were no preventive remedies and there was absolutely no hygiene. The prisoners in the clear-up *Kommando* were affected but they had it easier than most, because they were not starving and had soap to wash with. Many prisoners tried to hide the fact that they had typhoid so that they would not be put in Block 7, for the way out of the sick bay ended in death.

In Birkenau SS doctors experimented on prisoners with medication against spotted fever. Some prisoners were invited to have themselves vaccinated. They were not told against what. It was like any other preventive vaccination. I too had to go to the sick bay, where an SS doctor gave me an injection and told me to report if I got worse or developed a temperature. After a few days I did run a high temperature but I did not go to the sick bay because I had found out in

Mikuláš Šteiner,
prisoner number 64565

Adalbert Deutsch,
prisoner number 65082

My friends helped me to survive

the meantime what would happen there. So what could I do? Finally I even lost consciousness. My mate Mikuláš Šteiner helped me in my distress: he succeeded in getting the clerk of the typhus block to give him written confirmation that I had recently been suffering from frostbitten feet. Then I was moved to Block 8, for those not seriously ill. The SS carried out a weekly 'selection' there and the weakest were sent to the gas chambers. Due to my 'supplementary diet' in the clear-up *Kommando*, I no longer looked like a skeleton and was saved. After I recovered I returned to the clear-up *Kommando*, which helped me to get back to full strength. I had enough to eat, which meant I survived. The prisoners in our *Kommando* helped me too whenever they could.

After being cured of typhus it was not as difficult to get back into the clear-up *Kommando* as it had been in Auschwitz, because in 1943 the number of prisoners working in it was increased daily and even then the work could scarcely be done.

In Birkenau, as in the base camp at Auschwitz, we had to do the same work in two shifts. Twenty, thirty or more lorries rolled in every day, laden with parcels, bags and suitcases, which we sorted. I was one of fifteen prisoners who worked in the store. There were big piles two to three metres high of the stolen belongings of the newly arrived deportees, for sometimes 3,000–5,000 Jews arrived at any one time. By the time we had sorted their belongings most of them were dead, murdered.

By 1943 the Nazis had refined their murder machine. Even the clear-up *Kommando* was done away with. Big tipper trucks took the booty away.

'Nacht und Nebel' Process

NN=Under cover of darkness.

Any prisoner who had these letters on his file card was isolated from the world and no one found out what became of him. An NN prisoner disappeared from his family and he was exploited in Nazi economic enterprises such as Krupp, I.G. Farben and others.

Finally he became a '*Muselmänn*' and ended up in the gas chambers

13

Extermination Policy

Extract from an Address by SS Heinrich Himmler to the Reichsleiter and Gauleiter in Posen on 6 October 1943

In this close circle of fellow party members I can advert to a problem which you have all taken for granted but which has become the most difficult issue in my life: the Jews. You have come to take it for granted that there are no longer any Jews in your district (Gau). All Germans – with a few exceptions – are convinced that we would not have been able to withstand the bombing and problems of the fourth and even now the fifth year of the war, and who knows maybe a fifth and sixth year if we still had the subversive plague in our midst. It is easy to say 'the Jews must be exterminated'. It is the hardest task on earth for whoever has to carry it out.

I beg you to listen and never to speak of what you are about to hear in this company. We have been faced with the question: what about the women and children? I have decided to find a solution. I did not consider it right to exterminate the men – that is to kill them (!) or have them killed – and to leave their avengers in the form of children to grow up and confront our sons and grandsons. The hard decision had to be taken to eliminate these people from the face of the earth. It was the most difficult decision to date for the organisation which has to carry it out. It has been carried out without – I think I can say – our men and women suffering spiritual damage.

When I read this speech by Himmler I still feel the same horror as if it were yesterday.

In the death factory in KZ Birkenau the Nazis used the most up-to-date technology. I will never forget the deportees from Riga. When the transport, consisting of almost 80 wagons, stopped at the ramp and the SS opened the doors, about 5,000 children got out accompanied by escorts and doctors. They were Jewish children. SS-Hauptsturmführer (HSF) Dr Mengele inspected the long column of children standing five abreast. The children were thirsty, and wanted water. Mengele stroked their heads and said: 'You will be going for a bath, then you will get tea.' Then he picked out twins for his criminal experiments. When he had chosen about ten pairs of twins an ambulance drew up and the twins were taken off to his laboratory. Then SS thugs gave the order to march off without there having been a selection; the children went to the washrooms with the escorts and the doctors. They were really gas chambers. After barely an hour the white smoke could be seen rising from the chimney of the crematorium.

All who arrived at the ramp at Auschwitz were beyond human help and abandoned by God. That was the reality of Auschwitz, which I had to face day after day, working in the clear-up *Kommando*. That was the price I had to pay to survive.

During selections Dr Mengele stood on the ramp and contentedly whistled Cavarodossi's aria and 'E lucevan le stelle' from *Tosca*. It did not cost him a thought to decide on life or death with a flick of his baton.

Josef Mengele, born on 16 March 1911 in Günzburg, doctor of philosophy and medicine, member of the Nazi Party since 1937, and of the SS since 5 November 1940, had been stationed in Posen in the Race and Settlement Headquarters (Rasse- und Siedlungs Hauptamt). He had served on the Eastern Front since 5 January 1942, in the 5th 'Viking' Panzer division. After he was wounded he was transferred to the Death's Head group in KZ Auschwitz. On 30 May 1943 he was appointed camp doctor, and worked there until the liquidation of the Gypsy camp. From August to September 1944 he was SS camp doctor in KZ Birkenau, section B.II.f and simultaneously senior medical officer of the outpatient department, responsible for sections B.II.a, B.II.b and B.II.d. His last rank was SS-HSF. During his service with the SS he was awarded the Iron Cross

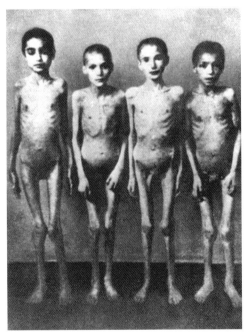

These twins were Mengele's guinea pigs. Very few children survived his terrible experiments

SS-Hauptsturmführer Dr Josef Mengele, the murderer of KZ Auschwitz–Birkenau

SS Brigade Leader Professor Dr Carl Clauberg. In Block 10 in KZ Auschwitz he carried out criminal experiments on female prisoners. He was trying to make women sterile using X-rays

Erwin Schönborn, former chairman of the German Veterans' Association

Leaflet, 1973

Kampfbund Deutscher Soldaten

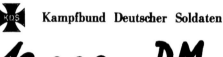

10.000.- DM
Belohnung

zahlen wir für jede einwandfrei nachgewiesene "VERGASUNG" in einer "GAS - KAMMER" eines deutschen KZ's. Wir akzeptieren keine KZ - Zeugen aus Polen, Israel oder den USA, die, wie in den NS - Prozessen, M E I N E I D E geschworen haben, ohne dafür belangt werden zu können.

Wir benötigen:
NAME, VORNAME, WOHNORT, GEBURTSTAG, GEBURTSORT, WO VERHAFTET, IN WELCHES KZ EINGELIEFERT UND IN WELCHEM KZ "VERGAST".

Verantwortlich ERWIN SCHÖNBORN (KDS) 1. Vorsitzender
6000 Frankfurt 56

German Veterans' Association

10.000 DM REWARD will be paid for objective proof of 'gassing' in the gas chamber of German concentration camp. No KZ witnesses from Poland, Israel or the USA will be accepted, who have perjured themselves in Nazi courts, thereby acquiring immunity from prosecution.

1st and 2nd Class and the Eastern Service Medal. After the war he was wanted for war crimes.

I wanted to survive to give testimony to the terrible truth of KZ Auschwitz and Birkenau. Thirty years later the denial of Auschwitz was spread by Nazis and neo-Nazis. Prominent in this movement is Erwin Schönborn, highly regarded in brown (Nazi) circles since his 'Veterans' association' announced a reward of 10,000 Marks to anyone who could provide evidence that gassings had taken place.

I witnessed the arrival of hundreds of deportations and countless selections carried out by SS doctors: Mengele; Dr Fritz Klein, doctor in charge of the women's camp; the professor of medicine, SS-HSF Dr Johann Paul Kremmer; camp doctor Friedrich Karl Hermann Entress; SS-OSF Dr Heinz Thilo and SS-Brigadeführer (BF) Dr Carl Clauberg.

The prisoners who worked in the clear-up *Kommando* on the ramp knew well what 'selection' meant. They knew that children, mothers, the sick and anyone over forty were not separated from the others to get better treatment, but so that the 'Final Solution' of the 'Jewish problem' could be achieved. We witnessed the most horrific scenes.

Bodies were often piled up on the ramp of people who had suffocated in the train and been dragged off it. One day two children, a boy and a girl, got up out of the pile of corpses. They stood up, staggered a bit and began to wander aimlessly around among the bodies. They were calling for their mother. An SS man saw the children. He beckoned the girl over, smiling. As she approached he drew his pistol, she ducked but the SS man stepped over the bodies, grabbed her by the hair and shot her in the back of the neck. Then he killed the boy in the same way.

Once a fourteen-year-old Polish girl tried to get round the SS men. She went on her knees in front of them, trying to prove that she was strong enough to work. An SS man grabbed her and threw her onto the lorry that was carrying the victims away. Such was her fear that the girl jumped off the lorry and pleaded with them again. In vain. She was grabbed by the hair and flung on to the moving lorry. That was how they murdered children.

After the selection on the ramp, all those who were 'unfit for work' were loaded onto lorries and taken to the gas chambers. An ambulance car always drove along behind. However, there were no doctors in this vehicle – it carried the Zyklon B gas. When the convoy reached the chambers the SS helped the innocent victims, tried to reassure them, telling them to take care climbing out of the lorry. 'You are going into the washrooms to shower, then you will go into the camp and your luggage will be waiting there.' On the left of the showers was the women and children's changing room, on the right the men's. The victims entered the changing room, where they had to undress. On the walls were hooks numbered 1 to 1,000. The SS told the women to hang their clothes on the hook and to remember the number so that they could get their clothes when they came out, and to tie children's shoes together so that they would not get lost. When the women were in the showers the SS pushed the men in.

Meanwhile the ambulance had gone round the corner. An SS man – wearing a gas mask – climbed onto the flat roof of the gas chamber and opened a tin labelled Zyklon B and poured the contents down the chute. As soon as the purple crystals came into contact with the air the poisonous gas was released.

The air in the chamber was warm so that the cyanide gas could spread more easily from the shaft in the ceiling. This deadly gas worked slowly. It took five to ten minutes, and then all the victims were dead.

The poisoned air was sucked out by fans in ventilation ducts. Then the special *Kommando* went into action. Two hundred prisoners worked there day and night. The hair was cut of the corpses. It was made available to industry. One of the uses was to insulate and seal torpedo heads. Dentists and dental technicians were roped into the crematorium special *Kommando*: they had the task of removing gold teeth from the victims' mouths. These were melted down into gold bars. In the space of three years, six tonnes of gold from dental fillings were delivered to the Reichsbank in Berlin.[1]

Finally the corpses were taken to the crematorium. During the mass murders there was always an SS doctor in attendance. The four crematoria at KZ Birkenau were long buildings with chimneys. Crematorium II and III had five ovens with fifteen cremation chambers. Crematorium IV and V had one oven with nine cremation chambers – in all there were twelve ovens and forty-eight cremation chambers.

Cremation ovens in the crematorium at KZ Birkenau

---

1   *This dental gold was discovered in Switzerland in 1999. Even though Switzerland was neutral during the war it accepted the gold from the Nazis in exchange for supplies.*

Crematorium II in KZ Birkenau was 100 metres long and 50 metres wide. It contained five ovens with fifteen cremation chambers

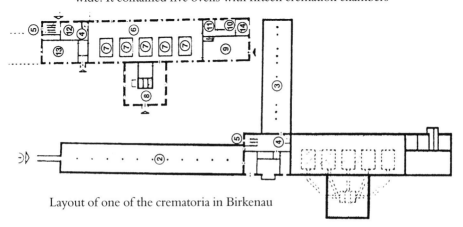

Layout of one of the crematoria in Birkenau

1 Steps to changing room **2** Changing room **3** Gas chamber • Concrete column • Gas shaft **4** Corpse lift **5** Slide for disposing of bodies **6** Crematorium **7** Ovens with three cremation chambers each **8** Chimney **9** Coke/fuel store **10** Toilet **11** *Kommando* leader's room **12** Execution chamber **13** Dental gold smelting (in Crematorium II, section room) **14** Accommodation for dental gold smelter in Crematorium III

The victims were killed with this gas. I.G. Farben delivered 19,000 kilogrammes of Zyklon B gas to Auschwitz in 1942/3

The SS doctor watched the gassing through this opening. He watched as 1,000 people suffocated in ten minutes

Cremation of the bodies took fifteen minutes. In twenty-four hours, 4,500 bodies were burned in forty-eight chambers. The ovens were on night and day. If there was not enough space the bodies were burnt in the open on huge bonfires.

Wedding rings of thousands of Jews who were gassed in Auschwitz

What was left of the murdered Jews – shoes

Reichsführer-SS Heinrich Himmler on his Inspection Visit to KZ Birkenau

The commander of KZ Auschwitz, SS-SBF Rudolf Höss wanted to demonstrate the death conveyor belt at its most efficient for the occasion of Himmler's visit, so he arranged a special deportation of 3,000 Polish Jews. When the 3,000 Polish Jews had been crowded into the gas chamber, waiting for water, an SS man climbed up on the roof, and poured the Zyklon B crystals down the shaft, where they turned into cyanide gas. The gas chamber was soundproof as well as airtight.

Himmler approached the door of the gas chamber, accompanied by Höss and other high-ranking SS officers. Höss invited him politely to look through the observation window. Himmler looked into the death chamber for a few minutes. He seemed satisfied with what he saw and laughed and joked good-humouredly with the officers. When the 3,000 men in the gas chamber were dead he showed a lively interest in the next stage of the proceedings.

The next day Himmler came back to the camp and watched expressionless as naked female prisoners were whipped for disobeying orders. In fact he personally had ordered an increase in punishment beatings for indiscipline on the part of prisoners. The beatings were administered to men and women on their bare buttocks. During this the prisoners were tied onto a wooden frame – the so-called 'buck'.

Reichsführer-SS Himmler. Inspecting the death factory KZ Birkenau

14

Women in Birkenau

IN BIRKENAU THE MOST WRETCHED creatures of all were the women, with their shaven heads and covered in dirty rags. They were cruelly tortured day in and day out by female SS wardens. They beat them for no reason. Often they would not even allow their fellow prisoners a drink of water to quench their thirst.

The women in the clear-up *Kommando* 'Canada' were quite different. They looked healthy and were unusually cleanly dressed. They had clean underwear every day: there was plenty of it available in the packages. Of course they dared not be caught taking it by the SS sentries in the clear-up *Kommando*. They found food too. But they were only a small number of women – 200 or 300 female prisoners in the clear-up *Kommando* – out of the 15,000 women in the camp. All the other women vegetated and starved in the dirt.

This was where my wife Gisela had ended up. I had been trying to find her for a long time, to get news of her, to send her a sign that I was alive. One day I recognised someone I knew, working amongst the women in the clear-up *Kommando*. It was Vali Kohn from Trenčín.

Gisela's sister, aged nineteen. She was sent to be gassed by an SS doctor during a selection

I tried to contact her. It was dangerous because contact between the sexes was forbidden, under threat of terrible punishment. However, I found an opportunity to take booty down to the women's sorting hut. When I thought the sentry wasn't watching I spoke to her and asked about Gisela. She told me that she had met my wife and even been talking to her.

This is what Vali Kohn told me: 'When Gisela arrived in Birkenau, she found her two sisters. Both of them were like skeletons, who could scarcely move and had lost the will to live; Gisela witnessed their cruel death and martyrdom. It had been very difficult to calm her. On top of that she had been assigned to the corpse *Kommando*. Every day ten women had to carry out the bodies of those who had died during the night. She suffered terribly, her strength dissipating, until one day she just could not work anymore. It was on a Sunday in December, she was rubbing her cheeks to give them a bit of colour, when an SS doctor pointed to her in a selection. That meant the gas chamber.' One week before Christmas, Gisela Burger was murdered – she was only twenty-two years old.

The women often looked death in the face. At first the SS only liquidated the sick. Later they proved their sadism at the selections. The lives of the captive women depended on a wave of the hand of Dr Mengele or the other SS doctors. The prisoners who were to be gassed were put on one side. Whoever was on the other side still had hope. On Sundays there were selections instead of rest. The women pinched their cheeks to look livelier and smiled in order to stay alive.

The women worked for ten hours a day in various *Kommandos* – road-building, demolition of houses and agricultural work. Their diet consisted of so-called

Women with shaven heads after 'delousing' in the 'sauna'

400 to 600 women 'lived' in a stable in the most terrible unhygienic conditions

The female SS wardens who tortured the women prisoners most cruelly day after day.
They were captured by the British at the liberation of Bergen–Belsen
(amongst them are some wardens from KZ Birkenau)

coffee in the morning, a litre of turnip soup at midday and in the evening 300 grams of bread and a little piece of sausage or margarine. On this inadequate diet their health deteriorated rapidly. Because of the filth in which they lived terrible epidemics broke out. Most of the women fell victim to spotted typhus.

Anyone who could not walk to work had to go to Block 25, the death block. There the 'assembly list' was drawn up for the gas chambers. All women unfit for work were sent to this block. During their last moments they suffered terribly here. They were beaten, kicked, given nothing to eat or drink. For quite a distance around the block, screams, crying and cries for help could be heard but no one dared to go near it.

15

The First Deportation from Slovakia – 1,000 Jewish Girls, 23 March 1942

Edith Goldmann née Rose
born 17 July 1924,
now living in Australia

Lea Holzberg née Lenke Gröschler
born 11 January 1919,
now living in Israel

EDIT ROSE-GOLDMANN AND LENKE GRÖSCHLER-HOLZBERG made the following statements after liberation:

'My name is Edit Rose-Goldmann and I was only eighteen years old when the disaster happened. I lived in Spišské Matašovice in the Stará Ves district of Slovakia. In March 1942 the HG assembled 1,000 Jewish girls in the Slovakian army barracks in Poprad. It was terrible to be separated from home, not knowing what was happening, or what the future held.

'I am not very tough, but luckily I met Lenke in the barracks and she was older and much braver than me and stood by me in moments of despair.'

'Yes, it was really hard,' said Lea Holzberg (née Gröschler). 'I was twenty-two years old then, four years older than Edit, but I was not as brave as I seemed. I was terrified, like all the others, but I did not show my feelings. In the three terrible days after we were captured, I remember talking constantly about what they might do to us.

'On 23 March 1942 – the date is burned into my memory – we were herded to Poprad railway station. There were cattle trucks drawn up ready. The HG militia drove us into the trucks, beating us like animals. Edit and I stayed together, we were inseparable. There were about fifty to sixty girls squeezed into each truck, we could scarcely move or breathe.

'After travelling for one day and two nights non-stop the train came to a halt late in the morning of 25 March 1942. When the doors were opened we saw no Slovakian HG men, only armed SS guards. We had reached our destination, the ramp at Auschwitz.'

Her voice faltered as she swallowed her tears. You could see that the memory still affected her after fifty years. Edit continued her statement:

'On the ramp we were lined up five abreast. I stubbornly held on to Lenke. She was my only security. Then came the order to march off, escorted by SS on both sides. We marched along like that for one and a half kilometres, till we saw a big gate with *Arbeit macht frei* over it and behind it buildings that looked like a barracks. It was all surrounded by a barbed-wire fence about two and half metres high. We went through the gate into the concentration camp and were driven to a building that was a delousing station and washroom for the deportees. Everything went according to their perfect plan.

'They took our luggage from us and gave us numbers. I was given number 1371. We had to put on trousers and blouses of murdered Soviet prisoners without any underwear. On our feet we wore wooden clogs and no socks. We could not keep even the tiniest item of personal belongings.

'We were woken at 4.30 a.m. by a roar and at 5 a.m. everyone got a half-litre of "tea". It was more hot water than tea. Then we were herded into the yard where we had to stand until 7 a.m., thinly dressed, our shaven heads bare. We were waiting for the so-called roll call, the head count and torture of prisoners. In these hopeless moments I would think about my family and wondered whether we would ever see each other again. I used to think of Lenke too and hoped she was still alive.

'We were frozen and lived without the slightest hope, and the only thing left was our lives and now we would have to constantly put up a fight in order to stay alive. The separation from Lenke was another source of distress because she was in another block and had been assigned to a different *Kommando*. I saw her from time to time all right but in the end I lost sight of her completely. Our fate had separated us.

'In spite of all this misfortune it was not too bad for me. I had been allocated to a *Kommando* building a farm. As soon as the farm was up and running I was one of ten girls who continually worked there. It was a matter of surviving the tough regime in the camp.'

'I was still alive,' chipped in Lenke. 'In September 1942 I was moved to KZ Birkenau. There I lived in terrible conditions in a stone building, with 400 other girls. We had to do heavy work in a quarry and demolish houses. I lost a lot of weight and soon weighed only 40 kilogrammes and got typhoid fever. What saved me was being put in a *Kommando* working in potato fields, where Polish civilians

Prisoners lived here in terrible conditions – 400 girls to a hut

worked too, who secretly gave us bread when the SS guards were not looking. So we got some additional food that helped us in the struggle for survival. Every four to six weeks we had to line up for selection. This sadistic method of selecting prisoners who were to be killed was the most terrible aspect of KZ Birkenau. Thousands of Jewish prisoners, women and girls, had to line up naked and the SS doctors would send those weakened by starvation and hard labour to the gas chambers. The martyrdom lasted until the end of 1944 then the murder machine was stopped and there were no more gassings after that.

'In January 1945 the Nazis began to liquidate KZ Birkenau. I was put in an evacuation column and we were force-marched for three days and nights. Many girls did not survive this torture and exertion; anyone who stopped marching was shot. When we reached the station we were driven into cattle trucks and taken to KZ Ravensbrück in the freezing cold.

'Then we were evacuated again and the journey ended in Neustadt, near Hamburg. There the Wehrmacht took over. By that time we knew that liberation was only a question of time. On 2 May 1945 finally the day came when we were liberated by the Americans.

'I went back home to Poprad and searched for my family in vain. Not one of my entire family came back from Auschwitz. Then I went to Israel.'

Edit said the same as Lenke: 'I will never forget what fear of death meant. I tried to help someone and it nearly cost me my life. Once I was sent into Birkenau camp to collect provisions. A Polish prisoner, Wanda Jakubovska, a registrar in the sick bay in Birkenau, asked me to take a letter for a Polish girl who was working with me. This was forbidden, but I wanted to help Wanda. When I was searched at the entrance gate to the camp, the SS guard found the letter. I was brought straight to the office of the female registrar, Drechsler, and was interrogated in the presence of Mandel, the female camp commander. First they wanted to know who had given me the letter. Of course I knew I could not betray Wanda. I maintained that I did not know I was doing anything that was forbidden. I said I did not know the prisoner because it was the first time I had fetched provisions and had only taken the letter out of kindness. I suggested the name might be in the letter. I don't know whether they believed me or not, but they let me go. I got nothing to eat that day.

'Next day I was taken to the camp commander SS-SBF Schwarzhuber. When I repeated my statement, he hit me on the side of the head and shouted, "Clear off, you bitch." As a punishment I was put in a penal *Kommando* where the treatment was the equivalent of a slow death by torture. We worked all day, up to our knees in ice-cold water. Many girls died each day. I got a fever too. Wanda Jakubovska saved my life, by bringing me medicine, and she helped me get out of the penal *Kommando*. Anyway, after that I was taken to the infamous bunker in Block 11 where the *Kapo* Jakob was in charge. He led those who were condemned to death to the black wall where the SS shot them. My luck lasted and I escaped that too.

'In January 1945 the evacuation began for me and thousands of other prisoners, the death march from Auschwitz–Birkenau! We were hungry and had to keep up a pace of 40 kilometres a day in hard frost, dressed in thin clothes. Anyone who could not keep up and fell was immediately shot by the SS.

'In Leslau we were accommodated in a barn with other prisoners. There I met my friend, Melania Hertz. She told me, "I was deported to Auschwitz on 2 April 1942 in the third transport from Slovakia. I was twenty-two years old then. The number 3684 was tattooed on my left forearm. Then I vegetated for three years in KZ Birkenau."

'I hardly recognised her and was happy that she was sitting beside me. We were looking forward to liberation. The next day we were transported in open wagons to KZ Mauthausen. From there all the women were taken in lorries to Lenzing, where we were put up in a disused factory. It was here we celebrated liberation by the Americans on 5 May 1945, the day we had longed for.'

My twenty-two-year-old sister Isabella was supposed to have been deported to Auschwitz on the first transport from Slovakia to work in forced labour in Germany. She escaped this fate by a miracle. When my mother received the notice from the HG militia on 20 March 1942, saying that her daughter Isabella was to report the following day for work abroad in Germany, she showed the letter to her neighbour, Mr Šeliga. When he saw it, he was horrified and said: 'Your daughter has to disappear today. Since she is the same age as my daughter,

I will give you her ID papers, so that Isabella can get away across the border into Hungary.' The extraordinarily humane action of this Slovakian saved my sister's life and spared her the dreadful experiences Edit endured.

Isabella succeeded in illegally crossing the border into Hungary. She lived there, using Šeliga's identity papers until 1944. Then she had to flee again. She reached Romania and from there made her way to Palestine, where she still lives in the Kfar Masaryk Kibbutz.

Jafa Krausz née Isabella Burger,
born 18 January 1920.
Photo from 1942

Melania Schein née Hertz,
born 11 July 1920.
Photo from 1941

16

Bunker – Block 11

ANYONE WHO TRIED TO ESCAPE, obtain food, break the rules or attempted to speak to any of the women working nearby was taken to the political department, the bunker under Block 11.

Sometimes it happened that a prisoner would recognise his wife or daughter and could not resist speaking to them. Anyone who was caught so doing, or caught escaping or planning an escape would be taken to the bunker.

This was an underground concrete cell where the prisoner had to lie or sit on the damp floor. Because the cold, damp concrete ceiling was only one metre high, you could not stand upright. The food in this hole was water and a small piece of bread. There were no blankets, not even in the worst frost. This is where Edit Rose, prisoner number 1371, spent the worst hours of her life – here you waited for death.

This cell was only slightly better than the one for serious offenders, where the dimensions only permitted the prisoner to stand, not sit or lie at all. Prisoners were taken from these cells for interrogation. In the office where the interviews

Entrance to the standing cell in Block 11.
It measured 90 cm by 90 cm and was 1 metre high

took place, the accused had to sit on a special chair to which the torturers tied his hands and feet. The chair was in the form of a swing. As it swung, two SS men hit the prisoner who was to be interrogated from the front and from behind till his strength gave way. From time to time the prisoner was asked if he would confess to the charges. Whether he confessed or not the punishment continued; no prisoner left the political department without receiving a beating.

There were two main punishments: work in a penal *Kommando* and execution. The prisoners in the penal *Kommando* had to work so hard that they collapsed dead in three weeks. If a prisoner was condemned to death, the *Kapo* led him, naked from the waist up to the so-called 'black wall'. There he was made to face the wall and an SS man shot him in the back of the neck. Sometimes there were mass executions – then sub-machine guns were used.

About 20,000 prisoners were executed at the so-called 'black wall' beside Block 11

17

General Selection

THE MEN'S AND WOMEN'S CAMP was divided into nine sections, and each SS doctor had his own section. The doctors were: Josef Mengele, Fritz Klein, Johann Paul Kremmer, Karl Endress, Heinz Thilo, Professor Carl Clauberg and three other doctors.

Every four to six weeks, on a Sunday, all the Jewish prisoners in Birkenau had to line up five abreast, naked, accompanied by the block-wardens and registrars for the SS doctors to walk up and down as if inspecting a military parade. They would point a finger now and again at someone and the registrar would write down the prisoner's number. This selection meant they were unfit for work even though many of them were still fit. Thus were they condemned to death; they were gassed the next day.

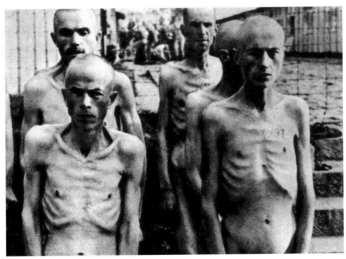

Waiting for selection

I wanted to survive at all costs. I kept looking for a way out. One day it occurred to me that my stepfather might be able to help me because he was not a Jew. That evening I said to Miki Šteiner, my best friend, 'Miki, I am going to the political department and tell them that I am not Jewish and that I can prove it if they allow me to write to my mother in Poprad.' In Birkenau Jews were forbidden to write letters according to the Nacht und Nebel laws. 'My mother will understand what lies behind this letter and persuade her husband to claim me as his illegitimate son. That would mean I would be classified as "mixed race".' Miki answered, horrified: 'Are you mad? Anyone who goes to the political department voluntarily never comes back.'

But I had made up my mind and went. Two SS officers there asked me what I wanted. I told them that I had to wear the Star of David on my prison clothes, even though I was not Jewish. The SS men looked at me amazed and asked me how I could prove it. I said my parents could send on the Aryan certificate if I could write a letter asking for it. They gave me the usual KZ letterhead and I wrote to my mother.

After about six weeks I was called back to the political department and was told by the SS men: 'According to this document you are of mixed race. You need not wear the Jewish star. We will give the instructions.'

After a few days I actually got a new badge to wear on my prison clothes, the red triangle with 'S' printed on it, which reclassified me as a Slovakian political prisoner. So I had achieved my aim. I no longer had to line up for the much-feared selections. It was another positive step in my struggle to survive.

Adolf Burger's record card from KZ Mauthausen.
He was categorised as mixed race – see upper right

18

Theresienstadt Ghetto

The fortress at Theresienstadt – thousands of prisoners were murdered here by the SS

THERE WAS A RAY OF hope for prisoners in Birkenau in September 1943. A transport of 5,000 Czech Jews arrived from the ghetto in Theresienstadt – and there was no selection. The new arrivals were accommodated in KZ Birkenau section B.II.b, which had been transformed into a family camp. The news that there had been no selection spread like lightning. But the hope that the murder would end lasted only a few hours, because Dr Mengele sent the majority of a transport from France, which arrived the following day, straight to the gas chambers.

Three months later another transport of 5,000 people arrived from Theresienstadt and they were also taken to the family camp. Why? Why were they spared?

The Nazis were expecting an international commission and were intent on showing off good camp conditions, so entire families from Theresienstadt were lodged in the family camp. The SS men convinced them that nothing would happen to them there. There were even schools for the children. But the inspection commission never came.

In fact, on 11 May 1944 Himmler had given permission for representatives of the International Red Cross to visit the ghetto in Theresienstadt and another labour camp. The preparations had already started in Theresienstadt in February 1944. They wanted to demonstrate a model labour camp, so a place of worship, a cinema, a music pavilion and a park were built.

After all this careful preparation the visit of the International Red Cross team took place on 23 June. The inspection was satisfactory to both parties and the Nazis succeeded in convincing the commission that things were exactly the same in the other work camps and that further inspections would not be necessary.

However, the prisoners in the family camp in Birkenau did not know about this. On 5 March 1944 the prisoners in the family camp who had come on the transport of September 1943 were ordered to write to their families or to friends. The letters were to be post-dated 23 March 1944 as the post had to go through Berlin. The camp commander Schwarzhuber went into the family camp and told the inmates that some of them were to be sent with their relatives to Heydebreck to work.

On 7 March 1944 the 3,793 who were still alive out of the 5,007 people from the Theresienstadt transport of September 1943, were moved to the quarantine camp B.II.a. The people from the December 1943 transport stayed behind in the family camp.

First the September group had to go into the 'sauna' and be disinfected, which was the usual practice when prisoners were being moved to another camp. This must have reinforced their belief that they really were being moved to Heydebreck.

On 8 March the prisoners lined up as usual for the head count. Nothing indicated the horror that was to come that night. But suddenly at 7.30 p.m. the order 'Return to huts,' came over the loudspeakers. This order applied to the entire complex. The block-wardens made sure that none of the 10,000 prisoners were allowed to leave the huts.

Shortly after that a convoy of lorries drove into the quarantine camp, escorted by armed SS units with dogs.

It was terrible because the families knew where they were being taken. Anyone who arrived by train and went straight from the ramp to the gas chambers believed that they would be allowed to shower before going to the camp. But the men, women and children of section B.II.b knew exactly what was going to happen to them. The SS thugs and murderers drove them out of their huts, beating them with sticks and set the dogs on them. Their screams could be heard in the neighbouring camps and far into the countryside. Finally the lorries drove off.

It was already dark when the heavy lorries drove through the entrance gate to the crematorium. The prisoners found out where they were as the lorries screeched to a halt. The SS men let down the tailgates and started wildly beating the prisoners out. More than fifty SS men formed a corridor along which they chased them. They paid no heed to the old, or the sick, or children, but beat and chased them all. The faint hope that the family camp was protected by the International Red Cross faded into thin air.

The SS did not bother with the usual performance on the ramp when Dr Mengele carried out a selection and people were taken to 'wash' before being led calmly to the courtyard of the crematorium. Anyone in the family camp who had watched the smoke rising from the chimneys of the crematoria day and night for six months was not going to be fooled by this performance. That is why these Czech Jews were treated with such brutality on their last journey. It was not long before the first 600 from the first convoy were down in the underground chamber where they had to undress under the glare of floodlights. They were to wait there for the next group. The SS paid no attention to them; they had them where they wanted them. There was no way out of this room.

Schwarzhuber and Dr Mengele appeared in the doorway. They stood looking at the prisoners without pity and seemed pleased with the process so far. When they came in there was quiet for a while then everyone shouted, 'Let us live, let us work.' They still hoped to be saved. Suddenly the men streamed towards the door. Schwarzhuber had said they were going to Heydebreck to work, hadn't he? They intended to remind him. Then shots rang out. The SS men – Buntrock, Kurtschuss, Georges and others who were standing near Schwarzhuber – opened fire on the orders of USF Berger.

The prisoners were ordered to undress and they knew their last hour had come. The weeping and screaming mingled with the orders to undress. The prisoners would not take their clothes off so they were pushed into the gas chamber fully dressed. Suddenly a voice sang out – it grew stronger and others joined in. The Czech national anthem, 'Kde domov můj', rose from the choir. Then they sang the 'Hatikvah', which is now the national anthem of Israel. Singing was their last protest.

The Zyklon B was shaken through the shafts and began to work. The singing turned to screams, the prisoners pounded the doors with their fists, began to cough and the coughing faded into groans in a few minutes. Ten minutes after the crystals were shaken into the shaft there was deadly silence.

Nothing could be heard through the thick walls of the crematoria but prisoners who worked in the special *Kommando* told us how 3,793 Jews from Theresienstadt were murdered in Crematorium II and III in Birkenau on the night of 8/9 March 1944.

Before the special *Kommando* opened the door of the chamber the SS men left Crematorium II and went over to Crematorium III where the remaining groups from Czechoslovakia were driven in to the gas chamber. Evidently the 5,000 Jewish prisoners from the transport of December 1943 left living in the family camp would be enough to satisfy the International Red Cross delegation. Between September 1943 and May 1944 17,517 prisoners from the Theresienstadt ghetto were deported to Auschwitz. Only 1,167 of them survived to be liberated.

On 10 July 1943 special parcel stamps were given out in Theresienstadt. There were four small stamps on a sheet. No parcels were given out in the camp without one

On 1 January 1943 receipts were issued in Theresienstadt for 1, 2, 5, 10, 20, 50 and 100 Crowns. Prisoners from German-occupied European countries had to exchange their money for these receipts

19

Paraguay

GOVERNMENT DEPARTMENTS AND THE SS vied with each other to plunder the belongings of their victims. The Security Ministry of the Reich (Reichssicherheitshauptamt – RSHA) had drawn up a particularly treacherous plan. Eichmann had organised the apparent resettlement of Jews to Paraguay. Enormous sums in money and jewellery had to be paid for a valid passport. But a transport of 1,000 of these settlers bound for Paraguay ended up on the ramp in Auschwitz. The preparations had taken much longer than usual. The ovens of Crematorium II were lit in the morning. In contrast to his usual routine, Voss and his SS entourage paid a visit to the prisoners in the special *Kommando* in the crematorium to check that everything was in order. The concrete floor in the gas chamber, which was usually wet, had been carefully dried. Some sort of perfume had been sprayed in all the gas chambers to disperse the mouldy smell that pervaded them. Everyone was to get the impression that they were in normal showers. Signs were put up saying, 'Entrance to bath and disinfection area'.

A convoy of lorries drew up in front of the crematorium. The SS escorts jumped off the running boards and ran round to let down the tailgates. Then they invited people to get out in a manner that had never been seen in the camp before. They helped when necessary. Within a short time the 1,000 new arrivals were standing in the yard, looking round curiously. The camp leader Schwarzhuber stood up on a wooden box and welcomed them very politely and explained that it was his job to prepare them for emigration via Switzerland. A representative of the Ministry of Foreign Affairs would explain in greater detail. Then a civilian in Gestapo uniform spoke. This was none other than SS-OSF Hösler, who proceeded equally graciously and in great detail to explain that the Swiss authorities required all deportees to be disinfected and carry a certificate to that effect. This would now be done and then they would go straight to the border.

The speech and the good treatment by the SS reassured the people so that at first many went willingly into the changing rooms on the ground floor. To make the deception of the changing rooms and disinfection more convincing prisoners from the special *Kommando* were standing around the walls with signs in large print, while the man from the Ministry urged people to note the letter of the alphabet so that they would return to that position after disinfection. Some began to undress quite calmly and were led into the gas chamber without realising what was happening. But not all were fooled. The situation grew more and more tense.

Many hesitated, refusing to get undressed. Their nervousness affected the polite, well-behaved SS men. Some of them took out their truncheons and started to flail about them, hitting everyone in sight as usual. Now everyone realised it was a trap. They drew back, horrified, and the SS men, including the sadists SS-OSF Quackernack and Schillinger, strode up and down in front of the humiliated people.

A strikingly beautiful woman with jet-black hair attracted the attention of the SS men. She threw them coquettish glances, and with a winsome smile pulled up her skirt to show her suspenders. The two SS men paid no attention to anything else. Their eyes were fixed on the woman, who was taking off her blouse and stood there in her bra. Then she took off her shoe and with a swift blow, hit Quackernack full on the forehead with the heel. He instinctively covered his face with both hands, she dived on him and took his pistol – there was one shot – Schillinger cried out and sank to the floor. A second shot aimed at Quackernack missed, even though he was only a few feet away. There was chaos in the changing room. The young woman with the gun vanished into the crowd but she might turn up anywhere and start shooting again; the SS men fled in panic. At first no one saw to the wounded Schillinger. As a few SS men tried to drag him towards the door a third shot rang out and one of them was hit. Then the lights went out and panic increased. The prisoners from the special *Kommando* pushed their way to the door to get out at the first opportunity. Nevertheless there was time to talk to some of the new arrivals, which was how they found out that the SS had tricked these people, who had paid enormous amounts of gold or jewellery in order to emigrate to Paraguay via Switzerland.

When the special *Kommando* prisoners opened the doors to the changing room on Voss' orders and squeezed out first, they saw two mounted machine guns, which fired into the changing room in a horrendous bloodbath. The few who had succeeded in sheltering behind the concrete pillars were later taken to another room and shot. Meanwhile the 'disinfection mechanism' started to spray out the deadly Zyklon B gas into the gas chamber, where the people who really believed they were only going to be disinfected, had gone. The SS doctor on duty that night was SS-OSF Heinz Thilo.

All promises and pretence of emigration to Paraguay were nothing but shams in which Eichmann, the police, RSHA, the Ministry of Foreign Affairs and the government of the Reich were involved.

The next morning word spread that Schillinger had died on the way to hospital and that another SS man, USF Emmerich, had actually been wounded. The prisoners greeted the news of Schillinger's killing with rejoicing because he had been one of the most brutal of the SS men. The body of the woman who had shot him – she had been a dancer – was laid out on the dissecting table in Crematorium II and the SS men had to file past her as a warning to them of the consequences of a few minutes' carelessness.

20

The Gypsy Camp in KZ Birkenau

One of the few survivors – Antonia Donga,
with her tattooed prisoner number, Z-32557, KZ Birkenau

Berlin, 29 January 1943

RSHA (Reich Security Department)
V A 2 No.59/43g
Express Letter
[. . .]
Re: Deportation of mixed-race Gypsies, Roma-Gypsies and members of Gypsy families
of non-German descent and of Balkan origin to a concentration camp.
I. By order of the Reichsführer of 16.12.1942 . . . the above groups are to be selected
according to certain guidelines and to be deported to a concentration camp within a few
weeks.
These people will be categorised as 'Gypsy persons' and will be transferred to KZ
Auschwitz/Gypsy camp regardless of degree of mixed race.

APART FROM THE JEWS, GENOCIDE was also perpetrated on the Gypsies (Sinti
and Roma). Since 1936 they had been deported to the camp in Marzahn, Berlin.
The RKP (from December 1939, Section V of the RSHA) was responsible for
the persecution of the Gypsies. In December 1938 Himmler had ordered 'the
solution of the Gypsy question to be taken in hand'. From May 1940 Gypsies
were deported from all Reich territory. In the spring of 1942 the systematic
deportation of Gypsies from all German-occupied European countries began.
Especially in Poland and the Soviet Union, deported and native Gypsies were
killed by special units or in extermination camps. Five thousand Gypsies were
killed in Kulmkof (Chelmo) extermination camp in gas vehicles.

On 29 January 1943 the RSHA instructions went out to carry out Himmler's
'Auschwitz Order' of 16 December 1942: mixed-race Gypsies, Roma Gypsies and

Balkan Gypsies were to be sent to KZ Auschwitz. Gypsies from all over Europe were put in a 'Gypsy camp' in Auschwitz. Their fate was sealed: this was their final destination. Without selection on the ramp they were put into the Gypsy family camp B.II.e, in wooden stable blocks.

Lucie Adelsberger, a doctor from Berlin, arrived with a transport on 19 May 1943. From 21 May she worked as a doctor in the Gypsy camp. She described the terrible conditions there, where people just stagnated. Her day began at 4 a.m. The hospital block was exactly like the other huts: a former stable, without windows, only dimly lit by narrow strips of glass under the eaves. Cold winds and heat passed through the gaps in the planks and rain streamed in through the holes in the badly tarred roof, soaking the clay floor and the patients. Three-storey wooden bunks ran along the side walls, where 800 to 1,000 patients lay huddled together on thin straw mattresses with ragged blankets. Two wooden tables and a long stove completed the furnishings. The stove constituted a broad brick ledge and two holes for stoking it.

Doctors and clerks sat on the brick seat that ran along the hot stovepipe, neatly filling out patients' charts. Any patients who could crawl out of bed, dressed only in short shirts or wrapped in ragged blankets, could sit there too. New arrivals from the camp were deposited there, unwashed, in their dirty, vermin-ridden clothes. The sick were examined on the stove because there was no couch. The cauldrons of soup were placed there for distribution and bread was cut on the unwashed brick ledge. Everything was done on the stove – people crawled under it to get to the other side of the hut, 'meals' were cooked and eaten, abscesses lanced and wounds treated. It was used for 'washing' in the yellowish, rusty, contaminated water that stained everything. People slept on it more comfortably than in the overcrowded bunks.

There was perhaps an average of 900 people in the hut at any time. Emaciated bodies, with raging temperatures, lay pressed together in their bunks; on top of, under and beside each other, ten to a space designed for three or at most four. On the top tier, where the more mobile patients lay, it was possibly more bearable, except that the rain soaked through the blankets and straw mattresses and dripped down onto the middle bunks, so that they were never dry. Lower down, where the seriously ill patients could no longer crawl out to the toilet or even sit up, was a morass of filthy blankets soaked in urine. People in their death throes tossed and turned among dead bodies, emitting terrible groans and cries that sounded like animals dying in a primeval forest.

There was not much time to treat patients. Medicines were scarce: two ampoules of camphor and a bottle of infusion of digitalis constituted a week's supply. Only bolus alba was plentiful, stored in giant sacks. It was a white powder, an all-purpose remedy administered internally for diarrhoea, for stomatitis it was sprinkled around the mouth, and for skin complaints affected areas were powdered with it. It was even used as whitewash on the walls and bunks, so that they gleamed in all this misery.

All the doctors could do was comfort the patients, who were either emaciated skeletons or bloated due to starvation and delirious. They did not improve but continued to die like flies. Amongst the groans of the sick and the plaintive 'Yaaah' of the dying came the voices of Gypsies calling out 'Mulo, Mulo' – 'Someone dead.' There was nothing but death, prisoners were dying at the rate of twenty or thirty a day in each hut, in all the blocks.

The children's block was much like the adult one. The suffering of these little ones went to your heart, maybe because their faces had lost all childlike features and their hollow eyes stared out of aged faces. Like the adults, the children were all skin and bone, no fat; their skin, thin as parchment, was stretched over the hard-pointed bones and opened in festering sores. Their undernourished bodies were covered in scratches from head to toe and were exhausted. Many suffered from Noma ulcers round the mouth, which ate into their jaws like cancer, leaving holes. These children continued to eat and drink, some of them got better and seemed to recover. Those who could not move swelled up into shapeless lumps. Diarrhoea, lasting for weeks, dissolved their bodies, which no longer had any resistance, until nothing remained.

At night the children could not sleep for hunger, thirst, cold and pain. Their moans and cries were unbearably loud and echoed around the hut till they would fade away in exhaustion and start up again after a short pause. Night after night the sound of the crying rose and fell in endless torment. If those responsible could have experienced three nights of the children's block, where Lucie Adelsberger and the other doctors slept, or if they had been present in the morning when the children were being washed, to see them pulled from their beds in the filthy blankets, off the rotting straw mattresses that were crawling with maggots, to see them lying on the clay floor or on the cold ledge of the stove and be washed together and all put back to bed, the wet, sick children in the damp blankets, they would surely have taken pity on them.

On the night of 31 July 1944 the SS announced 'Seal blocks', which meant everyone had to stay in. Hours pass until it is dark. Then trucks drive up. By the reflection of the searchlight on the wall, they all know it has stopped at their hut. The engine is switched off, the doors are thrown open. The SS appear. Names and numbers are called out. Forearms of patients and carers are checked by blinding torchlight. They scarcely dare to breathe or turn their heads. Who is next? When will their number be called? Will it be half an hour or a few minutes or seconds until the door is shut again and the truck drives off? They do not know.

The next morning, 1 August 1944, the Gypsy camp that had held 3,500 to 4,000 people the day before was empty and silent, in contrast to the usual babble. A woman who had hidden and was discovered later was brought before the camp commander. Two children, aged three and five, who had slept through it all, wrapped in their blankets, came out of the orphans' block, hand in hand, crying because they had been abandoned. They too were taken to the gas chamber.

Account of the Survivor Elisabeth Guttenberger

I was born in 1926 into a family of four children, long settled in Stuttgart. We lived in a very nice leafy part of town with lovely gardens and parks. My father dealt in antiques and stringed instruments. We lived peacefully alongside our neighbours and did not experience any discrimination. Everyone was kind to us. When I think back on this time I have to say that it was the best time of my life.

My teacher was opposed to the Hitler regime . . . Thanks to her; I finished primary school at eighth grade, which enabled me to do clerical work in Auschwitz, otherwise I would not have survived . . .

We were arrested in March 1943 in a large family group. The police came at six o'clock in the morning and loaded us onto lorries. I was just seventeen years old then. I was deported to Auschwitz together with my parents, four brothers and sisters, a three-year-old niece, my eighty-year-old grandmother and many other relatives. My other grandmother was also deported with her daughter and nine grandchildren . . .

While we were being deported our train stopped for some reason. Another train came from the opposite direction and stopped exactly beside ours, so close that we could see the driver's face. My cousin asked him, 'Tell us, where is Auschwitz, what is it?' I will never forget the expression in the driver's eyes. He stared at us and did not say a word. Because he was one of the people who had to drive the deportation trains, he could not say anything, just looked through us. I only realised in Auschwitz why this man could not give us an answer – it was as if he had turned to stone.

Our first impression of Auschwitz was terrible. It was dark when we arrived, but we could only see the lights in a vast area. We had to spend the first night on the floor of a big hall. Early in the morning we had to march into the camp. There we had our numbers tattooed on our arms and our hair was cut off. Our clothes, shoes and the few things we had brought with us were taken away.

The Gypsy camp was in the Birkenau camp between the men's camp and the prisoners' hospital building. There were thirty stables that were called blocks. Kitchens, sick bays and washrooms were in an extension. There was only one toilet block for the entire camp. More than 20,000 'Gypsies' were accommodated in the other blocks. The huts had no windows, only air vents. There was a clay floor. In a hut for 200 people there were often 600 and more. This overcrowding was martyrdom in itself.

My aunt was walking beside me. We looked at each other and began to cry. It was a terrible sight. People sat motionless in the stalls, staring at us. I thought I was dreaming I was in hell.

After about a fortnight we were assigned to labour gangs. I was assigned to a building *Kommando* with many other women and had to carry heavy stones. The men had to build the road to the camp, even old men, whether they were sick or not. It did not matter, they were roped in. My father was sixty-one at that time and they did not take that into account, or anything else for that matter. Auschwitz was an extermination camp.

Birkenau camp was not yet finished then. The hunger was the worst. Sanitary conditions were indescribable. There was scarcely any soap or washing facilities. When typhoid fever broke out, the sick could not be treated because there was no medicine. It was sheer hell. It could not have been any worse . . .

First to die were the children. Any who were born there died within a few days of birth. Day and night they cried for bread. They starved quite quickly. The SS were only concerned that the newborn were tattooed with a number according to regulations. There was no nursing care, no milk and no hot water, not to mention powder or nappies. The bigger children had to carry stones for the road on those rations and were dying of starvation.

Then there was SS brutality. They beat people to death every day. In our *Kommando* we had to do everything at the double. An SS block-leader would ride along beside us on a bike. If a woman fell because she was faint, he would beat her with a stick. Many died of this ill treatment. The block-leader was called Konig . . .

After about six months I got into the prison office. There I had to set up a card index of the deportations and keep records in the big register of the men in our camp. Every day I had to enter the names of those who had died. The names were brought to the office from the sick bay.

I entered thousands of names into that book. I had just been working in the office for a week when a death notice came in with my father's name on it. I seemed to be paralysed and wept. Just then the door flew open. OSF Plagge stormed in and shouted: 'What is she bawling about in the corner?' I could not answer but my friend, the registrar Hilly Weiss, said, 'Her father is dead.' The SS man answered, 'We all have to die sometime,' and walked out . . .

The Sinti defended themselves against the 'liquidation' of the camp. That was a tragic story. Our Sintis made knives out of tin. They also fought with sticks and defended themselves to the last. I know an eyewitness of the dissolution of the camp – later she told me through her tears about how the Sinti had fought with such despair because they knew they were to be gassed. And then the rebellion was put down with machine guns . . .

The camp doctor in the Gypsy camp was called Dr Mengele. He was one of the most feared doctors in Auschwitz. As well as all his other crimes he did experiments on cripples and twins. My cousins, who were twins, were his guinea pigs. After he had taken various measurements and given them injections, they were gassed. When the last Sinti and Roma were sent to the gas chambers in the final batch, they gassed the twins. Their bodies were dissected on Mengele's orders before they were burned. He wanted to see how identical their internal organs were.

In 1944 2,000 people fit for work were deported again. The remainder, only about 3,500, were the old and weak and children and others who could not do heavy work. They were gassed on 2 August. Of 30,000 Sinti and Roma Gypsies who were deported to Auschwitz, only about 3,000 survived. I found this out through my work in the office.

I myself lost about thirty relations in Auschwitz. Both my grandmothers, and an aunt who had ten children, two of whom survived. Another aunt with five children did not survive. Another aunt was gassed at the end. My father literally starved to death in the first few months. My eldest sister caught typhoid and died of it in November 1943. Of course it was due to starvation and malnourishment too. Then my youngest brother died. He was thirteen and had to carry heavy stones, until he was like a skeleton. My mother died a few months later. They all starved.

There is nothing to compare with Auschwitz. If you said: 'The hell that was Auschwitz', that is no exaggeration . . .

Extract from the Memoirs of Rudolf Höss

. . . I can no longer remember the number of Gypsies and mixed-race Gypsies who were in Auschwitz. Their section of the camp was designed to hold 10,000 and it was full. In general, conditions in Birkenau were suitable for anything but a family camp. There was no adequate provision of any sort, considering that the Gypsies were to be held there for the duration of the war. It was even impossible to feed the children. I secured a supply of food for the young children by wangling, quoting the orders of Reichsführer (Himmler), but this aid ceased when the Ministry of Food refused all supplies of baby food for concentration camps.

Himmler visited the camp in July 1942. I conducted him on a thorough tour of inspection of the overcrowded huts, the inadequate sanitary conditions and the packed sick bays. He saw everything exactly as it was; the patients suffering from contagious diseases and the emaciated children with Noma ulcers, which made me shudder, as they reminded me of lepers I had once seen in Palestine, wasting away, with big holes in their cheeks that you could see through. They were decaying alive. He heard the mortality rates, which were still quite low compared to the overall rate in the camp. I do not think that any newborn infants survived the first week. When he heard these child mortality figures, which were extraordinarily high, he gave orders to exterminate them like the Jews, after selecting those fit for work. I pointed out that the Gypsies were not the category of people for which Auschwitz was designed. Then he gave orders that the criminal police were to carry out more detailed scrutiny as quickly as possible. It took two years to reselect them. Gypsies who were fit for work were transferred to other camps. By August 1944 there were about 4,000 Gypsies left, who had to be gassed. Up to this point they did not know what was ahead of them and only realised it as they were marched hut by hut to the crematorium. It was not easy to get them into the gas chambers . . .

21

Extermination of 450,000 Hungarian Jews

THE RED ARMY WAS ONLY a few hundred kilometres away from Auschwitz and getting nearer every day. In Birkenau they were working feverishly. A few hundred prisoners moved the railway tracks close to Crematoria II and III. They built a new platform so that the transports would go straight to the place of extermination. The crematoria were carefully prepared. Civilian workers from nearby factories were brought in. A former farmhouse, which was separated from the camp by a little wood, was converted to 'Bunker V'. New living quarters were built and the clear-up *Kommando* Canada was increased to nearly 1,000 prisoners. These works at the beginning of May 1944 were supervised personally by SS-HSF Moll himself. He was to direct the extermination of the Hungarian Jews.

Moll was an incredibly brutal, cynical man of exceptional organisational ability and energy. As soon as he was put in charge he redeployed a series of lower-rank SS officers. USF Steinberg was put in charge of crematoria II and III and below him OSF Muhsfeldt; RF Holländer and Eidenmüller were below him. The newly converted Bunker V was under the command of USF Eckardt, who was Hungarian and therefore spoke the language perfectly. The commanders of Crematoria IV and V were strengthened by USF Seitz and later by SF Busch.

The largest number of prisoners was to dig trenches behind Crematorium V so that bodies could be burned near the three gas chambers. This was the most

From May 1944 the railway tracks led straight to the crematoria

strenuous work. They had to keep digging the heavy earth out of the trenches without a break, with SS men roaring and *Kapos* harassing them. The earth was loaded on to wheelbarrows and taken away at the double. The deeper the trenches, the harder the work. It took a few days to finish the trenches, which were forty to fifty metres long, eight metres wide and two metres deep. Moll had thought up a few more gruesome details. In the middle of the trench the prisoners had to dig a channel 25–30 cm wide into the ground, sloping from the centre towards either side, so that the fat from the bodies would run off and be collected in basins at the sides. The prisoners had to work through the night until Moll was satisfied that water ran out into the basins.

A fuel store was prepared and huge lorries delivered great quantities of material for burning: railway sleepers, fir branches, dead wood, beams and rags, quantities of methylated spirit and empty grease barrels. Behind the crematoria an area 15 m by 60 m was concreted over, on which the ashes were to be flattened. There were lots of coarse and fine wire nets, cement and barrels of calcium chloride – in short everything necessary for the disposal of such a large number of bodies. Moll had thought out the extermination of the Hungarian Jews – in all, five trenches, the crematoria, Bunker V with four gas chambers and a further four trenches for burning bodies were made ready.

The first transports of Hungarian Jews arrived in mid-May 1944. Twelve trains a day, each consisting of about forty to fifty cattle trucks, arrived at the newly built ramp at Birkenau. They were literally packed to capacity with Hungarian

A transport of Hungarian Jews shortly after their arrival on the ramp at Birkenau

Jews. These people had suffered terrible thirst on their four- or five-day journey and many of them did not survive the transport.

Those who were 'selected' on the ramp for the gas chambers, trailed along in long lines on the dusty road, exhausted. Mothers pushed prams, leading bigger children by the hand. Younger people who helped with the old and sick had evidently only been let join this group because they had begged not to be separated from their debilitated families, who needed their help.

What they saw on the way made a depressing spectacle. There were emaciated prisoners in striped prison clothing standing behind long barbed-wire fences, and SS guards with machine guns on the turrets of the watchtowers. This made them even more apathetic. Then the raging thirst on the hot summer day drove them nearly to despair. When they finally reached the yard in front of the crematorium they were barely a hundred metres from the cremation trench. The high wall hid it from their sight. There was a great fire, hissing, sparkling and glittering. A grey cloud filled the air with a sweet smell.

Moll made sure that the deception was played out, so that the new arrivals would think they were going to their quarters after disinfection. He took care to pacify the impatient and thirsty by encouraging them to be patient. They had to wait till the gas chambers were ready to take them after the arrivals from the previous transport had been gassed.

First the bodies had to be dragged out of the gas chambers and stacked in a yard behind the crematorium. The prisoners had to remove all the belongings

After selection by Dr Mengele and other SS doctors they walked to the 'showers'

left behind in the changing rooms. The area had to be cleaned up a bit; this all took time. The idea was to further weaken any resistance by leaving them waiting about and thirsty, in a state of uncertainty. While they were waiting the whistle of a train announced the arrival of another transport. After a short while another weary column of deportees trailed along the road through the camp, showing the same confusion, fear and apathy as the others. The timetable had to be adhered to; Moll himself would turn up at the burning trenches and even the SS men were afraid of his rebukes.

Later, the bodies, which had been dragged out of the gas chambers, were carried to the burning pits where the prisoners hurriedly broke off their gold fillings and cut off the women's hair. When that was done the bodies were thrown in three layers on top of the fuel, and when about 2,500 bodies were piled up the fuel was set on fire. The fire had to be fed constantly because the pile, which at first was over the trench, collapsed inwards as it burned and there was not enough air circulating. So the fire had to be fed with oil, methylated spirit and fat, which ran out of the channels at the sides – the fat from the burning bodies. There was a constant stink of oil, fat and burning flesh.

A grandmother and her grandchildren on the way to the gas chamber

Prisoners in the special *Kommando* carrying the bodies
of gassed Hungarian Jews to the cremation pits

The SS guards at the pits were mostly drunk, while the recently recruited guards in the watchtowers were visibly horrified. It was a truly terrible sight. The bodies moved in the glowing fire, rising and bending. The entire cremation process took two hours. What was left of the bodies at the end only filled one-third of the trench. There were countless bones and skulls scattered about. Water was poured in from all sides to cool it down a bit. A white cloud of steam rose hissing out of the trench, covering everything in a thick, warm damp fog. As soon as the surface was cooled, boards covered in lead were thrown into the trench.

Now the worst job began. The prisoners had to stand on the boards and shovel out the burning hot ashes. Even though they wore gloves and flat caps, they were badly burnt about the face and especially their eyes. During the day shift an average of 110 prisoners were deployed around Crematoria IV and V alone: about twenty-five for carrying bodies, ten pulled the gold teeth and cut off the hair of the dead, twenty-five placed the bodies in layers in the pits, fifteen prepared the fuel for the fires and thirty-five shovelled the ashes out of the pits after the fires had been extinguished.

The ashes were taken in wheelbarrows to a special area. There they were piled up in a mound, often the height of a man. Body parts, which had not burned, were taken out and put in a small pit for cremation. The ashes were stamped and sieved so that all that was left was fine dust. This work was done almost exclusively by Greek prisoners. Their sad songs and the monotonous stamping created a ghostly atmosphere. A small group of prisoners took away clothes, shoes and the other belongings of those who had been murdered. All this work was planned and strictly organised. Changes were only made if more prisoners were needed to help with dragging the bodies away. At night fires could not be lit in the trenches for fear of air raids, so the number of stokers was reduced by half. They prepared the cremation in the early hours of the morning. Everything had to be done at a terrible pace.

The SS had used about 100 railway carriages to transport the 10,000 Hungarian Jews. Several lorries were enough to take all the ashes to the bank of the Weichsel, where they were tipped into the river. With every transport from Hungary there was an open wagon carrying wooden beams. The Hungarians were supposed to think that this was to be used to build their accommodation. None of the deportees knew what was in store for them. You could tell that from their luggage too. After they were killed it was taken by lorries to the effects store. In spite of the heat most of them had brought their winter coats and even furs, which meant that they expected to be away at least through the coming winter.

In the gas chambers of the four crematoria about 10,000 people could be killed in one day and their bodies cremated inside, and in the pits. That was how more than 450,000 Hungarian Jews were liquidated in the space of a few weeks.

The statements of the two young Slovakian Jews Walter Rosenberg and Alfred Wetzler, who succeeded in escaping from Birkenau, led to US intervention. The Allied Military Command threatened the Hungarian dictator (Reichsverweser), Döme Sztójay, that the Budapest Industrial Bank and other industrial centres would be bombed, if any other Jews were deported to Auschwitz. Sztójay gave in and the transports stopped. The threat by the American government saved more than 300,000 Hungarian Jews, even though 450,000 had already been killed in May 1944.

22

Escape

IN SPITE OF THE FACT that the camps in Auschwitz and Birkenau were so tightly guarded that escape would appear impossible, prisoners were always trying to escape. Their intention was not just to save their own lives but above all to tell the world about the mass murder and to get help for the 10,000 or so prisoners under threat of extermination. During my time in Auschwitz there were several escape attempts, hardly any of which succeeded.

Five prisoners – a Slovakian, a Frenchman, a Pole, a German and a Dutchman – made one failed attempt with the help of an SS man, who then betrayed them. The five dead prisoners were sat on a bench at the gate of the camp and we had to file past them as if on parade, as a warning. Nevertheless there were further attempts – one by two Slovakian Jews was successful.

I can clearly remember 7 April 1944. The clear-up *Kommando* I was in was getting ready for the night shift. It had been a 'normal' day. The day shift was back in camp and we had filed out and lined up waiting for the head count. This time we all waited in vain – everyone, the entire camp, tens of thousands of prisoners. At 6 p.m. the sirens sounded in Birkenau, three short bursts, repeated for ten minutes. The shrill sound, with short intermissions, could be heard for miles around.

Escape.

Two Slovakian Jews were missing. Although thousands died every day in this place, not a single prisoner was allowed to go missing. Twelve hundred SS men went after them. They combed the entire district metre by metre. They formed a circular ring and went through all the huts and washrooms with dogs, turning everything upside down.

From time to time we heard orders being shouted: 'You have two hours to bring me the two of them.'

And we stood there, waiting, freezing, and feeling afraid but quietly hopeful.

'They'll never catch them,' someone said.

'Maybe they are being interrogated already,' said another.

The nervousness of the SS men gave us new strength. We heard the slow heavy steps of the prisoners coming back from their shift in the special crematorium *Kommando*. The search was only stopped after midnight. Our *Kommando* had to start work. The others were chased back to their huts, hungry and exhausted.

The SS raged for three days and nights, in vain. The two escapees had got away without trace. They were twenty-five-year-old Alfred Wetzler, prisoner number 29162, and twenty-one-year-old Walter Rosenberg, prisoner number 44070.

Alfred Wetzler, born 10 May 1918   Walter Rosenberg (Rudolf Vrba),
in Trnava, prisoner number 29162   born 1924 in Topolčany,
     prisoner number 44070

Escaped from Birkenau, 7 April 1944

After the war I heard the details of the escape from Wetzler and Rosenberg.

They had both been in Auschwitz since 1942 and were block-registrars. They used to sit together planning their escape. One day Fred said, 'I have important information for you. Four of the men from the mortuary want to attempt an escape, they need our help.' Walter knew the prisoners well. They had the job of collecting the dead, so they could move about the various sections of the camp unhindered. This gave them a distinct advantage in planning an escape.

'You know the planks that are stacked for building the new camp?' Fred continued. Walter nodded. 'They are for Birkenau III. It is going to be built beside Birkenau II, to accommodate the large numbers of Hungarian Jews.'

He said, 'They have bribed some *Kapos* to stack them so that there is a space underneath. It is big enough for four men to hide.'

Walter knew immediately what they were up to. The planks were in the outer camp that was not guarded at night, because all the prisoners were in the inner camp, which was surrounded by a high-tension barbed-wire fence and the watchtowers. If they succeeded in hiding for three days while all the guards were swarming about they would have a very good chance of getting away, because it would be assumed that in three days they would have got out of the Auschwitz area. Then other authorities would have the task of finding them. The sentries, who would be positioned around the entire camp for three days, would withdraw, then the prisoners only had to wait until nightfall to creep past the unmanned outer watchtowers.

'How can we help, how come they asked us?' asked Walter.

'Sandor Eisenbach is one of them. He trusts us.'

Walter smiled. Sandor was a Slovakian, much older than him, who knew his parents and had kept a fatherly eye on him since they had met up in the camp. 'They are not asking much, only to keep an eye on them and tell them what's going on in the camp.' Fred and Walter had freedom of movement because they were registrars.

A few days later the sirens sounded and they watched anxiously as the SS began to search the camp with dogs. They ran past the stacks of timber a few times, never thinking that the escapees could be crouched in the hollow space inside.

Some time later, while the search was going on some distance away, Walter passed casually by the hideout and said in a low voice, without looking in, 'Can you hear me?'

'Yes.'

The voice was faint but distinct. Walter pretended to be looking at papers and continued: 'Everything is fine. They are over by the crematoria. They have passed by here a dozen times, but didn't look at the wood.'

'Right, thanks.'

The following day the search was intensified. The two men took turns to keep the others informed. As evening drew in they knew the chances of the four getting away were increasing, because the SS men in the search parties were convinced that they had been given the slip. The third day and night were more or less a formality; on the fourth morning when Walter stopped at the woodpile and called out softly, there was no answer. They had got away. The four escapees had a long journey ahead of them.

So Walter and Fred decided to let two weeks go by before they did anything. By then, they reckoned, the others would be either dead, or recaptured, or have reached safety. The more days passed, the more hopeful they grew.

Nevertheless they were cautiously optimistic, and rightly so as it turned out. Barely a week after his last visit to the woodpile, Walter noticed unusual activity at the camp gate. He watched as the four men were led back into the camp surrounded by grinning SS men.

The capture of the four men from the mortuary was not the only drama in the camp that day. A few hours later two French Jews, a *Kapo* and his helper, tried to escape and were immediately recaptured by the SS. Walter and Fred were convinced that this gave the camp commander the excuse to put on a big show. Never before in the history of the camp had six escapees been recaptured. He had never had the opportunity to make an extreme example of them to the other prisoners as a warning that there was no point in trying to escape. So no one was surprised when a few days later a portable gallows was rolled in. The SS was lined up with drums and guns.

Schwarzhuber gave a speech before the execution. He held forth for a few minutes, warning the prisoners of what to expect if anyone tried to follow in the footsteps of the six prisoners standing in front of them with their hands bound behind their backs. He announced with obvious satisfaction. 'They will be hanged. But first they will get fifty strokes.'

An SS man stepped forward, holding a multi-tailed whip. The condemned men had to bend over the punishment block and for ages nothing could be heard but the dull thump of the whip, cutting into their flesh. This was only the prelude; the real show was to be the hanging. The two Frenchmen stepped onto the gallows to a roll of drums. The executioner, who was a prisoner, worked quickly. The trap doors opened and thudded against the sides of the platform and the terrible jerking began.

After a few minutes the bodies hung motionless. Everyone waited for them to be taken down to make room for the next victims. Fred and Walter had to grit their teeth at this spectacle, which no one can get used to, no matter how often they see it. But nothing moved on the gallows. Walter heard an SS man barking an order and saw the four men who had escaped from the hideout being led back to the punishment block.

They were being spared for another time, but why? What for? To be tortured again? Did this mean that the SS still did not know how they had got out? That evening Fred and Walter considered every aspect of the situation, and decided that their chances were very slim. It was only a matter of time before their friends gave in. They were sure of this because the human body and spirit can only take so much. After all, when it came to torture, the SS were specialists.

To Walter's astonishment, the four men turned up alive in the camp a few days later. Sure, they had been taken to the dreaded punishment block, but they were still alive. Fred and Walter tried to figure out a reason for sparing them but they were really nonplussed.

Nevertheless it did not take long to find out whether they had found the hideout in the woodpile. The punishment *Kommando* was isolated from the rest of the camp, but Walter soon found an excuse to go over to it. He passed close to Sandor Eisenbach and whispered to him without looking at him. 'Do they know about it?' The prisoner was working in a squad digging a trench with his bare hands and carrying the earth away in his striped cap.

'No,' he grunted, without stopping or raising his head.

'Are you sure?'

'I swear by your father's memory. You will get away soon.'

He picked up his capful of frozen earth and trotted away to empty it. Walter went back to Fred, confident that he could trust what Sandor said – he felt great respect for the strength of this man and his three comrades.

The next day he saw him again and thanked him. 'Don't be silly,' murmured Sandor.

'What went wrong, how did they catch you?' whispered Walter.

'In Porebka we ran straight into a military patrol. Give the place a wide berth. It's not a big town, but for some reason it is teeming with soldiers, and the sky is full of barrage balloons.'

Even the tiniest scrap of information was useful. Fred and Walter were ready to make their escape. The 'department store' of the Canada *Kommando* had provided them with expensive Dutch suits, overcoats and heavy boots. Their Russian tobacco had been soaked in petrol and dried. And most importantly they had engaged two Poles to replace the planks over their heads, as soon as they had climbed into their hideout.

Finally Fred and Walter set the date: 7 April 1944 at 2 p.m. Although they had freedom of movement there were still dozens of things that might prevent them from arriving at the woodpile at the same time. Walter thought about Fred and the Poles who were there waiting for him. Then he saw the Poles working on the woodpile and Fred was there too. No one spoke. The Poles moved the planks and gave them the nod.

This was it. Fred and Walter hesitated for a minute, because they knew that there was no going back once the hideout was sealed up. Then they climbed up and slipped down into the hole. The planks were replaced over them. It was dark and quiet. Their eyes got used to the darkness and they could just make each other out in the faint light coming through the gaps in the planks. They hardly dared breathe, much less speak. It took them about a quarter of an hour to calm down.

Their provisions were very meagre: three cubes of margarine, three loaves of bread, a watch, a razor, a torch, a plan of the camp, labels from Zyklon B gas canisters and a list of names of the SS personnel and doctors who had decided the fate of thousands of prisoners with a wave of the hand.

Walter took out his Russian tobacco, crumbled it and stuffed it in gaps between the planks while Fred watched anxiously.

It took them an hour to seal their improvised prison against sniffer dogs. Then Walter sat down, leaning against the rough wooden wall and tried to think positive. He forced himself not to think of their recapture, but repeated over and over to himself, 'There will be no more roll calls now, no hard labour, no crawling to the SS. You will soon be free.' Free or dead! He fingered the sharp edge of his knife and swore that if they were found, he would not be taken out of the hideout alive.

Time stood still. He looked at his watch; it was only 4 p.m. – the alarm would not be raised until 5.30. Suddenly he realised that he was dying to hear it. He feared the wailing siren, but could hardly stand the wait.

They could not stand up and grew stiff from sitting. The familiar sounds of the camp drifted in. Finally, after what seemed a week, he heard the sound of marching feet and every fibre of his body tensed. It was the prisoners returning from work. Soon they would line up in tidy rows of ten for roll call. Soon they would be missed, and then there would be the sirens, barking dogs and the stamping of SS boots.

They heard orders being shouted in the distance by the *Kapos* and wardens. Walter thought of what was before them and suddenly he realised that they would be free by 10 April. He looked at his watch again. Five minutes to go till the siren. The *Kapos* must have missed them by now. They were almost certainly discussing what to do and wondering whether the two registrars had just been held up or had actually fled. Should they raise the alarm and risk looking foolish or wait and bring the wrath of Schwarzhuber on themselves, if it turned out that they had escaped.

5.30 p.m. . . . still all quiet.

6 p.m. . . . the quiet was getting on their nerves.

Then the sirens tore through their thoughts. Orders echoed from one hut to the other and the dogs barked like mad. The search was on – a long, thoroughly exhaustive search that would last three days, until every inch of Birkenau was examined and every possible hideout turned inside out.

They could hear the thugs getting closer. The voices were very near now. Walter heard USF Buntrock growling: 'Look behind those planks, this is a search party not a stroll. Use your heads as well as your eyes. Damn it!'

Boots scraped on the planks over their heads, and some sand trickled down. The movement caused dust to rise and they covered their noses in case they had to sneeze. They heard more boots and men panting, dogs snuffling and panting, their paws scraped along the wood as they slipped and jumped. Walter held his knife ready. Fred crouched, all tensed up. Then the noise died away. Stillness enveloped the hideout, giving them a strange feeling of security. They had won the first round.

The search party soon came back, however, chasing through the entire area, going into every nook and cranny, their search growing more frustrated. They heard the boots and the dogs again and the curses of disappointed men. So it continued all through the night: the noise rose and fell, died out and surged round them again. They had bread and margarine, but could not eat anything. Even when their pursuers went away they only dozed; it was not proper sleep. Their nerves were strained.

The second day brought a critical phase. The camp commanders knew that time was against them and they drove the searchers mercilessly. They swarmed around the hideout and all over the woodpile. The voices sounded rough and strained. The intervals of stillness grew shorter. As the tension rose outside, it seeped through to the pair in hiding, because they could not see what was really going on. Their nerves were strained to cracking point and their stomachs contracted. They could neither eat nor drink even though they had had nothing for twenty-four hours, not even liquids.

Night brought no relief. Men stamped and stumbled hurriedly on top of them, the pressure only eased towards morning.

'Only one and a half days more and it won't be so bad,' said Fred. 'They must be pretty sure by now that we have got away.' To a certain degree he was right, because on the third day everything was more relaxed. In fact, it was the quietest day. The next twenty-four hours passed quietly. The search was continued but it was not so determined. The hours went by slowly and they grew more and more tense as they waited for the signal that the sentries had been withdrawn, which would give them the go ahead.

They knew the procedure. An SS man appeared in the closest watchtower. Then the order was passed all the way round the camp from tower to tower. This was an admission of defeat for the time being, as the towers emptied. The sentries would march back into the camp and the coast would be relatively clear from then on. The call was relayed on like an echo, as it was passed on from tower to tower: 'Sentries stand down!' It grew fainter and fainter till it could not be heard, then it came back after it had gone round the entire camp, growing louder and louder and finally fading away.

It was 6.30 p.m. on 10 April. Fred and Walter heard the stamping of marching feet, then nothing but the sounds of reduced activity in Birkenau. Officially they were outside now.

They still did not budge. 'We would be better to wait another while. It could be a trick. They could be lying waiting for us to appear.' said Walter. So they waited . . . 7, . . . 8, . . . 9 o'clock. Without a word, they got up at the same moment and began to push the planks back a few inches.

Panting, tense and sweating, they used their last reserves of strength. Very gradually the planks rose a few inches until they could grip the rough sides. They pushed them sideways and suddenly they could see the stars above them in a moonless sky. They climbed out into the cold air.

A huge floodlight illuminated the main road. Thousands of lights along the fence lit up the trench behind the barbed-wire. There was not a single spot in shadow. In front of them was the centre of the camp and on the right the crematoria. They sat motionless on the pile of wood, staring in at the camp. They were determined they would never see it again.

For the first time Walter saw the camp from the outside. The bright lights formed a soft, yellow haze in the darkness, bathing everything in a mysterious light that looked almost beautiful. They both knew what a terrible beauty it was and that people were starving and dying in the huts and that death lurked everywhere.

They turned their backs and slid down from the woodpile until they hit the ground, and, throwing themselves flat on their stomachs, began to inch their way forward, away from the now harmless watchtowers towards the little birch wood, with the disused cremation pits. They reached it, running bent over until they came to open ground, where they crept along flat again. Thus they fled, but then they came across a new obstacle.

At first Walter thought it was a river: it was a whitish strip, about eight metres wide, stretching away on both sides as far as the eye could. He knelt down, stretching out his hand to find out what it was. Sand . . . that was all. A strip of sand, surrounding the entire camp.

Escapees had to cross this fence and death strip

It was worse than water because if they stepped on it, their footsteps formed directional arrows, which the search parties could follow at daybreak. They crossed the mini-desert and came out on an open moor, covered in thick fern. There were signs on boards here and there saying: 'Achtung! KZ Birkenau. Any persons crossing this ground will be shot without warning!'

So they were still within the camp perimeter, and the wood seemed a long way away. As it grew light they still had not found cover. The moor ended at a field. They stopped to get their bearings, looked round quickly and threw themselves on the ground. Five hundred metres away they saw a group of female prisoners with SS guards.

They lay there panting for a minute, then raised their heads carefully. The column was on its way to work, and they had not been seen.

Nevertheless they did not dare get up, but continued crawling along on their stomachs using every dip and hollow they could find. It would have been folly to rush, so it took them another two hours to reach the shelter of the trees. They rested for a while, then pushed on through the thick pine forest. The green canopy was reassuring. They marched on. The ground was soft under foot, but their boots were good and strong. Rain pattered down on their bare heads but did not penetrate their good Dutch overcoats.

Finally Walter said, 'It's time we slept. We have to find somewhere to hide.' They searched for half an hour until they found a thicket and lay down among the ferns, feeling safe and sure that no one would find them. The Slovakian border is about 100 kilometres from Auschwitz as the crow flies and the way before them led through dangerous territory.

All German military personnel and civilians were under orders to shoot obvious strangers on sight. The Poles were told in no uncertain terms that they and their families would be shot if they helped escaped prisoners. Indeed, many who did paid with their lives. Even if the two men did not put a foot wrong, there were still the plenty of pitfalls ahead.

The forest saved them: foliage, pine needles and branches made a great bed. They awoke because they were cold. They decided to keep going till dark in the direction of Beskiden. By evening they reached Bielitz-Biala. They skirted the village. It took them six more days and nights to reach the mountains on the border. A cold wind was blowing up there. They had to avoid open ground; the mist helped but made navigation difficult. Their provisions ran out.

Another evening came and went. They crossed a railway line, then a river. The village of Milowka lay before them, so they were on the right route approaching the border. Suddenly all seemed lost – a woman and child appeared out of the mist. Would she help them or hand them in? Could they trust her?

She came closer, looked them up and down and handed them a piece of bread. After a minute she said, 'There's a hay barn a bit further on, wait there! My brother-in-law will come after ten and guide you further on.' She disappeared into the fog just as she had appeared.

Should they wait? Tiredness made the decision easier. They decided to risk it. After 10, a tall lean fellow arrived with hot soup, bread and a few cigarettes. As they ate their fill he whispered, 'I know who you are. There are wanted posters stuck up everywhere. I will take you to the border, then I have to go back to the factory . . .'

This Pole helped them, even though he knew that he and his entire family were threatened with death if he was caught in the act or if it came out that he had hidden them and taken them to the border. They walked in a single file, the Polish guide leading the way. The night seemed endless. Finally dawn came and they hid in undergrowth at the edge of a cleared area. The border stretched before them. How easily they could be seen by a guard. Their guide pointed in the direction of Slovakia. He had to go back quickly himself.

'Bye now, and watch out!' he said and shook hands with them. 'Your pictures are everywhere. They are looking for you in all the villages. I hope you make it!' He turned on his heel and disappeared into the safety of the forest.

After crossing the border they reached Žilina by way of Čadca on 25 April. The two brave escapees from Birkenau informed the illegal Communist Party in Slovakia and the International Red Cross about the mass murder in the concentration camp and about the new plans.

Their report reached the Kremlin, the Vatican and Pius XII, the British Prime Minister, Winston Churchill, the American President, Franklin D. Roosevelt. Cordell Hull, the US secretary of state, sent a Diplomatic Note to the Hungarian Dictator Döme Sztójay, protesting about the deportations to Auschwitz.

The transports were stopped as a result of his powerful threats. The world had heard the truth about Auschwitz, but the railway lines to Auschwitz and the gas chambers were never bombed. Why not?

Other prisoners who succeeded in escaping from KZ Birkenau were:

Vítězslav Lederer, prisoner number 29162, arrived on a transport from Theresienstadt in December 1943. He had been in camp B.II.b. He fled with the help of a Romanian ethnic-German SS man, Viktor Pestek, on 6 April 1944.

Rosin Arnošt, a Slovakian Jew, prisoner number 29858, escaped from Birkenau and arrived in Slovakia on 6 June 1944.

The world found out about the cruel deeds of the Nazis and the extermination of millions of people, thanks to these prisoners who risked their lives to tell.

Rosin Arnošt, prisoner number 29858

Escape route April 1944

Telegramm Aufgenommen Staatl.Kriminalpolizei   Befördert

Tag Monat Jahr Zeit   Stelle Hohenfalze   Tag Monat Jahr Zei

9 April 1944 1237   Eingang 11.April 1944

       durch W   Egb.Nr. 2334/44   an   durch

                                        Verzögerungsvermer
                                            203

Hohenfalze Nr.2037 Telegramm-Fernspruch-Fernschreiben-Berufspruch

KL AUSCHWITZ WRY 9433 8/4.44 0833 - KA.-
AN DAS RSHA, IV C 2, BERLIN.-AN DAS SS WYH., AMTSGRUPPE D,
ORANIENBURG.-AN ALLE GEST.STAPO /LEIT/ - KRIPO /LEIT/.
STELLEN UND GREKO.----
BETRIFFT: SCHUTZHAFT JUDEN 1./ R O S E N B E R G   WALTER
ISRAEL, GEB.11.9.24 ZU TOPOLCANY, EINGELIEFERT AM 30.6.42
VON RSHA.-2./ W E T Z L E R   ALFRED, ISRAEL, GEB! 10.5.18
ZU TRNAVA, EINGELIEFERT AM 13.4.42 VOM RSHA.----
ROSENBERG UND WETZLER SIND AM 7.4.44 AUS DEM KL.-
AU.II. BAUABSCHNITT IIA UND IIB, ENTFLOHEN. DIE SOFORT
EINGELEITETE SUCHAKTION HIER BISHER OHNE ERFOLG. ES WIRD
GEBETEN, VON DORT AUS WEITERE FAHNDUNGSMASSNAHMEN
EINZULEITEN UND IM ERGREIFUNGSFALLE DAS KL.-AUSCHWITZ
UMGEHEND ZU BENACHRICHTIGEN.---ZUSATZ FUER DAS RSHA.
DIE AUSSCHREIBUNG DES ROSENBERG UND DES WETZLER IM
SONDERFAHNDUNGSBUCH BITTE ICH VON DORT AUS ZU VERANLASSEN.
ZUSATZ FUER DAS SS WVH,: MELDUNG AN DEN REICHSFUEHRER
IST ERFOLGT. WEITERER BERICHT FOLGT.DAS VERSCHULDEN EINES
POSTENS WURDE BISHER NICHT FESTGESTELLT.

KL.-AU.-AUT.II/44070/8.4.44 DV.---
GEZ.HART.JENSTEIN SS-STUBAF.+++

                                 FAHNDUNGSKARTEI

                                 SUCHVERMERK LIEGT NICHT VOR

                                 KEINE PERS.AKTE:

Copy of the original telegram to the RSHA section IV C 2 in Berlin announcing the escape of prisoners Wetzler and Rosenberg

Telegram received   State criminal police
9th April 1944 at 12.37 hrs.
11th April 1944
Egb. no: 2334/44   Delay stamp 203
Hohenfalze no: 2037 Telegram

KL Auschwitz WRY 9433 8/4.44 0833 - KA.-
To RSHA, IV C 2 Berlin. TO SS WYH. GROUP D,
ORANIENBURG. -TO ALL GESTAPO /Commanders/ Criminal
police chiefs
RE: JEWISH DETAINEES 1. ROSENBERG WALTER ISRAEL
DoB 11.9.24 IN TOPOLCANY, DETAINED BY RSHA on
30.6.42 - 2.WETZLER ALFRED,ISRAEL, DoB 10.5.18 IN
TRNAVA DETAINED BY RSHA on 13.4.42
ON 7.4.44 ESCAPED FROM KL AU.II SECTION IIA & IIB.
SEARCH SO FAR UNSUCCESSFUL
STEP UP SEARCH. INFORM KL AUSCHWITZ IF CAPTURED
TO BE ENTERED IN SPECIAL SEARCH RECORDS AT CAMP
FÜHRER HAS BEEN INFORMED.
FURTHER REPORTS TO FOLLOW.
SO FAR NO SENTRY BLAMED.

KL.-AU.-AUT.II/44070/8.4.44DV. - - - - - -

                    SEARCH FILE
                    NO SEARCH STAMP
                    NO PERSONAL FILE

A prisoner is led to the gallows, condemned for attempting to escape.
The camp band had to play 'Alle Vögel sind schon da' during the execution

PART II

THE FORGERY WORKSHOP
IN KZ SACHSENHAUSEN

1

From KZ Birkenau to KZ Sachsenhausen

Gate of KZ Sachsenhausen

IT IS EARLY EVENING ON 12 April 1944. The most wretched of the wretched walk in rows of five, wearily dragging their feet, forcing themselves to march, using up their last effort of will. The presence of SS guards flanking the marching column forces them to continue marching.

There are 15,000 of them. They are coming back through the gate of KZ Birkenau after a day of hard labour. The prisoners think of only one thing: survival, the only way to achieve this is never to stand still. You must stick it out – everything. The SS too has only one objective: exterminate and destroy, for these prisoners belong to an inferior race and have no place in the Nazi world order.

So everyone is on the move, prisoners and SS men, all marching along. Each *Kommando* pulls a cart behind it piled high with the bodies of those who will never walk again, who will never smile at their loved ones, never stroke their children's heads, never again experience the sweetness of love. They lie stiff; their dead eyes staring up to heaven to the God who abandoned them. On the right of the gate is a prisoners' band playing a German folk tune 'Auf der Heide blüht ein kleines Blümelein'. As they march into the camp the *Kapo* roars: 'Attention! Eyes left!'; the prisoners have to show respect for the SS men by marching in step.

The individual columns of prisoners march to their blocks, where they have to line up for the head count. A new order is shouted: 'Caps off!' The prisoners have to stand and wait till the head count is done. Suddenly a voice calls out nine prisoner numbers, among them is mine: 64401. The nine prisoners are to report to the camp commander the following day.

So the next day after roll call I report there. I, Adolf Burger, Slovakian political prisoner, who had already vegetated for a year and a half in KZ Birkenau. The number 64401 had been tattooed by the Nazis on my left forearm. The distance from the roll call yard to the camp commander seemed endless to me. What did this mean? What fate was in store for me? A penal *Kommando*, deportation or maybe even the gas chamber?

Hesitantly I entered the camp commander's office. In accordance with the regulations I presented myself: 'Prisoner 64401 reporting.' The SS officer looked at my file card.

'Prisoner Burger?'

'Yes, sir.'

'Occupation – typesetter?'

'Yes, sir.'

His rough voice softened, became kindly.

'You are going to Berlin, Herr Burger.'

So I was not prisoner number 64401, but Herr Burger, yes indeed, Herr Burger, I was not hearing things.

'We need experts like you. You will have good working conditions, you will get on well. I can give you no other information. You will find out everything else when you get there. I wish you all the best.'

Now I am Herr Burger; a few minutes earlier I was prisoner number 64401. I staggered out of the camp commander's office, stunned. I thought I had been dreaming. What I had just experienced was simply incredible. Was I entitled to be pleased? Or maybe it was only a devilish trap, a 'game' that the SS official was enjoying at my expense.

I went back to my hut. I told my friend Mikuláš Šteiner everything. He said, 'You're lucky, you'll escape the gas chamber.' Then the block-registrar came and said: 'Get yourself fresh prison clothes. You are going away tomorrow.' Only then did I believe that a miracle had really happened and that I would get out of the hell that was Birkenau.

The following day, everything turned out to be true: I was no longer allowed to go to work. On the third day we lined up to march off in front of the camp administration block, waiting for the SS men who were to escort us to the station and take us to Berlin. There were nine of us:

Eduard Bier	born	19 June 1910	stateless
Adolf Burger	"	12 August 1917	Slovakian
Symcha Fajermann	"	20 January 1915	Polish
Leib Gafne	"	6 January 1915	Polish
Mozes van Prag	"	3 May 1910	Dutch
David Lubetski	"	15 March 1905	Polish
Herman Salzer	"	16 November 1912	Polish
Ascher Schipper	"	9 January 1915	Polish
Roger Weill	"	23 September 1918	French

Finally the guard arrived. We walked to the station, or so we thought. But instead of the express train to Berlin we went to KZ Auschwitz. That was a bitter disappointment. So it was a trick! But why? Why are they moving us from camp to camp? If they were going to kill us they could have done it in Birkenau with less fuss. Our uncertainty increased with every second. Our nerves were in shreds.

At the gate of Auschwitz we were ordered to halt. We stood and waited. An SS man appeared and ordered to us to go to the quarantine block. 'You will be kept in quarantine for four weeks. We need to be sure that you are not carrying infectious diseases.' After all we had been through in the last few months in Birkenau, quarantine was like a holiday. We did not have to work and were not beaten by SS men.

On 21 May, a couple of days after the quarantine ended, six SS guards from Berlin came for us. We were given marching rations, and we were off! We were taken to the station, where we waited for the train to Berlin. It was an indescribable feeling: we felt like normal people again. We still did not know what was in store for us. Might we even be set free?

The express steamed in. We got into a reserved compartment, which was only separated from the other passengers by a sliding door and windows with the blinds drawn. Slowly the train moved off. We made ourselves comfortable and looked out of the windows. Villages and towns flew past. The woods were a glorious fresh green. Here and there people were working in the fields, mostly women. Some waved to the speeding train as it flew past. When I saw them I was painfully aware of everything I had lost.

We arrived in Berlin early in the morning. The station was packed with people: men on leave from the front with their kit, Red Cross nurses rushing about, women laden with suitcases with small children by the hand. We felt the curious stares.

'Ma, are they criminals?' shouted a little boy pointing at us. The woman, who was obviously embarrassed and upset, just drew the boy aside and said, 'Be quiet!'

The guards took us on a local train. On the way we saw Berlin in 1944: bombed-out buildings, ruins, rubble. It was the same everywhere. So that was all that was left of the capital of the 'Thousand-Year Reich'.

The journey took an hour. Imagine my sense of horror as we saw the name 'Oranienburg' and marched from the station to the small town, nine prisoners and six SS men. Our wooden shoes clattered on the pavement. We saw goods displayed in the shop windows: bread, margarine and milk. The people we met acted as if they did not see us, half-starved creatures that we were. They were obviously used to prisoners being marched through their little town. There was no pity in their eyes. After half an hour we reached the gate with the name KZ Sachsenhausen above it. So we were in another concentration camp! Berlin, a printing works, work at my own occupation – everything that the camp commander in Birkenau had promised us seemed to have vanished. It was 22 May 1944.

First we had to go through a series of formalities in the camp. File cards were filled out. We were registered, and assigned new numbers. Herr Burger became a prisoner again with the number 79161. After all our personal details had been recorded we thought we would have a 'normal camp life'. But it turned out to be quite different. We were taken to a hut, the quarantine block.

Sachsenhausen concentration camp was situated 35 kilometres north of Berlin. It was laid out in 1936 and built by German prisoners, dissidents of the Nazi regime. At first it only covered an area of 31 hectares, surrounded by a barbed-wire fence. In 1941, there were 10,577 prisoners vegetating here. By May 1944 it was four times that figure: 47,709 and covering an area of 388 hectares, twelve times the original size.

More than 200,000 prisoners were held at KZ Sachsenhausen, of whom 100,000 were killed. In a three-month period in the autumn of 1941, 18,000 Soviet prisoners of war were shot. In all there were more than 20,000 Soviet POWs, very few of whom survived.

In the autumn of 1941 alone
the SS killed 18,000 Soviet POWs

Soviet POWs were shot in the neck in this frame as
their body height was measured

KZ Sachsenhausen was shaped like an equilateral triangle. The camp was surrounded by a wall 2.70 m high with nine watchtowers and a 1,000-volt electrified wire fence. The window of the quarantine block gave on to the roll call yard. Around the yard was the 'shoe-testing track'. The SS military clothing department had the so-called shoe-testing track built in order to test the durability of footwear for the German army and Waffen-SS.

Prisoners had to run this 700 m long track for eleven hours a day, carrying a satchel full of sand. The course was over concrete, ploughed earth, field tracks, gravel, sand, cobblestones, cinders, and through waterlogged drains. That amounted to 40 kilometres a day. Prisoners who could go no further had dogs set on them.

We had now been in the quarantine block of Sachsenhausen camp for three weeks. Why were we quarantined again? What was in store for us? What would they do to us in the next hours and days?

Shoe-testing squad (drawing by prisoner)

Ausweis

Der Häftling

Nr. 68 852 Helmut Tulatz   Block: 4

hat für Tragversuche und zu Prüfzwecken von der
Schuhprüfstelle im K. L. Sh. leihweise erhalten

1 Paar   Standard-   Schuhe Nr.   E 31

Die Schuhe bleiben in jedem Falle Eigentum der Schuhprüfstelle.
Irgendwelche vorkommende größere oder kleinere Reparaturen dürfen
nur von der Schuhprüfstelle durchgeführt werden.

K. L. Sh., den 5.10.44

Leiter der Schuhprüfstelle

1 0 1 5

Prisoner No. 68 852 Helmut Tulatz Block 4 was issued with loan of:
1 Pair Shoes size: E 31 for purposes of wear and durability tests
at K.L.Sh. footwear-testing centre. Shoes remain the property of the
testing centre.
Any repairs arising, whether major or minor, are to be carried out
by the centre.
K.L.Sh 5.10.44

                    Director testing centre

                    Identity card

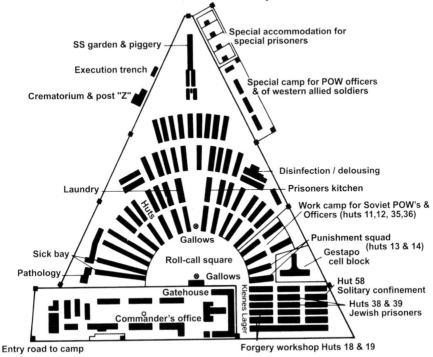

KZ Sachsenhausen
Prison and Command camp 1944

SS garden & piggery

Execution trench

Crematorium & post "Z"

Special accommodation for special prisoners

Special camp for POW officers & of western allied soldiers

Laundry

Huts

Disinfection / delousing

Prisoners kitchen

Work camp for Soviet POW's & Officers (huts 11,12, 35,36)

Punishment squad (huts 13 & 14)

Gallows

Gestapo cell block

Roll-call square

Sick bay

Gallows

Pathology

Gatehouse

Kleines Lager

Hut 58
Solitary confinement

Huts 38 & 39
Jewish prisoners

Commander's office

Entry road to camp

Forgery workshop Huts 18 & 19

1944 ground plan of KZ Sachsenhausen prison camp and administration

View of Blocks 18 and 19

SS-Scharführer Sommer invented 'pole-hanging'

These four SS men took part in the killing of the Soviet POWs

The Forgery Workshop

Forgery block

AT LAST, ON 5 MAY 1944 the uncertainty was over. An SS officer came into the hut. He introduced himself as Kurt Werner and informed us that from now on we were under his command. He led us out of the quarantine accommodation through the south side of the camp to Blocks 18 and 19, which were separated from the other blocks by an additional barbed-wire fence.

We had noticed the barbed-wire from a distance. So this was our destination. We still did not know what secrets were hidden inside the huts that looked like a camp within a camp. Huts 18 and 19 were like a proverbial cage. Barbed-wire was wound tightly around them. Even our view of the sky was blocked by barbed-wire strung over the huts; the small windows had been painted white so that no other prisoners could see into our strange cage.

We stopped at the gate. Werner ran the bell. We heard the sound of machinery. An SS man opened the gate and we went into the block. As we entered we saw a whitewashed room with modern printing machinery and prisoners working. Their heads were not shaven and they wore clean prison clothes. SS-HSF Werner said, 'This is where English banknotes are printed, you experts will work here.'

He handed us over to the block-warden, Artur Lewin, a political prisoner from Berlin. First Lewin took us into the dormitory. We gazed in astonishment at the double bunks with white sheets, pillows and blankets. Compared to the terrible

conditions in KZ Birkenau it seemed to me that I had come into heaven from
hell. Everyone was allocated his place and a locker for personal belongings. What
a luxury. But at the same moment I realised the terrible truth: I would never
get out of here alive. A forgery workshop established by the Nazi state is a state
secret and death awaits any witnesses. Then the warden led us to the recreation
room. There were long tables and benches. He brought us bread, sat with us
and said: 'There is no way out of here, my friends. We can only be saved and get
out alive by chance. We have to hope for that. I am warning you that sabotage is
impossible. Only one man tried it. He hid a £50 sterling note. He was found out
because the security service bookkeeping is very exact and all serial numbers are
registered. There was a roll call and SS-HSF Werner demanded that the thief
own up. But everyone kept mum. So the SS searched the workrooms and living
quarters and found the note in Hermann Gütig's locker in Block 19. First they
tortured him as punishment. Then they locked him in the air-raid shelter, which
they used during bombing. They called an ambulance and an SS doctor gave him
a lethal injection in the heart. So I am warning you. I have been in this death
block since 1942.'

There were prisoners in the forgery *Kommando* who had built the workshop.
Among them was Oskar Stein, a Czech who was one of the first political prisoners
in the workshop. He told us how they had set up the machinery and started
printing banknotes in August 1942. The printing of English banknotes was top
secret. The prisoners could only leave the huts to go to the showers, escorted by
SS men.

We newcomers were grateful for every scrap of information. We soon realised
how perfectly organised the workshop was. Our block was totally isolated from
the rest of Sachsenhausen camp. We had our own doctor and technical staff.
Prisoners carried out repairs and maintenance. It was not just a forgery workshop
but also a factory for the production of forged notes, passports, documents and
English stamps. It was technically perfect. A book-printing works with the most
up-to-date machinery, a collotype department, offset, a darkroom, a retouching
department, bookbinders, setting and engraving rooms, and a control room for
the forged banknotes. We even had our own diesel-powered generator in case of
power cuts.

It was a devilish idea to establish a state forgery operation in a concentration
camp near Berlin. The idea of using exclusively Jewish political prisoners to
forge banknotes was really macabre. It was a strictly kept secret. Even the camp
commandant, OSF Kaindl, was not privy to what went on in Blocks 18 and 19.
They were directly under the control of the RSHA, the Security Ministry of the
Reich.

In the evening I lay on my bunk and could not sleep for hours, even though
it was eerily quiet and the camp seemed peaceful. There was no way out – and
that was terrible. Because these special blocks inside Sachsenhausen camp were
so secure there was no thought of escape. And on the other hand it was out of the

question that anyone would ever set us free. For we now guarded a state secret of the Third Reich. As we found out later only very few people – Hitler, Himmler, Kaltenbrunner, Schellenberg and some selected security personnel – knew about this forgery operation. In Auschwitz and Birkenau it was only my will to live that kept me going: the will to survive all this, to be able to tell how the Nazi criminals treated their opponents and victims. Now I wondered, was my struggle to survive to have been in vain?

The next day was my first working day. We were wakened at six. After washing and dressing we had plenty of time for breakfast. We got the same rations as the other camp inmates, only bigger portions. After breakfast, which did not have to be swallowed hurriedly, like in Auschwitz, we went into the workshop together. I was put to work at a machine that made coloured banknote paper.

It was about 10 a.m. when the door opened and SS-SBF Bernhard Krüger came in, the man who gave his name to the operation. The nine new 'recruits' had to line up. SBF Bernhard Krüger, head of section VI F 4 of the RSHA, the officer in charge of the forgery squad, smiled and looked us straight in the eye as he addressed us from the raised platform built by prisoners in Block 18.

'If you work hard and do a good job, you will have nothing to fear. Some day the war will be over, then you will be able to leave this block. Of course you must understand that we cannot give you your full freedom. Your work must remain a secret forever. But I repeat, do not be afraid! You will be well looked after. But you may not have contact with the outside world. I wish to make it clear to you that I have saved you from certain death and you can see that you have a good deal. Work hard and victory will be your reward.'

He paused and continued in the manner of one who would decide our life or death: 'I want to make it quite clear that if you do not work hard you will be shot without mercy.' The head of forgery left the workshop, smiling cynically. So now we newcomers had been told officially what we had realised ourselves. There was no way out of here. We were condemned to death after completing the job. What was the point of making any effort and slaving away?

We knew our task would not be easy and that any of our SS guards could become our murderer one day. We knew too that the SS guards had orders to shoot us down if necessary.

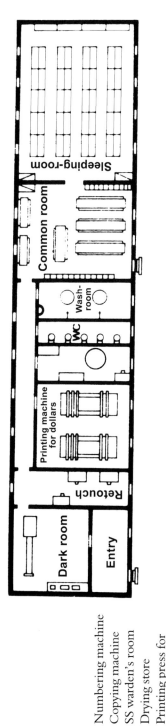

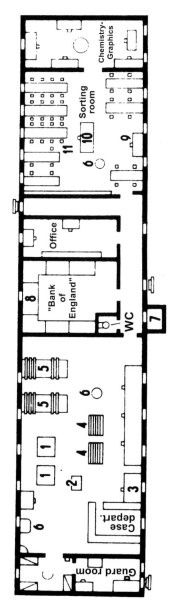

Sleeping-room

Common room

Washroom

WC

Printing machine for dollars

Retouch

Dark room

Entry

Courtyard

Chemistry-Graphics

Sorting room

11 10 9

6

Office

"Bank of England"

8

WC

7

5 5

6

4 4

1 1

2

3

Case depart.

Guard room

Ground plans of Blocks 18 and 19

1   Numbering machine
2   Copying machine
3   SS warden's room
4   Drying store
5   Printing press for
     English banknotes
6   Stove
7   Dynamo
8   Storage shelf for
     forged notes
9   Foreman's desk
10   Sorting stations
11   Work tables.

Members of the Reich's Security Service who Directed or Guarded the Forgery Operation

Bernhard Krüger, SS Major, director of Sonderkommando Secret Service, born 1904, Chemnitz

Kurt Werner, Battalion Sergeant Major, head of the forgery workshop, born 17 July 1912, Egeln

Herbert Marock, SS Company Sergeant Major, born 24 December 1913, Kiel

Hans Jansen, SS Company Sergeant Major, born 1912, Cologne

Alexander Jessen, SS Company Sergeant Major, born 16 June 1888, Hamburg

Hansch, SS Lieutenant, Krüger's replacement; Heinz Beckmann, SS-HSF, Chemnitz; Edwin Heizmann, SS-HSF, Kaiserslautern; Bruno Psoch, SS-USF; Träger, SS-SF, Tachau; Willi Schmitt, SS-OSF, Petrovagrad; Heinz Weber, SS-OSF, Nordhausen; Hoffman, SS-HSF, Berlin; Alfred Kramer, SS-USF, Oldenburg; Willi Wildfang, SS-OSF, Ludwiglust; Heinz Buckelmann, SS-OSF, Güstrow; Fritz Heider, SS-USF, Cologne-Deutz; August Petrick, SA-SSF, Berlin, Blumenstrasse 99

Previous Forgery Operations

THE NAZIS WERE NOT THE first to circulate forged enemy money. They merely copied the use of forged money as a weapon of war. From 1790 to 1796 Great Britain had flooded France with large quantities of forged paper money (*Assignats*) in an attempt to sabotage the French Revolution.

No wonder the German Imperial Secret Service (Reichswehr) was already forging foreign reparations payments in the 1920s with the aim of revenge for defeat in the Great War and in order to damage the young Soviet state. With the knowledge of some members of the government, Reichswehr General Max Hoffmann had recruited former officers and criminal immigrants from Russia to print French franc notes and Soviet Tscherwonez notes. The reparations to France, among others, were to be paid with the forged banknotes. They attempted to weaken the Soviet economy with the Tscherwonetz notes and support the counter-revolution in Russia. By chance, the police in Frankfurt-am-Main confiscated 1,200 kilogrammes of forged Tscherwonetz notes to the value of 12 million roubles. This developed into a major international scandal.

This forgery operation had started in Hungary in 1925. There was a unit of the German secret service active there, led by Prince Ludwig zu Windischgratz, a Hungarian minister, the chief of police Emmerich Nadossy and Jankowich, a retired Hungarian colonel. They had received their orders, equipment, and machines from General Max Bauer.

The operation went wrong due to Jankowich's carelessness. He was caught in the Netherlands with huge amounts of forged money. There was a scandal and, as a result of the pressure exerted by indignant public opinion in Hungary, all three were tried and given prison sentences.

The influence of the German government was sufficient to help its workers. As soon as the affair was forgotten, Jankowich was secretly pardoned and the head of state (Reichsverweser) Horthy reappointed him to the rank of Major (Honvéd).

In spite of these embarrassing events the German secret service, the Reichswehr, continued its forgery operation. But in the summer of 1927 a gigantic rouble forgery was uncovered. The case came to court in spite of attempts to keep it quiet.

Thanks to pressure from the press and the Soviet government in 1930, two of the captured forgers were sentenced to long terms of imprisonment on appeal, and two others received large fines. The two émigrés, Karumidse and Sadathierschwilli, both notorious men, who had fled there from the Soviet Union, succeeded in reaching Switzerland unhindered.

4

'Operation Andreas'

SS-SBF Alfred Naujocks and the Greatest Forgery Operation in History – Hitler's Paper Weapon: 'Counterfeit Money'

SS-SBF Alfred Naujocks, in charge of agents and
head of intelligence in Heydrich's secret service

ALFRED NAUJOCKS WAS BORN ON 20 September 1911. He studied engineering for a short period in Kiel. He was typical of the young bully boys employed by the Nazis in their 'struggle phase'. He was a well-known amateur boxer and was often involved in street fights with Communists. He joined the SS in 1931 and three years later the secret service, where he soon became one of Heydrich's trusted entourage.

Naujocks was head of Section VI of the RSHA and had special assignments such as obtaining forged papers (passports and ID cards) and forged banknotes for security service (Sicherheitsdienst – SD) agents working abroad. Acting on Heydrich's orders, Alfred Naujocks had faked the Polish attack on the German transmitter at Gliewitz, which was situated near the Polish border. Naujocks was the leader of a small troop of SS men dressed in Polish uniforms, who occupied the transmitter for a short time on 31 August 1939 and announced that it was time that Germany and Poland should go to war. To make the attack look more plausible, SS-SBF Naujocks left the body of an executed concentration camp prisoner dressed in a Polish uniform at the scene, giving the impression that he had been killed in action. Nazi propaganda presented this as an act of Polish aggression and the justification for bringing forward the invasion that took place. The very next day after this staged 'Polish provocation', the Wehrmacht invaded Poland.

In November 1939 Naujocks was given another assignment. Walter Schellenberg, who was subsequently head of Section VI of the RSHA, had invited Major Stevens and Captain Payne-Best, two members of the British secret service, to a meeting of agents in the Dutch border town of Venlo. There they were set upon by the SS men under Naujocks' command and taken to Germany in their own car. The German press named the British officers as the perpetrators of the failed attack on Hitler on 8 November 1939 in the Bürgerbräukeller in Munich. Hitler survived the attempt because he had – unexpectedly – already left the Bierkeller shortly before the timing device set off the explosion.

The actual assassin was Georg Elser, a German cabinet-maker, and he was caught by the SS as he was trying to escape to Switzerland. Elser, a socialist, had been a Communist sympathiser in the late 1920s and was a member of the Red Front Veterans' association. During the Sudeten crisis he decided to assassinate Hitler. On 8 November a time bomb set by him exploded in the Bürgerbräukeller. Eight people were killed.

Elser was arrested the same evening and was interrogated by a special team of Gestapo and criminal police investigators. Finally the Gestapo took over the

Johann Georg Elser

investigation and Elser was interrogated from 19 to 23 November in Prinz-Albrecht Street in Berlin. After this he was sent to the same concentration camp as the two British officers, KZ Sachsenhausen, and later to KZ Dachau. He was executed by SS men on 9 April 1945 on the orders of the Gestapo.

Naujocks was rewarded for his criminal act with the Iron Cross, 1st class. The seized car became his property. Naujocks then told his chief Reinhard Heydrich about his plan for forging English banknotes.

'Forgery': The Paper Weapon

The first plan for a large-scale project to forge foreign banknotes was conceived by SS-SBF Alfred Naujocks. English notes were to be forged and then were to be either dropped over England or distributed indirectly through neutral states in such large quantities that the English currency would be destabilised. Heydrich took Naujocks' plan a stage further. He intended to forge not only sterling banknotes but also American dollars.

As head of the secret service, Reinhard Heydrich set out his plans in a detailed memorandum that he passed on to Hitler through Reichsführer Heinrich Himmler. He agreed to the plan immediately, defying German law.

Law Against Production and Sale of Forged Currency

Forgery and circulation of native or foreign currency, whether coinage or paper currency carries the penaltyof penal servitude for life.

German Law (DSGB 1940)
Art.146 and 147

Murderers and Forgers of the Third Reich, 1941–5

Adolf Hitler,
Führer and Chancellor of the Reich

Heinrich Himmler,
Reichsführer-SS, Chief
of Police, Minister of the
Interior

Reinhard Heydrich,
SS-Lieutenant General,
commander of security
police, secret service and
Gestapo protector of
Bohemia and Moravia

Dr Ernst Kaltenbrunner,
SS-Lieutenant General,
general of police, head
of security police and of
secret service

Walter Schellenberg,
SS-Major General,
major general of police,
head of Section VI of RSHA

Otto Skorzeny (Engineer),
SS-Major,
head of RSHA espionage training

Dr Josef Goebbels,
minister for information and propaganda and from
1944 in complete charge of war effort, one of those
chiefly responsible for Nazi crimes and the 'Final
Solution' of the Jewish problem

Department of Security of the Reich – RSHA

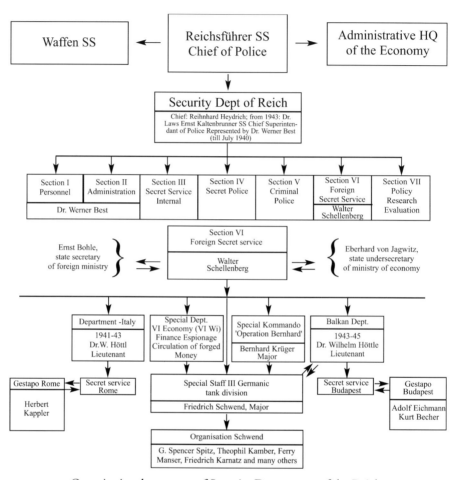

Organisational structure of Security Department of the Reich

Only the top echelons of the Third Reich and the heads of secret service knew about the forgery operation in KZ Sachsenhausen. Reinhard Heydrich, as head of the security police and the secret service, and SS-BF Otto Rasch took part in the secret meetings in October 1939 about the realisation of the forgery plan. Naujocks was then tasked with the management of the forgery operation whilst Krüger, the forgery expert, was charged with the technical planning.

The first details were contained in instructions declared 'top secret', which Naujocks received from Heydrich. 'This is not a question of forgery or imitation in the usual sense but it constitutes unauthorised production [of sterling notes]. The notes must be so close to the original that even the most experienced sterling note specialists would not be able to detect any difference.'

This called for something extraordinary. It was a task that could only be completed with comprehensive technical expertise and with the greatest circumspection. When 'Operation Andreas', as it was first called, started in 1941, it was without precedent.

This production of duds demanded the following:

1. First, paper had to be produced that exactly replicated that on which English notes were printed.
2. Printing plates had to be made up that could reproduce the tiniest details.
3. Mathematicians would be needed to work out the numbering system used by the Bank of England on its notes.
4. A worldwide distribution network would have to be set up.

Krüger encouraged Naujocks to 'look for the best people you can find in Germany. You are fully in charge.' Naujocks was faced with greater difficulties than he had imagined. Even the production of the paper to print the English notes seemed to present an insurmountable obstacle, a problem that had to be solved first and foremost.

Naujocks' men cut up real English notes and had them analysed in the laboratories of several third-party institutions. The results of this analysis did not always tally. There was only one point that comforted the forgers: the paper was not made from a particular type of reed that only grew in Burma and other Asiatic states, as they had thought, but from linen rags. These rags were shredded in special machines. The English did not use ordinary linen, but a type that was only obtainable in Turkey. Naujocks ordered several tonnes, which were promptly delivered. But the first attempts failed – the 'raw material' used by the English must have been something special.

Naujocks' workers realised that the banknote paper – like other costly paper – was produced by pulping by hand. So 'Operation Andreas' would have to use this method too. The specialists experimented with chemicals; they tried special additives and altered details of the process. If all the tests were positive they had got it right. However, thorough examination under a microscope and special lamps proved that there was still something wrong. It could only be the rags . . .

Further analysis indicated the solution: the English did not use new rags but old ones. He had the linen from Turkey made into cloths, gave them to factories for cleaning machinery, then collected them again, had them washed and then made into paper. Now the paper withstood the most exacting tests.

The problem of the complicated watermark was also laboriously solved. These secret markings covered the entire note with parallel wavy lines, interrupted in three places by the letters and numbers on the notes. The wire used to press the watermark into the paper mass had to be exactly 0.02 mm thick.

The right paper and watermark for the greatest forgery operation in history were finally achieved in December 1940. Naujocks combed Germany in his search for the best craftsmen who would be able to do this work. They were conscripted and designated 'essential workers' and sworn in. They set to work in separate buildings in the paper factory at Eberswalde, north of Berlin.

The Production of Banknote Paper at Hahnemühle Paper Mill, Near Dassel

Robert Bartsch

Statement of Robert Bartsch, formerly managing director of Hahnemühle paper mill, April 1983:

> The manager of the pulp paper mill in Hahnemühle, Herr Richard Schüll, was summoned to the RSHA headquarters in Berlin-Dahlem. After signing an undertaking to observe strictest security, he was informed that the Reich urgently needed foreign currency because of the war situation from 1 September 1939. As the pound sterling was a leading world currency at the time – rate £1 = RM20 – a German paper mill was sought that could reproduce the currency. As has been said, the paper for the English notes produced in England (by the company Portals) was thought to be made by a mechanised pulping process. So the mill would have to be able to produce handcrafted paper. The manufacturer would also have to generate the necessary raw materials and refine them further.

Herr Schüll was given some English notes of various denominations as samples to help the Hahnemühle experts solve the problem. Evidently the men from RSHA knew all about the facilities at the mill because they made references to the many types of fine-quality watermarked paper with horizontal dark and combined light and dark watermarks, which our firm had been producing for decades and exporting to other countries as cheques and currency exchange dockets. The raw materials used for it, fresh white linen and cotton rags, were provided by their own rag-processing department. There were ample facilities available for further processing, such as rag shredders, boilers, grinders for mixing fibres and bleaching machines.

After Herr Schüll returned from Berlin, I was summoned to his office. I was scarcely in the room when to my astonishment he shut the doors and windows. Then he came towards me and said that he had been sworn to secrecy by the RSHA in a high-security matter and he would require the same of me. Then he showed me English notes, which were quite different from German notes. They were larger and had very little black print; however, they had an impressive, distinctly attractive, excellently executed watermark of varying depth.

More tests and discussions took place during the remainder of 1941. Because of the tight security I had to carry out the analysis myself. In addition I had to take on the most important task of identifying the Bank of England 'security features' and check that they were accurately reproduced. If we had not done this it would have been pointless continuing. It was clear to me from the beginning that in this case it would not be enough only to use well-known criteria of the paper industry to establish surface weight, composition of material, ash content, coating and gloss, because those duds would only have a short exchange life.

While it took me some time to identify the details and analyse the paper used by the English, Schüll had found a suitable producer of the watermark patterns in the Duren area, with the help of the RSHA. This firm then started to prepare the first samples of watermarks. As everyone could see, it was not just a matter of making a simple Velin sieve with moulded dark watermarks or combined light and dark marks; in this case it had to be wire of varying thickness, a very fine network and counter pattern of wavy lines, which was very difficult to reproduce.

Meanwhile we had obtained a clearer picture from the analysis of the raw material. We found out that the raw material was composed of special fibres, especially quite fine ramie fibres from the Far East, mixed with first-class broad-weave linen fibres, which formed the embossed pattern. For security reasons we had to base our forgery on these features. The RSHA would see to the supply of ramie fibre. Ramie (China grass) is a fibre from a type of nettle – Boehmeria – with stalks about 2 metres high, found in East Asia, east and west India, Egypt, Algeria and Australia. The fibre is very strong, white, smooth and glossy. The breakdown of ramie fibres presented certain problems but we managed to overcome these by boiling, bleaching and pulping the mass. The fibrous material had to have certain characteristics to satisfy the requirements for producing watermarked paper. It had to be highly tear-proof and foldable. The watermark had to be distinct and unwrinkled. In addition, crushablity, fibre length and coating were important features. We had to be sure of smoothness, take into consideration the quality of the wet pulp and the peculiarities of the moulds and the relatively low surface weight of $40g/m^2$ – it was actually not at all easy to reduce everything to the lowest common denominator. While the sheets were being coated there could not be the slightest air bubble, wrinkle or fold. Since every frame did eight runs, from the outset we had to do everything in our power to ensure that wastage was not too high.

Finally the experts working on the project succeeded, as early as 1942, in producing top-quality paper, which corresponded in every respect to the English samples. In the meantime we had succeeded not only in identifying the security features, which were not visible in daylight, but also in reproducing them exactly. Basically it was a question of particular translucence under UV light and a particular type of translucence round the edges, for example after a little drop of water has dried. This was an important feature of the coating used in the paper manufacture.

After all the conditions for smooth-running production had been created and replicability was guaranteed, the frames for £5, £10, £20 and £50 notes could be made. The Hahnemühle paper workers who were on active service, many of them on battlefronts, were recalled by the RSHA and brought back to work.

From 1943 handmade paper was in full production. The workers needed more training time than usual for the process to run smoothly because of the $40g/m^2$ surface weight, the high density of the material and combined ingredients, but also for the particular formation of the watermark. Age-old ways of doing things had to be altered and new techniques introduced. The original sheet contained eight watermark runs, which were laid out on a fine surface separated by fine perforated tear-lines. In order to make the edges like the originals these lines were roughened after the printing process and not too sharply cut. Every hand-made sheet of paper had to be stacked after coating in piles of approximately 110 sheets, to be carefully flattened in a hydraulic press and drained. Only then could the pulper remove the wet sheet from the stack and place it on a so-called giant stack of about 500 sheets.

Handmade paper requires several additional processes, so that the structure is right in the final set-up. So in this case the wet stacks of paper were laid over each other in several lengths, individually separated by metal plates and put in a hand-press to flatten the surface. After the stack had been successfully loosened by moving the sheets to a new stack, the mechanical drying could take place over drying drums. Transport within the firm was in specially numbered, sealed crates, containing an exact description of the contents.

After the first drying, the sheets were stored in the crates for a time before a coating of animal glue was applied in a dipping process, followed by pressing out the surplus glue. After lying for a week, the sheets were again dried mechanically on drums, but at a fairly low temperature. The fine surface coating was particularly important with regard to maintaining the security features of the notes. After drying naturally for a few weeks, the fine paper sheets were smoothed on rollers so that the surface pattern could best be compared with the sample.

Then came the final process: sorting the usable and half-usable sheets and the separation of the inside tear-lines on the frame. Every sheet or frame was thoroughly tested against the light for impurities or other flaws. The A1 sheets had to be absolutely perfect, which meant that even the tiniest speck of dirt could not be allowed.

Hahnemühle provided the quality assurance whilst all the security measures demanded by the RSHA were observed in the paper mill. All areas used in the production, equipment and storage were sealed off and locked. Only the people working there had access, and of course their security guards from Berlin. The group of people who had been sworn to secrecy was also checked regularly by the Gestapo from Hildesheim, who had probably received a list of personnel from the RSHA.

Once the RSHA was satisfied with our product, it meant they could buy the necessary quantities of fibres anywhere in the world without any concerns about currency. It meant too that the secret service had plenty of currency at its disposal.

In the meantime, in April and May 1945, the end of the war was approaching. Hahnemühle had to raise the white flag and surrender on 20 April 1945. All paper still in the store had been destroyed by Good Friday, either by pulping or burned in the boiler house. We also had to destroy some frames, all files in my possession as well as some original English banknotes, including the printed comparison samples produced at the mill.

Production of handmade paper ceased in Hahnemühle in about February 1945.

Dassel, April 1983

Robert Bartsch

Photo from 1943 showing Robert Barsch, then managing director, conducting quality control, which began by cutting up the original sheet; all the necessary equipment was in another room

In this old office building, built in 1906 and demolished in 1961, the handmade paper for the sterling £5, £10, £20 and £50 notes was sorted and prepared for printing in KZ Sachsenhausen

Watermark on the £10 note (produced in Hahnemühle). Each mould could print eight runs of four, separated by fine perforated lines. A replica deckle edge was achieved (surface weight 40 g/m²)

Spechthausen paper mill – Ebart Bros & Co. – near Eberswalde, 1932

Former administration building of the Hahnemühle pulp paper mill in Dassel – it was the headquarters of paper production for the forgery operation from 1941 to 1945

Hahnemühle paper mill in Dassel

According to Robert Bartsch's statement, the following quantities of notes were produced from 1943 to 1945:

Raw production of English notes 1943–5

Tub	Sheets 1943	Sheets 1944	Sheets 1945	Total sheets
V	235,000	284,000	26,000	545,000
VI	307,000	319,000	26,000	652,000
VII		239,000	25,000	264,000
Total	542,000	842,000	77,000	1,461,000

Note: one sheet covers eight banknote-runs

Distribution of denominations

	£5	£10	£20	£50
Sheet	731,000	380,000	225,000	125,000
Run	5,848,000	3,040,000	1,800,000	1,000,000
= £	29,240,000	30,400,000	36,000,000	50,000,000
50% rejects = total £	14,620,000	15,200,000	18,000,000	25,000,000

Calculation total of pounds net in Reichsmark

	Value in £ stg	Value in Reichsmark
£5	14,620,000	292,400,000,-
£10	15,200,000	304,000,000,-
£20	18,000,000	360,000,000,-
£50	25,000,000	500,000,000,-
Total	72,820,000	1,456,400,000,-

Production of English Notes Begins

PRODUCTION STARTED IN 1942. NAUJOCKS had issued the contract for top-quality paper to be developed for the forgery of English notes. It had to correspond in every respect to the English samples. The printing plates were not so much of a problem. The complicated engraving process went on simultaneously with the paper manufacture. Printing could only begin when the 60 to 160 most important features of each note had been identified. The engravers worked on these in three shifts almost without interruption. They were all essential workers under oath.

They had the greatest difficulty with the ornate lettering and with Britannia's flowing robes, in which there was a particular security trap. After seven months the 'false' Britannia was indistinguishable from the real one and a few months later all other details had been expertly reproduced.

Colours were part of the printing process too. They were obtained from the Reich's printing works and chemicals were added so that they penetrated the

'Britannia', a motif on English notes that was difficult to forge

paper faster and the fine lines appeared blurred – the sign of an old note. Unless the colour composition had been altered, the notes would have looked too new.

Several mathematicians worked out the English system of registration numbers with the help of complex formulae.

The first notes printed by the security service in 'Operation Andreas' in Delbrückstrasse, Berlin, had to be put to the test for authenticity. To this end they were presented for exchange in Switzerland in late 1942. The person charged with this task even asked the Swiss bank official to check the notes, saying he had got them on the black market.

This 'industrialist' presented not only a bundle of forged notes but also a letter from the forgery department of the Reichsbank, which had been forged in Naujocks' workshop. The letter stated that it was possible that the notes were forgeries but that they had not the facilities in Berlin to check their authenticity. After three days the results came back. After thorough examination by experts the banknotes were declared authentic.

The middleman continued his bluff. He wanted to be absolutely sure and asked the Swiss to telegraph the Bank of England and check whether the serial numbers, dates of issue, etc. were correct. The answer came back: 'Everything in order – stop – banknotes with dates given are in circulation.' Naujocks was jubilant. Heydrich was delighted. Now the mass production 'Issue A' of the forged notes could go ahead.

Although Alfred Naujocks had had the 'brilliant idea', he fell into disfavour. Very shortly after his great triumph over the Swiss experts, he was demoted, on the orders of Heydrich, to the rank of a mere SS man and transferred to the front to the SS regiment 'Adolf Hitler's Bodyguard' (*Leibstandarte*) because he had bugged the rooms in Kitty's, the notorious Berlin brothel, and recorded diplomats and officers. He had even recorded Heydrich in bed.

Naujocks' successor as head of Section VI F 4 in the RSHA was SS-SBF Hermann Dörner. SS-SBF Bernhard Krüger, an engineer, was appointed director of banknote production. So the cover name was changed to 'Operation Bernhard' after him.

One of the greatest supporters of 'Operation Bernhard' was never to see the realisation of his novel utilisation of 'prison work': Heydrich, who had been protector of Bohemia and Moravia since 27 September 1941, died of injuries sustained in an assassination attempt by the Czech resistance on 4 June 1942. SS-Obergruppenführer (OGF) Dr Ernst Kaltenbrunner was appointed his successor as chief of security police, the secret service and thereby of the entire RSHA.

Management Structure of Secret Service for the Forgery Operation 1943–5

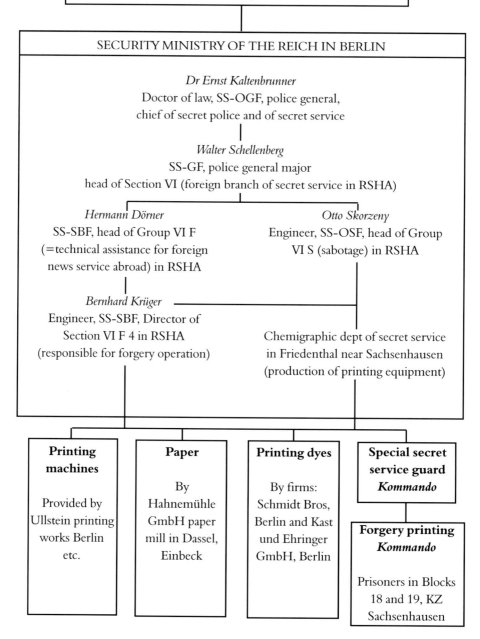

Heinrich Himmler
Reichsführer-SS, chief of police,
minister for the interior, head of armaments

SECURITY MINISTRY OF THE REICH IN BERLIN

Dr Ernst Kaltenbrunner
Doctor of law, SS-OGF, police general,
chief of secret police and of secret service

Walter Schellenberg
SS-GF, police general major
head of Section VI (foreign branch of secret service in RSHA)

Hermann Dörner
SS-SBF, head of Group VI F
(=technical assistance for foreign
news service abroad) in RSHA

Otto Skorzeny
Engineer, SS-OSF, head of Group
VI S (sabotage) in RSHA

Bernhard Krüger
Engineer, SS-SBF, Director of
Section VI F 4 in RSHA
(responsible for forgery operation)

Chemigraphic dept of secret service
in Friedenthal near Sachsenhausen
(production of printing equipment)

Printing machines	**Paper**	**Printing dyes**	**Special secret service guard** *Kommando*
Provided by Ullstein printing works Berlin etc.	By Hahnemühle GmbH paper mill in Dassel, Einbeck	By firms: Schmidt Bros, Berlin and Kast und Ehringer GmbH, Berlin	

Forgery printing *Kommando*

Prisoners in Blocks
18 and 19, KZ
Sachsenhausen

'Operation Bernhard'

Recruitment of Jewish Prisoners Qualified for the Printing Trade

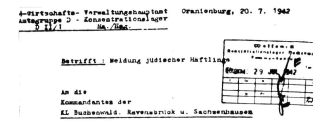

Department of the economy and administration
Oranienburg 20.7.1942
Group D — concentration camps
D II/1   NA. /Hag.
Re: Recruitment of Jewish prisoners
To: Commanders of KZ Buchenwald, Ravensbrück & Sachsenhausen
Prisoners in the camp who are qualified in the printing trade,
such as paper manufacturing, printers or suitable craftsmen
(e.g. barbers) are to report to me immediately.
If these Jewish prisoners are foreign nationals they must
speak German and state their nationality.
Closing date: 3 August 1942
Head of Section D II
Signature
SS Lieutenant

Only Jewish prisoners were to work in the secret service forgery block

ON 20 JULY 1942 A telegram was sent out from the central office for the economic administration of concentration camps in Berlin (SS-WVHA) to the commandants of KZ Buchenwald, Ravensbrück and Sachsenhausen with the following orders: Jewish prisoners in the camp who are qualified printers, paper experts or skilled workers (e.g. barbers) are to report immediately to this office. The prisoners may be foreign nationals but they must speak German. Nationality must be given when reporting. Deadline 3 August 1942.

3.August 1942.

Az.: AE-20/3-8.42.-Gr/Si.

Betreff: Meldung von jüdischen Fachkräften.
Bezug: Dorts.Schr.Az.: D/II/1-Ma./Hag.v.28.7.42.
Anlagen: -o-
Termin: 3.8.1942.

6

An das
SS-Wirtschafts-Verwaltungshauptamt
Amtsgruppe D - Amt II
Oranienburg.

Zu obigem Betreff meldet das K.L. Buchenwald:

         Friseure   11 *)
         Graphik   13
         Papierfach   3
                 27

Bei der vorstehenden Aufstellung handelt es sich ausschließlich um Juden. In der mit *) versehenen Zahl sind die Blockfriseure nicht einbegriffen.

                                 Der Lagerkommandant:

         I.A.:

                     SS-Obersturmführer.u.
                     Arbeitseinsatzführer.

```
                                        3 August 1942
File no: AE-20/3-8.42. -Gr/Si               6
Re: Recruitment of Jewish labour
Ref: Communication file no: D/II/1-Ma./Hag.of 28.7.42
Enclosures: -0-
Closing date: 3.8.1942
To: SS Department of Economy & Administration
Group D - Office II
Oranienburg.
With reference to above from KZ Buchenwald
                Hairdressers 11*)
                Illustrators 13
                Paper        3
The above prisoners are all Jewish. Typesetters are not
included in the figure marked *).

Camp commander
Initialled
Lieutenant & Head of Workforce
```

List of Jewish workers, qualified for the printing trade from KZ Buchenwald.
They were to work in the forgery workshop

On the basis of this order printing experts were selected from Buchenwald, Ravensbrück, Mauthausen, Theresienstadt and Auschwitz and transferred to Sachsenhausen. Krüger directed the preparations and carried out the forgery operation.

Thus began our journey to Sachsenhausen. Prisoners were transferred there from several concentration camps. In civilian life they had been printers, engravers, former bank executives or people with technical qualifications. The printing machines came from the Ullstein printing works in Berlin and other firms. Paper was delivered from the Hahnemühle paper mill in Dassel, Einbeck district. The printing inks were provided by Schmidt Bros of Berlin and by Kast und Ehringer, also in Berlin.

The *Kommando* began work in September 1942, at first with a team of twenty-six prisoners. By December 1942 the machines and equipment were set up in Blocks 18 and 19, which were surrounded with barbed-wire fencing. In January 1943 'Production B' started, i.e. the production of forged £5, £10, £20 and £50 notes. August Petrick, a civilian wearing the gold Nazi Party badge supervised the prisoners, who were also guarded by sixteen secret service guardsmen.

In the course of 1943 and the spring of 1944 further groups of prisoners arrived. By the autumn of 1944 there were 144 prisoners. The guards were constantly changed. Some were sent to the front and were replaced by wounded and invalided men. Work was organised under the orders of the RSHA. Prisoner number 46834, Artur Lewin, a fifty-four-year-old typesetter from Berlin, supervised the paper section at first, and later the printing section. He was eventually appointed block-warden. The prisoners started on tear-resistance tests of various types of paper under the direction of the foreman, prisoner number

Detail of code number AO937, series K54791187

Hans Kurzweil, prisoner number
46853, from Vienna

Victoria-Tiegel.
Millions of pounds worth of sterling notes
were printed on this type of machine

46853, Hans Kurzweil, a bookbinder from Vienna who was one of the most skilled of all the prisoners.

Meanwhile everything was ready for the forgery of the sterling pound notes. When there was a lot of work there were round-the-clock shifts in the paper room. One day a lorry delivered cases of paper with the watermarks of English banknotes.

The stacks of paper, which arrived from the Hahnemühle mill, measured 50 cm by 60 cm. They had to be cut in two vertically. Four notes were printed on each half sheet. The pattern of watermarks on a sterling note is a thick network of horizontal wavy lines and a wider network of vertical wavy lines further apart. The words 'Bank of England' are worked into this pattern along the upper and lower edge of the notes. In the middle is a watermark, stating the value of the note e.g. TEN or FIVE. In each corner the same value is given in figures. In the upper left corner is the outline of an oval shape standing on its end without a watermark. Above the lower words BANK OF ENGLAND, set in a frame, a four-figure number indicated (to the initiated) the date the paper was produced. The first two figures gave the week, the third and fourth figures the year. The real watermarks were separated from the narrow rim of the note by a wavy line. The edge was slightly ragged.

The printing plates (letterpress) for the printing of the English notes were made of copper in a secret workshop run by the RSHA under SBF Skorzeny in Schloss Friedenthal, 2 or 3 kilometres from Oranienburg. Here SF Heinz

Schloss Friedenthal near Sachsenhausen.
The printing plates were produced here

Gebhart, the civilians Herbert Paul and Rau and two female photographers (who were SS members) worked. In this workshop there were hydraulic presses, installation equipment for a galvanoplastic facility, and a store for the materials needed for the forgery workshop in Sachsenhausen.

The printing blocks that were produced by photography were passed on to the copper-engraving workshop in Blocks 18 and 19. The copper engravers there had the task of exactly reproducing every line and every dot on the printing plate for the banknotes. The following engravers did this work: Felix Cytrin, prisoner number 14898; Severin Tiefenbach, prisoner number 67865; David Bialer, prisoner number 102445; Leib Fried, prisoner number 102441; Laib Italiener, prisoner number 67866; Leib Zyberski, prisoner number. 67869.

Oskar Stein, the Czech anti-fascist, also kept his own list of the banknotes produced and delivered. This was very dangerous, of course, but it was thanks to him that we had exact details of the forgery. Leo Krebs, prisoner number 46681,

Engineer Oskar Stein, prisoner number 47832. Drawing by Leo Haas, 1944

Krüger's favourite item, the £5 note.
It was forged to the value of £19,729,330 sterling

The total value of £10 notes printed was £23,989,800

Total value of £20 notes printed was £26,746,680

Total value of £50 notes printed was £64,145,000

was appointed foreman of the printing department and Max Bober, prisoner number 46855, the foreman of the setting room.

The notes were printed four at a time onto the watermarked sheet in an automated process. Then the serial numbers were printed with the help of a counter. For example, on the £5 notes, the word FIVE was printed on the left hand side in special black dye in a separate process. On the lower half of the note there was a number in the watermark. This number was linked to the printed numbering on the note. The RSHA knew this code. The printing works were under direct surveillance of the SS and we all worked under constant guard.

All printed forgeries were entered in registers according to denomination, series and numbers. Forgeries that were delivered to the RSHA were also recorded in these books. Oskar Stein, prisoner number 47832, a Czech from Tábor, was in charge of the registers. The printed sheets were passed on to the sorting and cutting room. Dr Kaufmann was foreman of the cutting room and Oskar Stein was sorting foreman. Each sheet of four forged notes was cut with rulers. The forged notes were then put in the press in batches of a thousand, where the edges were rasped to make it look like handmade paper. Finally the printed forgeries were laid out for inspection.

The inspection section was in the same room as cutting. The prisoner assigned to this work had to be particularly careful. He knew all the secret marks on the English notes and had to compare every detail with the real notes. He had to ensure that he did not miss the slightest flaw in the paper. The checkers, former bank officials, sat at a table in front of a small inspection box. These were the size of a banknote, with an opaque glass lid, lit from below by a very strong light. This way the entire note could be checked. The prisoners doing the checking worked relatively slowly. Their daily total was 300 notes. The prisoners who did this work were often changed around because very good eyesight was required.

The finished notes were divided into four categories. First-class forgeries went into the first category. The second contained notes with slight, almost invisible flaws. In the third category were notes with printing errors: these were to be dropped over England by German planes and would serve to devalue English currency. The fourth category was for poor-quality forgeries, which were destroyed. The selected notes were then dirtied and crumpled, to make them look like used notes. Then they were put in bundles of 500 and entered in the register again.

The English used to carry money loose in their pockets, with notes held together by a safety pin. So in the forgery workshop a special group of prisoners was formed with the task of pinning notes together with safety pins. The prisoners would pierce the notes in the upper corner, where Britannia was depicted. Notes were never pinned like this in reality. They did it in case we ever succeeded in smuggling out news of the forgery from our 'gilded cage'. Then the forgeries would be easily distinguished from the real notes. But the opportunity never arose.

The forged notes were stored in a special room. Once a week they were taken away by Krüger. Millions went through the forgery camp and the secret service kept track of them all. Krüger's only interest was to maintain the schedule of the forgery programme. Whenever the prisoners reached their target he treated them in a fatherly manner, rewarding their 'good work' with cigarettes, which he always carried in his pocket. Before he left the block with the forged money he would check the books carefully. Then he would disappear for another week.

Oskar Stein kept his own personal list of the banknotes produced and delivered. The following tables are based on his statement.

Value of sterling notes produced and delivered

Denomination of note	Value of printed banknotes	Value of (good) notes delivered
£5	19,729,330	1,324,310
£10	23,989,800	1,765,600
£20	26,746,680	2,820,920
£50	64,145,000	4,457,600
Total value in £	134,610,810	10,368,430

Number of sterling notes produced and delivered

Banknotes	Printed and numbered	Taken to RSHA	Percentage of (good) forgeries delivered
£5	3,945,866	264,862	6.7
£10	2,398,980	176,560	7.3
£20	1,337,334	141,046	10.4
£50	1,282,900	89,152	6.9
Total	8,965,080	671,620	7.5

Summary/overview of good forgeries according to denomination

Banknotes	Value in £	Total value of low denominations	Total value of high denominations	Percentage
£5	1,324,310	3,089,910		29.80
£10	1,765,600			
£20	2,820,920			
£50	4,457,600		7,278,520	70.20
Total	10,368,430			100.00

7

Into Liberated Yugoslavia with Forged Money

THE FIRST WORK I WAS assigned was relatively easy: forging Yugoslavian banknotes. Within 'Fortress Europe', as the Nazis called occupied Europe since 1941, there was free territory under the control of partisans. In the course of 1942, 1943 and 1944 the liberated parts of Yugoslavia covered larger areas than many of the smaller European countries (Austria, Switzerland, Hungary). The partisans controlled the administration of this free territory. The peoples' committees of local and district councils had their representatives who had joined together to form the Anti-Fascist Council of National Liberation of Yugoslavia (AVNOJ) in November 1942. The administration of the economy, agriculture and distribution of food was kept going with varying degrees of success. The liberation army needed money and it was necessary to raise a national loan through subscription.

On 13 January 1944 the executive committee of the AVNOJ raised the first general peoples' loan. The people saved whatever they could and handed in dinars, kunas, Reichsmark, lire, pengos, credit notes of the occupation administration – all currencies that were circulating in occupied Yugoslavia.

In Croatia two tranches of the national loan, a total of 250,000,000 kuna/lire, were distributed. The State Assembly of Slovenia announced a liberation loan of 50,000,000 Lire and later in Bosnia and Herzogovina a peoples' liberation loan of 300,000,000 dinar/kuna. In the space of one month, January 1944, large amounts of this loan were assigned as follows: 4,107,000 lire for the devastated Montenegro, the city of Split 7,746,400 kuna, Slovenia 33,968,000 lire, Croatia 248,129,366 kuna, to Bosnia 21,405,000 dinar/kuna. Loans and bonds were also earmarked by the partisans in the occupied zones. 13,500,000 Lire were assigned to Ljubliana, capital of Slovenia, which was surrounded by barbed-wire and air-raid shelters.

The material and financial help provided for the population by the loan was immediately noticeable. Considerable amounts were handed over to the peoples' committees and the army to support the people. The national bonds – the first 'partisan money' – was used as currency in the liberated territories. At the beginning of 1944 an issuing bank, Denarni zavod Slovenije, was established, which was the first free bank in occupied Europe. The first banknotes of a free people were printed in the heart of Hitler's 'Fortress Europe'. When the Gestapo became aware of what boost the partisan movement got from the loan, it prepared to retaliate.

In order to undermine the Yugoslav peoples' liberation loan, 'tricoloured' Tito banknotes were expertly forged in Sachsenhausen. The reproductions were so exact, down to the last detail of paper and print, that it was impossible to distinguish them from the real thing. The money printed on the machine I worked on was the very same as the money being circulated by the Yugoslav Peoples' Liberation Army. Hundreds of thousands of these banknotes had already been printed in the forgery workshop to destabilise the currency in liberated Yugoslavia.

Peoples' loan bond. The first partisan money in Yugoslavia

Peoples' loan bond

1944 – Yugoslav partisan money forged in Blocks 18 and 19, KZ Sachsenhausen

In 1944 this money was circulated in the liberated territory in Yugoslavia. The branch of the Gestapo in Agram (Zagreb), capital of Croatia, attempted to undermine the success of the peoples' loan that had been raised by the AVNOJ.

Meanwhile I had been working for half a year producing forged sterling notes. I had quickly got used to my surroundings and to my work. The total value of the sterling notes we were forging never occurred to me. I often wondered whose hands they fell into and whether some agent or other was picked up because of them. But there was not much time for reflection. Work took up most of the day. In the evening we were glad to go to bed, tired and happy.

8

Distribution of Sterling Notes

A MAN CALLED FRITZ PAUL Schwend was in charge of the distribution of the forged money. He started his career as a car mechanic in a petrol station in southern Germany. Because he knew a bit about aeroplane engines, he got to know the brother of Agnes von Gemmingen, which turned out to be a useful liaison.

When he married the twenty-four-year-old Agnes at the age of twenty-three, her family was bankrupt. He had to work as a salesman until Edouard Bunge, a relative by marriage, died in 1933 leaving a fortune of almost 32 million francs. The Schwend family inherited 120,000 francs. Fritz and Agnes Schwend bought themselves a house at Chiemsee and he tried his hand at arms dealing with Persia, without success. Bankrupt again, he decided to go to America to see Aunt Charlotte, Edouard Bunge's widow. She had become a recluse and with her money had joined the Mazdaznan sect. Aunt Charlotte lived according to the seasons (following the teaching of the ancient Persian religious philosopher, founder of the Zarathustran religion). She donated a great deal of her money to the sect, to the disapproval of the Bunge children, who lived in Switzerland. Aunt Charlotte became friendly with Fritz and Agnes and on 14 May 1936 she appointed Fritz to be her property manager.

Himmler's forgery distribution manager,
SS-SBF Fritz Paul Schwend, alias Dr Wendig

Schwend now had money to work with. He bought the Villa Rose-Marie in Abbazia, a sleepy little seaside town in Italy (now in Slovenia). It was there he started his currency and smuggling business. At that time it was legal to deal in currency and to possess foreign currency. There he met Germans who had buried money in secret accounts abroad. By reporting these people to the customs, he got richer by a few marks and because he had money at his disposal, he soon had many loyal helpers under him. He met pretty Hadda Neuhold on the beach – she became his secretary and mistress. Ferry Manser and his brother were two of his men, as was Alois Glavan (Capitano) and his mistress, the Yugoslavian Feodora Campanella, and the two Blaschke brothers, who were former bakers.

But soon the authorities were on the track of his illegal activities. He was arrested in 1941 and imprisoned in Klagenfurt. The head of the secret service in Rome, USF Dr Groebel, brought Schwend to the attention of the Italian representative in the secret service abroad, SS-SBF Dr Wilhelm Höttl, whereupon Höttl informed the RSHA in Berlin. Schwend's files were thoroughly checked and it was quickly agreed that Engineer Paul Schwend was a financial genius, and just the right man for 'Operation Bernhard'. Schwend was released from prison in 1942. Dr Arno Groebel took him under his wing and shortly after that Schwend got special ID passes and special authorisation. He was a free man again, working on top-secret Reich business.

He had connections across the world. He had travelled as a salesman all over Europe and the American continent, from Alaska to Tierra del Fuego. He built up an enormous distribution organisation and was promoted to SBF in the Waffen-SS. His headquarters were at Labers Castle near Merano and it bore the official title: 'Special Task General Commando III.Gemanic Panzer Corps'. Now he was no longer called Fritz Schwend but Dr Wendig. Schwend-Wendig was allocated a commission of 33 per cent of his 'turnover', from which he had to pay his agents 25 per cent. In turn the chief operators had to let their sub-contracted small-fry dealers have a share.

Schwend's organisation soon covered almost the whole world. He had his people in Africa, the United States, Argentina, Brazil, Chile, Honduras and Uruguay. His men operated in India, China and Japan, all over the Near East, and of course in all European countries. He maintained business links with the Vatican. His cover was as a technical assistant in the German Embassy in the Vatican. The secret service used people from all strata of society; business people, high-ranking officers and diplomats were initiated into his business. Trade attachés at the embassies of Hitler's Germany in Ankara, Berne, Lausanne, Lisbon, Madrid and Rome received large quantities of forged sterling notes.

The secret service used the forged notes – in occupied, allied and neutral countries, either on the black market or 'legally' in enemy countries – to procure gold, precious stones, jewellery or foreign currency. The financial distribution of the forged money was done by the special Section VI Economy (VI-W) in Section VI of the RSHA. The effects were noticeable throughout every conti-

Labers Castle near Merano (Italy), the distribution headquarters of 'Operation Bernhard'. From here the forged money was circulated all over the world

nent. In Europe the secret service traded its forged currency in Andorra, Belgium, Denmark, France, Greece, Ireland, Italy, Yugoslavia, Liechtenstein, Monaco, the Netherlands, Norway, Portugal, Sweden, Switzerland, Slovakia, Spain, Turkey and Hungary.

The members of the distribution network did extensive business in the employ of the secret service and of course for themselves. Many who were later respectable citizens founded their businesses, built their villas, or bought their wives jewellery with 'Bernhard' money. The sterling notes, all neatly packed and well guarded, made their way secretly from Sachsenhausen around the world.

Business was booming. They were a success everywhere. The stream of forged money reached Great Britain. By the end of the war the forged money would have amounted to 40 per cent of the authentic money in circulation. The 137 prisoners who were liberated on 5 May 1945 and who had been forced to work on the forgery of sterling notes informed the relevant authorities in England and the United States about 'Operation Bernhard'. As a result the Bank of England withdrew notes from £10 upwards. Later the £5 notes were withdrawn and replaced by new ones.

The sum taken by the Nazis must have been 48 million dollars (RM192 million). Because the transactions were done at black market rates the sum was in fact much higher. Between 1945 and 1960 the forgeries kept turning up and caused considerable problems in Czechoslovakia. In all more than 3,000 forged notes, which had been produced in Sachsenhausen, were seized by the banks to the value of £35,000.

After the war the American secret service was preoccupied with exposing the currency black market, but it only succeeded in seizing about 9 per cent of the

the entire quantity of forged money. The results are very revealing as we can see the distribution ratios of the forged notes:

Country	Forged sterling notes	Percentage share
Spain, Portugal, Switzerland	7,500,000	62.5
Denmark, Norway, Sweden	3,000,000	25.0
Turkey, Middle/Near Eastern states	1,500,000	12.5
Total	12,000,000	100.0

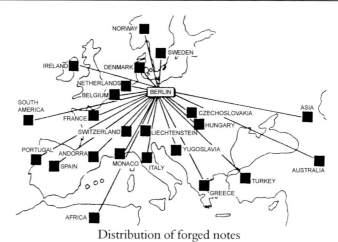

Distribution of forged notes

England had to issue new sterling banknotes

9

Salamon Smolianoff – Forgery Expert

ONE DAY OUR SPECIAL UNIT was increased by one. A man arrived who was said to be a forgery expert. The evening before he arrived, Krüger made an unusual announcement: 'Tomorrow a most experienced forger is joining us. We have known of him for a long time, but only recently managed to find out where he lived. He is just the man for this job and we have waited for him for a long time. With his help we will overcome all difficulties and complete our task.'

We had our own opinions about the man with the 'great reputation' whom Krüger was expecting. The next morning at 11 a.m. the door opened and a small rotund man came in, accompanied by two SS men. Krüger welcomed him, 'You must be tired; take a rest so that you can start tomorrow.' Then he turned to us and said: 'Now we have our expert.'

We prisoners gathered round our new 'colleague'. He made a good impression and seemed to be cheerful. The thinning hairline made us think he was going on fifty. His name was Salamon Smolianoff, born on 26 March 1887 in Poltawa, Russia. He was a Russian émigré, who was known to crime investigators as being respected among criminal forgers. He had had an interesting life.

He had shown signs of artistic talent at an early age and his father sent him to the Art College in Odessa, where he was a pupil of the famous Professor Eugen Zotoff who taught at the college and had made a name for himself in copper and steel engraving. In 1917 Smolianoff emigrated to Germany. In the imperial capital he met up again with Zotoff, who had also emigrated.

Both artists had to start from scratch. They did it their own way – art did not put bread on the table. Teacher and pupil used their combined skills to forge banknotes. They both became well known to Interpol. In 1923 Zotoff was sentenced to four years' penal servitude for forging coins. Smolianoff got off lightly because there was no evidence that he was involved in the Zotoff enterprise.

Smolianoff was arrested in 1927 in Amsterdam for forgery and distribution of the first £50 sterling notes, by the Nederlandsche Centrale in Zaken Falsificaten (the Dutch centre of Forgeries). Again he was lucky: on 12 July 1933 a Dutch court sentenced him to two years and six months' imprisonment for circulating forged money. He could not be punished as a 'producer' because there was no evidence. In 1933 Interpol succeeded in rumbling a new forgery ring of Smolianoff's accomplices, yet he managed to slip the net. He was only caught in 1936 in Berlin because he did not get away in time with his forged Swedish passport.

Salamon Smolianoff – master forger.

He was sentenced to four years' penal servitude by a Berlin court. After serving that sentence he was sent to KZ Mauthausen as an 'incorrigible criminal'. There Krüger finally discovered the 'King of the Forgers' and had him brought to Sachsenhausen straight away.

In Mauthausen his skill and reputation as an artist had saved his life. He did portraits of the SS men. In his new workplace in Sachsenhausen he was to work as a retoucher in the production of US dollars. He started work the very next day. Smolianoff, prisoner number 93594, was the only professional money forger of the 144 political prisoners in the forgery unit.

Kriminalkurrenden u. Kriminalberichte

„**ERKENNUNGSZEICHEN**"
Wien, I., Hohenstaufengasse 7

November 1927

| V. Abteilung |
| II. Gruppe |
| Nr. 16 |

Kriminalbericht Nr. 16

K. B. Nr. 1019

Verhaftung wegen Fälschung und Verbreitung gefälschter englischer Banknoten zu 50-Pfund

Wegen Fälschung und Verbreitung der in der I. Abteilung der „ERKENNUNGSZEICHEN" (Blatt E=n=1 vom Oktober 1926) beschriebenen Fälschungen von englischen Banknoten zu 50-Pfund, Type 1, wurde in *Amsterdam* (Holland) durch die *Nederlandsche Centrale in zake Falsificaten (Niederländische Falschgeld-Zentrale)* verhaftet:

S m o l i a n o f f Salomon, geboren am 26. März 1897 in *Poltawa* (Rußland) alias:

G ä r t n e r Nathanael, geboren am 21. Dezember 1899 in *Hamburg* (Deutschland), auch

V e r m e r Matheus, geboren am 21. Dezember 1888 in *Hamburg* (Deutschland), auch

B r e m e r L., Smolianoff gab an, in *Deutschland* (Leipzig, Berlin und Hamburg), *Ungarn* (Budapest), *Norwegen* (Oslo und Bergen), *Tschechoslowakei* (Prag) sowie in *Schweden* (Stockholm) und auch in *Holland* (Amsterdam) diese Falschstücke ausgegeben zu haben.

'Identification'
Vienna 1, Hohenstaufengasse 7

Section V

November 1927
  2nd Group

No. 16

Criminal record No.16
  K.B. No. 1019
Arrested in Amsterdam, Holland for forgery and circulation of sterling £50 notes.
(File ref: Page E=n=1 October 1926)
Smolianoff, Salamon, b. 26 March 1897 in Poltava (Russia) alias:

  Gärtner, Nathaniel, b. 21 December 1899 in Hamburg (Germany) and

  Vermer, Matheus, b. 21 December 1888 in Hamburg (Germany) and

  Bremer L., Smolianoff claimed to have circulated these forgeries in Germany (Leipzig, Berlin, Hamburg), Hungary (Budapest), Norway (Oslo, Bergen), Czechoslovakia (Prague), Sweden (Stockholm) and in Holland (Amsterdam).

Police report concerning Smolianoff, 1927

Kriminalkurrenden u. Kriminalberichte

„ERKENNUNGSZEICHEN"
Wien, I., Rockhgasse 4

Juni 1936

V. Abteilung
II. Gruppe
Nr. 12

Kriminalbericht Nr. 12[1]

K. B. Nr. 1196

Aburteilung wegen Herstellung gefälschter englischer Banknoten zu 10-Pfund, Type 4 und 6

Smolianoff Salomon, Kunstmaler, wurde am 12. März 1936 von der 20. großen Strafkammer des Landgerichtes Berlin als der Hersteller der gefälschten englischen Banknoten zu 10-Pfund, Type 4 und 6, festgestellt und wegen fortgesetzten Münzverbrechens verurteilt.

In Richtigstellung des Kriminalberichtes Nr. 18 (Jahrgang 1935: V. Abteilung, II. Gruppe, Nr. 18) wird mitgeteilt, daß der als Hersteller dieser Fälschungen bezeichnete russische Flüchtling Miassojedoff (Miassoiedoff), wie von den Behörden in Berlin festgestellt wurde, an diesen Fälschungsfällen nicht beteiligt war. Wie aus dem Urteil des obenerwähnten Gerichtes hervorgeht, kommt Miassojedoff als Hersteller dieser Fälschungen aus dem Grunde nicht in Frage, weil er sich vom 11. März 1932 bis 18. März 1934 ununterbrochen in Strafhaft befunden hat.

Siehe November 1927: Kriminalbericht Nr. 16 (V. Abteilung, II. Gruppe, Nr. 16), Jahrgang 1933: Kriminalbericht Nr. 23 (V. Abteilung, II. Gruppe, Nr. 23) und Jahrgang 1935: Kriminalkurrende Nr. 11 (V. Abteilung, I. Gruppe, Nr. 11) und Kriminalbericht Nr. 18 (V. Abteilung, II. Gruppe, Nr. 18), ferner Beschreibungen der Fälschungen Jahrgang 1933: I. Abteilung, E=n=2, Jahr-

---

[1] Nachtrag zu: Jahrgang 1935, Kriminalbericht Nr. 18 (V. Abteilung, II. Gruppe, Nr. 18).

'Identification'
Vienna 1, Rockhgasse 4

June 1936

Section V
2nd Group
No. 12

Criminal record No. 12

K.B. No. 1196

Smolianoff Salomon, painter, was found guilty in the Berlin Criminal Court (20 Strafkammer des Landgerichtes) of forgery of sterling £10 notes type 4 and 6 and of other forgery offences and sentenced.

Correction of criminal record No. 18 (1935 Section V, 2nd Group, No. 18) stating that the Russian refugee Miassoiedoff could not have participated in this forgery, as had been claimed by the authorities in Berlin, because he was in custody from 11 March 1932 until 18 March 1934.
See November 1927: criminal record no. 16.

Police report concerning Smolianoff, 1936

Salamon Smolianoff, master forger
(self-portrait)

Professor Eugen Zotoff, specialist
copper and steel engraver

10

Dollar Forgery

IN SEPTEMBER 1944 KRÜGER APPEARED in his forgery workshop and announced, 'Gentlemen, from today we are going to produce dollars too.' Krüger lived in Berlin and only came to Sachsenhausen to carry out his weekly inspections. He gave orders to his second-in-command, SS-HSF Kurt Werner, to choose eight prisoners who would work only on dollar forgery.

There was great excitement amongst us prisoners. Everyone wanted to be among the chosen few, because we all knew that there would be big problems forging dollars. To work on that would mean not having to work as hard and not being under constant surveillance. Who would be in the group? We waited expectantly for the decision. Finally Werner named the eight prisoners.

First and foremost, Smolianoff had the most important job. Then there were Norbert (Leonard) Levy, head of the photography section, Abraham Jacobson, head of copying, Leonard and Roger Weill as retouchers, the painters Leo Haas and Peter Edel and finally me, the printer.

I could only think of one reason why Werner had chosen me in particular for this 'assignment'. In the common room there was a table-tennis table for the prisoners. Sometimes the SS guards took part in the competitions. Of course the prisoners always let them win. Once Werner challenged me to a game. I was a good player and took my chance and won. My mates reproached me, 'You fool! That's all we need. He'll make you pay for it.' The next day Werner came back and challenged me to a return match. This time he won. From that day on he treated me with more good will and this was probably the reason he included me in the group.

There were special rooms set aside for the 'dollar group'. New machines and different paper arrived from Berlin. Soon after, Krüger brought in real $50 and $100 bills and gave them to Jacobson, the foreman.

Jacobson told Krüger on his next visit that dollar production would be unusually difficult. 'That doesn't matter,' he answered. 'Don't rush. We have plenty of time . . .' The problem was that Krüger wanted to produce the dollars using collotype, but the real dollar notes were produced by intaglio. Krüger would not hear of changing the process, because it would have taken a long time to produce the plate. The dollars were to be produced by collotype whatever the cost.

This photographic method can reproduce a drawing very sharply and is suitable for reproducing halftones. A matt glass plate is coated with a layer of gelatine, which is rendered photosensitive with a chemical (ammonium bichromate) and dried at 50 °Celsius. The surface then has a uniformly fine-grained finish. After illumination under a negative in the water-bath, the parts of the plate show up in varying strengths and correspondingly repel the greasy ink. By careful rocking a print emerges, with the image fully reproduced. This process has only one disadvantage: only a thousand prints can be produced from one plate. This did not matter once it worked – enormous quantities of the plates would be made in Sachsenhausen.

The eight of us worked in isolation from other prisoners. No one else was allowed to enter our three rooms in the back part of the block. First we learned how to produce playing cards and postcards by this process. We only produced sample dollars after that. The greatest difficulty lay in transferring the image of the banknote onto the glass plate. The dollar group did not need to create delays because the problems of forgery took up a lot of time anyway. We experimented for weeks on end and Smolianoff was in his element.

Trials were carried out continually and I had the job of keeping an album of all the special trials. This album was used to compare results.

Salamon Smolianoff at work, drawing by Leo Haas

The last project in the forgery workshop: production of $50 and $100 bills.
Only two hundred $100 bills were printed

11

Resistance

THE YEAR 1944 WAS DRAWING to a close and every day we grew more certain that the defeat of the Nazis was only a matter of months or even weeks away. So we decided to prolong the production of dollar bills so that they could no longer be used by the secret service. In spite of close surveillance and increasing threats, Abraham Jacobson had the moral courage to sabotage the work in a big way. He had been an officer in the Dutch army and was brave enough to put the SS off the trail without them suspecting a thing.

Smolianoff had taken charge of the most important task in the forgery process. He had to touch up the negative, so that the contours were sharply defined for the printing. Smolianoff experimented for four months without satisfactory results. At the beginning of January 1945 he completed his 200th unsuccessful attempt. Abraham Jacobson smiled mischievously to me and said, 'See, Dolfi, it's still no good.' He handed me a full sheet of poor-quality forged dollar bills, which he had just taken off the press.

'You are a master, Abi. If I'm not mistaken, the gelatine was off.'

'Of course. Smolianoff's negative was perfect as usual.'

'Yes, Smolianoff is very talented.'

'Indeed he is. And he is determined to prove his talent at all costs. Day and night he sits in his studio with magnifying glass, touching up. He really slaves away in every sense of the word. He is very proud of his reputation and intends to preserve it.'

'Do you think so, even here in Sachsenhausen?'

'Yes, because he wants to show off his skill to everyone, even the SS. He produces better and better work. But thank God we know how to go about the collotype: let in too much light, spoil the gelatine, everything is possible.' Jacobson grinned as he said these words.

It was easier said than done to sabotage the work, yet still we managed it.

Krüger stood in front of the clouded-glass window, his legs apart. 'Jacobson,' he shouted. Jacobson came rushing over from his machine, his dye-stained hands by his sides. Krüger pointed to the reproductions spread out on the table with a sweeping gesture, lifted up one, waving it under Jacobson's nose.

'Come on, out with it. Is this any use or not?'

'Not quite yet, in my opinion,' answered Jacobson quietly. His throaty Dutch accent seemed to rile the officer.

'"Not yet",' he imitated him. 'When then, H–Herr H–Hakobson?'

Jacobson dared to shrug his shoulders. He said we would continue printing, but so far the colours were not as intense as the original. Furthermore, he added, the decoration and ornamentation were blurred, as the Obersturmbannführer had seen for himself, which was not surprising, considering the original dollar bills were produced by intaglio and that the problem arose because they were attempting to achieve the same effect, and reproduce exactly the same details, by a totally different method, namely collotype printing.

'That's enough,' Krüger said dismissively. He had heard this litany of excuses before. 'Nevertheless I don't care how you do it. The main thing is to get it right.' Turning to Smolianoff, he asked, 'Well, have you anything to say about this? What do you think is causing the blurred colours?'

Before Smolianoff could answer, Peter Edel interrupted, unprompted. Shocked by his own courage, he even forgot the compulsory form of address: 'Permission to say something, sir.'

'Come on, out with it,' Krüger wheeled round to face him. Now there was no going back, now he had to give voice to the idea that had occurred to him like a flash of lightning during the discussion – a sudden idea. I don't know how he thought of it, nor why he said it so directly and clumsily. 'Maybe if they had very fine brushes instead of retouching pens for the tiny fine lines, the heliogravure and so on, fine pointed brushes, super-fine hair brushes, that would bend and curve at the slightest pressure . . .' Edel dried up.

Krüger looked at him with a strange smile, 'Brushes! Have you not got plenty of them here?'

Smolianoff butted in: 'Yes of course, but . . .', probably glad that that criticism was being deflected to materials.

'But what?'

'Brushes as pointed as needles, only more flexible; we have not got the type Edel means. Ours are bad, very bad.'

'And what kind of magic brushes are they? Where can you get them?'

'Maybe in Spitta und Leutz – they used to be available from an artists' suppliers in Wittenbergplatz,' suggested Edel.

'You used to be able to get lots of things before the war,' Krüger laughed, mockingly. 'The fine artists' suppliers shop was bombed long ago. But we could ask around. The man has to have what he needs. What are they called then, watercolour brushes or what?'

'Yes, sir. But they are different from these ones we have. They are called Chinese brushes, made of bamboo.'

'You are making a fool of me,' Krüger seemed to be suddenly enjoying this. Where on earth was he to get them from? Peking? Or did Edel really think he would send out a *Kommando* just to track down Chinese paintbrushes? That's a howl. 'But if that's true, do you think you can do a better job, Smolianoff? Haas, what do you think? Well, Burger, Weill, Jacobson, Leonard, is he right?'

Abraham Jacobson, foreman of the
dollar forgery group

Peter Edel – one of the youngest in
the forgery *Kommando*

We nodded, amazed at the turn the interrogation had taken. Well, we could try, it seemed reasonable.

'Sure,' Krüger grinned, ironically casual, 'I thought so. It's because of those little paintbrushes. Never short of an excuse. Hmm? Are you? And supposing I believed you. Where are we going to get them, without stealing them?'

'Maybe I know, I mean, where there might be some,' Edel burst out.

'Really, now! And you are only saying that now? So we have been wasting time beating round the bush here, holding everyone back. Why can't you just tell us, straight out? Come on! Where do you mean?'

'At home in my house, sir. I mean at my mother's. My painting things must be still there. But I don't know if they are or if my mother is. I've only just remembered. I thought, I wouldn't dare ask you about that.'

'You thought so, did you? I'll worry about that.' Krüger's mouth twisted into a cruel smile.

'Come with me,' he said. He crossed the yard with Edel and stopped at the door to the cutting room. He grabbed him by the lapels.

'Did you write to your mother?'

'Yes I did.'

'Any answer?'

'No. Not yet.'

'So that's it. You don't need your art stuff, it's just an excuse, so that we . . . well, you know the score. No lies now, let's have some straight talking. Well?'

'We could really use the materials.'

'Supposing you get what you want, that would be news!'

Edel said nothing. Krüger seemed to be considering the situation or at least he gave that impression. His questions proved to Edel that he had seen through the ploy straightaway, only it was clearer to him now than it had been when Edel came out with his spontaneous remark. What a stupid idea. Why should Krüger, this crafty man, who directed a million-dollar operation and was in charge of arsenals of materials of all sorts, why should he have to rely on a few art materials belonging to a prisoner? But obviously that was not the way Krüger thought. Without another word he pushed Edel through the door, walked casually past the block-warden, who shouted 'Achtung', and straight to the desk between the bookcases in the middle of the cutting room.

'Sit down there.' Krüger took the black cover off the rickety old typewriter and inserted a sheet of paper. 'Well, what's wrong? Do you expect me to type it too? You want something, don't you? So write it down.'

'About the paintbrushes?'

'Yes, of course. What else?'

Edel did not know what was happening to him. He had no way of knowing what might have moved Krüger to let him write to his mother, something he would not remotely have hoped for. Krüger looked over Edel's shoulder, reading what he was typing with two fingers: 'various Chinese brushes, particularly the fine and finest ones, sizes one to zero'. Krüger grabbed the sheet of paper, tore it out of the roller. What sort of rubbish was that? Did he think he was writing an order to a supplier? Or did he expect Krüger to draft a rough version for him?

Krüger quickly explained to him that he wanted instructions to his mother to give the bearer of the letter the materials – a proper letter with the right address, written like a real letter. 'What do we write: Dear Mother, Mum, Mama, well? what? – and sign off properly. Do you understand?' Krüger did not like the look of a basic list of certain types of paintbrush. He did not say why, although Edel could see why: it probably seemed too obvious and the recipient of the letter would wonder what was so special about those particular brushes.

'While we are at it,' he ordered, 'get the whole lot. Ask for all your art stuff. Your mother will be happy to know that we are looking after you so well. What does your stuff consist of?'

Edel was dumbstruck. Finally, he stammered, giving a full list: 'Oil paints, palette, outdoor easel, paintbox, compass case, mixing bowls, calligraphy pens, spraying apparatus and accessories and . . .'

'Spray, that's a good one,' interrupted Krüger, 'we can do with all that. Write it all down neatly, the whole lot.'

Edel wrote, as he was bid: 'KZ Sachsenhausen. Dear Mum, on the instructions of SS-SBF Krüger (who pointed at the key with the SS runes himself and did not object to the use of his name), I am writing to ask you to give the bearer of this letter the following materials . . .' And he finished off after the list: 'Many thanks for your trouble, love from your Peter.'

SS-OSF Heizmann arrived at Peter's mother's door with the letter. 'My name is Heizmann, ma'am, may I come in?' he said, holding up papers with the letter and the instructions above the door chain. 'This message is for you from SS-SBF Krüger, I am the bearer.'

She read it and hurriedly packed all the items requested. He was suddenly in a hurry and snatched the case and boxes. 'That's all.' He hardly let her walk down the hall with him. 'Please don't bother,' he reached the door, saluted and was gone.

Peter Edel was called into the guardroom where the lanky Werner, visibly irritated, told him he was to collect something at the wooden gate in the yard. Krüger's black Mercedes was parked and an SS man was just taking two large parcels out of the boot. They were wrapped in brown paper, tied and stamped with official stamps. 'Go on, open them, have a look, check them.' He was told to take them to his quarters. Werner followed him, shaking his head, with a slightly dense expression on his servile face: a complete set of artist's materials – that really was the limit. Krüger's ambition to produce dollars at all costs had made him go as far as sending to Peter's mother in Berlin for his painting materials.

12

Himmler's Orders – Success or Death

AFTER JACOBSON HAD SUCCEEDED IN destroying the work, in spite of two hundred attempts, Himmler's orders came through. 'The preparation of forged dollar bills will end in four weeks. If this deadline is not kept, the prisoners working on the job will be shot.'

Again we had to be extremely careful. Our lives were at stake. The Nazis were not to get the slightest hint of the fact that the printing of the notes had been delayed for months. The discovery of this sabotage would have meant certain death. The eight of us continued experimenting, without success. The SS were convinced that the prisoners in the dollar section were up to something suspicious. Time was running out. Finally there were only four days left. We could not postpone it any longer.

It was the 250th attempt. Smolianoff's finely touched-up negative was flawless as usual. Jacobson laid it on the glass plate coated with gelatine, which he exposed to light. Then he poured glycerine over it, rinsed it and pulled the image off onto paper. I put the plate in the machine, set the rollers going and turned on the machine. Twenty-four forged $100 bills rolled out, indistinguishable from the real thing. Smolianoff had proved that it was possible to forge dollar bills using collotype. All the initial shortcomings were ironed out, so that same night we printed 200 forged notes to the value of $20,000. Werner informed Krüger accordingly.

The next day Krüger appeared. Smolianoff above all relished the situation. Krüger first placed thirty real $100 bills on the table with the green cover, followed by the forgeries, which had been quickly doctored to look 'old'. Krüger and his companions took their time examining the notes closely. They checked each individual note, looked at both sides, let them slide through their fingers; in the end the SS men held and examined more than half of the forged notes.

On the same evening Krüger told Himmler of the success by phone and assured his boss that everything was ready now for the production of forged dollars.

After a few days Werner told the eight men in the dollar group about a plan that Himmler and Schellenberg wanted to see carried out without delay. 'A million forged dollars a day are to be produced, working in two ten-hour shifts.' It was then 12 February 1945.

But before the production could start, the prisoners heard bombing again. Berlin was being attacked by the Allies. Relays of planes flew over KZ

Sachsenhausen towards Berlin. It looked as if a black cloud was looming over the capital of Hitler's Germany.

The ultimate irony was that I then received an immigration certificate for entry to Palestine. My brother had been living in the Kfar Masaryk Kibbutz since 1933 and my sister had been in Maanit Kibbutz since 1935. They had done everything they could to secure the visa. It would have been my last hope for survival. The certificate had been sent from the Palestine Authority Office in Switzerland to KZ Birkenau, but by that time I was already in the forgery unit in KZ Sachsenhausen.

I did not know about the trouble my brother had been going to on my behalf. I was working at my machine as usual. Suddenly Krüger was standing beside me. I switched the machine off and he handed me a letter with an ironic smile. As I read the official entry visa to Palestine that really could have saved my life, he said: 'You must understand that I cannot let you emigrate to Palestine because you are high security.'

I still would not have believed it to this very day had I personally not been given the faded document by Krüger. When I showed the certificate to Abraham Jacobson, the foreman of the collotype section, he smiled and said: 'You can't leave us. It has taken three months to train you to forge US dollars. We can't do without an expert like you.'

All together in Block 18/19

OFFICE PALESTINIEN DE SUISSE

Téléphone : 5 12 10
Cte de chèques post. : I. 4889

GENÊVE, le 25.8.44
8, rue Petitot

Herrn
Adolf Burger
Birkenau bei Neuberun
- - - - - - - - - -
Stabsgebaude Nr.6/9901

Sehr geehrter Herr Burger,

    Wir teilen Ihnen hierdurch mit, dass Sie auf der
8. Liste der Spezialfälle von Veteranen-Zertifikaten für
Deutschland die

        Nr..M/438/43/H/9...

erhalten haben.

    Gleichzeitig geben wir Ihnen bekannt, dass diese
Liste dem Foreign Office, London, mit der Bitte um Wei-
terleitung an die Schutzmacht zur Verständigung der zu-
ständigen deutschen Behörden übermittelt wurde.

        Mit vorzüglicher Hochachtung

        משרד ארץ־ישראלי ז׳נבה
        Office Palestinien Genève

Prière de joindre un timbre-réponse pour chaque demande. – Nos renseignements, donnés après sérieuse étude, sont toutefois sans responsabilité.

Dear Herr Burger,
We hereby inform you that you have been allocated
No:........M/438/43/H/9

on the eighth list of special cases of veteran
certificates for Germany. Furthermore we are able to
inform you that the list has been sent to the Foreign
Office, London, in order to be forwarded to the relevant
German authorities.

This visa, issued on 25 August 1944 in Switzerland, arrived too late.
No prisoners were to be released from Blocks 18 and 19

'Pierre' – Elyesa Bazna 'Cicero', Top Nazi Spy

Elyesa Bazna, alias 'Cicero'

IF WE WANT TO FOLLOW up how the forged banknotes were used, we must not overlook a very important Second World War spy. This case is one of most famous espionage stories of our time, because of the extraordinary value of the intelligence. His documents were records of agreements about the future relationships between the Allies – photocopies of the proceedings of the Teheran Conference. The spy, who introduced himself as 'Pierre' and was really called Elyesa Bazna, was really a butler in the British Embassy in Ankara. He offered his services to Moyzisch, an envoy at the German Embassy. He brought fifty-two negatives to the first meeting, photos of the correspondence between the British Foreign Office and Sir Knatchbull-Hugessen, then British ambassador in Ankara. It consisted entirely of military information, guidelines and documents, which later helped to break the British secret codes. He demanded £20,000 for this information.

After Moyzisch had passed the documents on to Berlin, Ribbentropp sent £20,000. Then Kaltenbrunner took over the case and paid the reward himself – but using forged notes. He sent £200,000 to Ankara for Moyzisch. At the same time he demanded that the attaché meet 'Pierre' in secret, as he was the only one who knew him. The spy 'Pierre' acquired his cover name, 'Cicero', from the German ambassador, Fritz von Papen, in recognition of the extraordinary value of his services. 'Cicero' delivered photographs of top-secret documents such as minutes of meetings and negotiations between the British and Russian foreign ministers with Hull, the American secretary of state, in 1942. Other documents passed on included minutes of the conferences in Casablanca and Cairo, which were attended by Churchill and Roosevelt, and the proceedings of the Teheran Conference of 1943, including the strategic measures for the destruction of Germany from the east, west and south. Also in 1943, he delivered copies of numbers of RAF personnel in Turkey in October 1943. There were also intelligence reports on armaments delivered to the Soviet Union, reports concerning a secret mission of the Turkish president to Cairo for a meeting with Churchill and Roosevelt, and many other valuable documents. There was also the agreement of the Allied commanders on the date of air attacks on the capitals of states surrounding Germany. First Sofia was to be bombed, then Budapest and Bucharest.

Moyzisch described 'Cicero' as an intelligent, very cautious, person, who often changed the places they met and telephone numbers, times and days. 'Cicero' received almost £300,000 for his services. That was almost 6 million marks, but it was all forged money.

Julius Mader quoted Robert M.W. Kampner, one of the US chief prosecutors at the Nuremberg War Crimes Trials, according to whom Joachim von Ribbentrop, foreign minister of the Reich, attested to personally having issued payment instructions on 24 February 1944 in the following words: 'I request the secret service SD through the director of Group II Interior [of the Ministry of Foreign Affairs] to pay a lump sum of 250,000 marks in gold for "Cicero".' Mader stated furthermore that the secret service kept the gold and paid 'Cicero' with its own forged sterling notes.

When 'Cicero' tried to enjoy the fruits of his dangerous past in his South American hideout, the police informed him that his fortune consisted of forged banknotes. Typically, Bazna, alias 'Cicero', sought compensation from Germany in 1962.

14

Prisoners Held Hostage

IN 1944 AN ORDER CAME in to the workshop for 300 forged Soviet secret service (NKWD) identity passes. The inside of these documents was light green, the binding was red board with an embossed gold stamp. The inside pages were ready on time – we only had to make the hard covers.

When we received the red cloth board, it turned out that the impression on it was not identical to the original. There was feverish hunting for a replacement. The production of the passes was already delayed by a fortnight when the news came that it was impossible to produce an exact replica of the linen board.

The German secret service knew that if the covers were not indistinguishable from the original the Soviet secret service would capture all the German agents carrying the passes in no time. What was to be done? Tell Berlin that the order could not be delivered?

There was no question of this for Krüger. So far he had never failed to deliver, and he did not intend to start now. His career rested on his reputation of being able to carry out the most difficult orders promptly and to the satisfaction of his superiors. Was he now going to risk his future over a silly item of red linen board?

Krüger called the leaders of each section together. He described the problem with the red board: 'Since Berlin is demanding these passes within a week the only thing to do is alter the board to match the original. It is a tricky one but you must see to it that it is done.'

There was deadly silence in the room. The prisoners looked at each other. Everyone waited for someone else to have the courage to answer Krüger – the only answer was 'Impossible! Hitler's workshop is a printing works not a paper mill for producing hardboard' – we had never attempted anything of this kind. After we had got over the shock, Abraham Jacobson, the Dutchman, plucked up the courage to reply: 'We cannot produce that here. We have neither the tools nor the experience to alter the board. We are sorry but please understand that it is impossible.'

Krüger's face darkened, he glowered. He frowned and a nervous twitch started that was the sign of an explosion of rage. 'So you intend to sabotage this?' he screamed. 'Well, I'll knock the sabotage out of you.' He called four printers by name and said: 'These four are hostages. They will guarantee with their lives that the boards will be ready in twenty-four hours. If it is not ready by the dot of ten tomorrow they will be shot. It is up to you to save the lives of these four men.'

He left the room. The foremen of the sections stayed behind. Everyone realised the seriousness of the situation and knew that their comrades' lives had to be saved. But how? Was there any possibility of altering the board so that it corresponded to the original without the proper expertise and machinery? They sat there for three hours discussing and considering one suggestion after another and rejecting them.

Finally the engraver, Felix Cytrin came up with an idea. He suggested engraving the pattern of the one original sample cover they had on to a brass plate. This was the only possible way out of the situation. It was worth trying and we all knew that if it did not succeed, our comrades were doomed.

Felix Cytrin – drawing by Peter Edel

Cytrin set to work on this task. He started scratching lines on to the brass plate. The lines were very fine and his eyes hurt with the strain. He had to keep interrupting the work to rest his eyes. After he had worked all day at the engraving table, he was so tired in the evening that he nearly fell asleep. But our comrades' lives were at stake and that meant he had to work till he dropped. So he worked all through the night. His eyes got so sore that it was almost unbearable.

Finally he managed it. The hands of the clock were at 7.30 when he drew the last stroke. We still had two and a half hours before the deadline ran out. The completed plate was screwed on to the little hand printer; a piece of smooth board was placed in it, corresponding to the original. The plate was heated electrically and the machine set going. But as the stamp plate touched the linen board, it burned it.

We only had three-quarters of an hour left. No one knew what to do next. Just then, one of the bookbinders had an idea that saved the day. 'If we coat the plate with wax, when the plate touches the board, the wax will melt and before the electric current burns it, the plate will have detached from it.'

It was a good idea; we had to get hold of some wax. Luckily we found some. The plate was coated with it. At 9.30 we started the second trial. If this failed, all was lost. Everyone's eyes were glued to the machine when the press was set in motion. The four hostages were present too. Pale and tense, they awaited the decision on their lives. Then a sigh of relief went up: the wax had not even melted and the linen board was ready. It matched the original exactly.

Krüger appeared on the dot of ten. He grinned as he looked up at the clock and said: 'I knew you would not sabotage it, but I knew too that I had to threaten to kill you four or you would not have managed it.'

The board for the NKWD passes was embossed with
the right symbol in this type of printing press

Forgery of Documents

THE SPECIAL *KOMMANDO* IN KZ Sachsenhausen was overloaded with jobs. As well as forging banknotes we had to forge all kinds of documents. There was scarcely a country in Europe whose official and personal documents we did not reproduce.

Brazilian passports were among the documents printed, as well as Tunisian identity cards, English and American passports and patents, and various stamps were also produced. It might be Dutch baptismal certificates or certificates of French towns, or letterheads of the Palestinian Consulate in Geneva with Hebrew text, English marriage certificates, American military pay books, and many other printed documents.

Leaflets for agents of the Reich were also printed in Hitler's secret workshop. They were translated into almost all European languages and contained exact directions, for example, on how to blow up a bridge, derail a train or sabotage a weapons delivery. Although the money forgery took priority, all these 'special jobs' had to be done at very short notice and to a high standard.

One day an SS secret service man appeared in the workshop. He brought personal papers of an Argentinian who was in Germany on a visit. The documents had to be photographed and reproduced down to the last detail in twenty-four hours.

He said arrogantly, 'I will tell you why you are to do this. This Argentinian came to Germany on business. We arrested him on the excuse that his papers were not in order. Tomorrow we will give them back and let him go with an apology. That is why the papers have to be ready at such short notice. Then one of our agents will travel to South America as an Argentinian citizen and find doors open to him everywhere.' The officer smiled mischievously at his own ingenuity. 'Now you know why you are doing it. Hurry up now, because we don't like keeping innocent people behind bars!' With these sarcastic words he left.

I remember a Swiss passport, whose owner, a journalist, had been taken to the Gestapo under some flimsy pretext and had to hand in his papers. His passport arrived in our photography department, was photographed, touched up, reproduced on a gelatine plate and finally duplicated by collotype. The journalist got his papers back the next day and he probably never found out why he was locked up and let go so quickly.

Illness and Murder

I WAS WORKING ON THE production of sterling notes. This work was, of course, much harder than the forgery of the Yugoslavian notes. We never thought about the future while we worked, no one worried unduly about what was in store for us. But as soon as we left our machines, we were overcome by feelings of depression that were very difficult to snap out of. Some prisoners tried to cheer up their mates with black humour, others tried to banish thoughts of the future by reading novels, stories, newspapers and magazines, which were available to us.

Not everyone was so controlled. But in each national group there were a few who kept up the spirits of their mates, encouraging them and with the help of their wit and humour brought back their will to live.

In this special *Kommando* there were thirteen Czechoslovakians:

	Date of birth	Place	Date of arrest	Occupation
Adolf Burger	12.08.1917	Velká Lomnica	11.08.1942	Typesetter/printer
Karel Gottlieb	24.05.1917	Košice	19.11.1943	Joiner/carpenter
Leo Haas	15.04.1901	Opava	28.10.1944	Painter/artist
Victor Hahn	21.08.1909	Prague	26.08.1943	Bank clerk
Georg Jilovský	15.03.1884	Prague	26.02.1944	Artist
Jaroslav Kaufmann	19.01.1901	Benešov	20.08.1942	Dentist
Artur Klein	25.04.1907	Prague	03.12.1943	Electrician
Richard Luka	30.10.1913	Prague	25.09.1940	Architect
Alfred Pick	12.10.1906	Domažlice	20.08.1942	Dental technician
Max Stein	22.08.1899	Prague	29.11.1943	Weaver
Oskar Stein	05.08.1902	Tábor	23.08.1942	Paper expert
Stiastní Ernst	-	-	-	-
Artur Tuppler	10.06.1890	Nová Ves	23.08.1942	Builder/bricklayer

Dr Jaroslav Kaufmann from Hořice was neither a printer, nor a photographer, nor an engraver. Nevertheless the SS had put him in the special unit. He was a dentist, and because the prisoners could not even go to the SS prison doctor, in case they betrayed their secret work, Kaufmann had to treat all the prisoners. So that he would be 'fully occupied', the Nazis made him a foreman. In addition he had the job of crumpling the banknotes, so that they looked used.

Kaufmann was known for his irrepressible humour. He often distracted us from melancholy thoughts and was a moral support, especially to the Czechs and Slovaks. He would often shout loudly at the other prisoners to give the SS the impression that he was a strict slave driver.

Because we were 'high-security prisoners' we were even escorted into the sick bay by SS men. That only happened if someone was seriously ill. Dr Kaufmann looked after minor complaints. A seriously ill prisoner could not be sure that he would not get a lethal phenol injection into a vein. Anyone who was so ill that he could not leave our dormitory was more or less doomed. Generally he would be abandoned without hope because he could not be taken into the sick bay for security reasons, and if he had a contagious illness he was a source of infection to his comrades in the dormitory while he stayed there.

If we needed a dentist, and only if the pain was unbearable, we were taken out of Blocks 18 and 19 to the dentist because Dr Kaufmann could not do any complicated surgery. The SS guardsmen remained with the prisoner while he was undergoing treatment, to ensure that he would not speak about the forgery workshop.

Several of our group took ill and were murdered. One of them was a young student from the Soviet Union called Pjotr Sukienik who caught tuberculosis. Everyone knew it meant death if the SS found out. This good-hearted, gifted comrade knew what was to come, yet never a bad or bitter word passed his lips. We never heard him complain. He often told his closest friends, who would come and stand by his bunk in their free time, 'I would still like to see the end of the war. I'd like to know that my life had a meaning.'

As Sukienik's condition deteriorated the block-leader called Dr Kaufmann and ordered him to examine the patient. In the presence of an SS guard, the doctor made him cough vigorously and collected the phlegm in a test tube. This sample was to be analysed in the laboratory. In an unsupervised moment he switched the tube for another containing his own sample. Of course the SS doctors found that the patient did not have TB, so Sukienik was saved for a short time.

He did not see liberation. His condition got steadily worse. We and Dr Kaufmann did all we could to save his life and to help him, but in vain. One day OSF Heizmann called him out. We all knew what would happen. Pjotr said goodbye to everyone and went out. When Heizmann came back on his own he said: 'He was a danger to everyone else, so I had to shoot him. I offered him a cigarette. When he had nearly finished it I just put my arm around him and shot him from behind.' He paused: 'Although he knew he would be shot, he was so brave. He made a deep impression on me.' A prisoner had impressed a brutal SS man, a murderer, but to do it he had to die.

Heizmann was acting under the orders of Krüger, who was in turn acting under orders from his superiors. It was a vicious circle whereby they could all claim, 'I am not guilty! I am only carrying out orders.' On the basis of these orders, other sick prisoners from Blocks 18 and 19 were murdered: Abraham Fingerhut, Karl Sussmann from Vienna, Ernst Stiasní from Brünn and Abraham Kleinfeld were killed by OSF Edwin Heizmann.

The Czech doctor, Dr Jaroslav Kaufmann

Pjotr Sukienik, a student from Bialystok, shot by SS-OSF Edwin Heizmann
on the orders of SS-SBF Bernhard Krüger

17

Despair and Encouragement

APART FROM THE SS PERSONNEL, we in the special *Kommando* were the only people directly involved in this criminal activity who knew the scale of the forgery operation. As a result we were in effect condemned to death, and the SS did not worry about disclosing other secrets to us. We were not going to get out alive, so no unauthorised person would ever find out about them. The more we were initiated into Nazi practices, the more we longed for liberation – we wanted to tell the world about the incredible crimes and felt compelled to do so.

There were so many people who closed their eyes to the horrific deeds and boundless brutality, and did not want to know. We often talked about it in Blocks 18 and 19 and swore to each other that we would tell and warn people if we were liberated. Anyone who had seen helpless women and sick people being gassed, anyone who heard their agonised last screams, cannot and dare not keep quiet. We must struggle to prevent people forgetting. But who would see liberation day?

There were moments when prisoners experienced low points and were resigned to their fate. At times like these the strong ones had to step in. We encouraged each other and helped to overcome the despair. There were a few such strong personalities amongst us. It could be that they had privately come to terms with their fate and had grown fatalistic, but that was how they kept up their spirits up and allowed nothing to get them down. It was they who really helped us sustain the will to survive. Dr Kaufmann was one of them, and so was the Czech engineer Luka. They kept their heads even in the most difficult situations.

We made a big effort after that to make our existence more enjoyable. If one of us had a birthday we would decorate the table and present him with a gift. It was only something small but the recipient was always so delighted and often moved to tears. One day when we were setting up a celebration an SS man came in and wanted to know what we were doing. We told him that Kurt Lewinsky was celebrating his tenth year behind barbed-wire. The guard seemed to be indifferent to this. However, he went away and came back with a bundle of cigarettes. 'Anyone who has stuck it out that long deserves respect,' he said, leaving the cigarettes on the table. He left the room without another word.

Kurt Lewinsky, a German Communist, was one of the first prisoners in the forgery unit. He had come from KZ Buchenwald as early as the summer of 1942. He told how 'on a close August morning in 1942 an announcement bellowed out through the loudspeakers that "all Jews qualified in the printing trade were to report immediately to the office." Within a few days we were on a transport and I ended up in Sachsenhausen with twenty-two comrades. After the usual formalities the SS brought us to Block 19 on the outer edge of the camp. Shortly after that they started to isolate the huts with all manner of security: double fences, the thickest barbed-wire, even covering the roof of the hut. They sealed it off hermetically from the rest of the camp. Here Krüger revealed to us one day that we had been "selected" to form the forgery *Kommando*. He explained in detail and with dire threats before an audience of SS guards what we were to do. He threatened us with all conceivable punishments if we ever disclosed the secret to the outside world even by one word or gesture, by a note or any other means.'

Victor Hahn, prisoner number 75193, told how he was selected for the forgery workshop. 'I was on my last legs, in despair. Death was all around us; it dominated life. Krüger suddenly turned up in Auschwitz, confident, now and again he showed signs of sympathy for us and our lot. It was said he was looking for bookkeepers. I was an accountant with banking experience. When Krüger heard that he pricked up his ears. That is how I was chosen for Sachsenhausen.'

On 14 December 1943 Hans Walter celebrated his twenty-third birthday. We sat around the table in Block 18/19 and wished him well.

Jakow Plac, drawing by Peter Edel   Jean Lental, drawing by Leo Haas

Hans Walter's comrades

Bei Tisch 1 da habe ich 'ne Kummer,
Da sitz' ich gern und ohne Brummer
Die Leut' sind nett und sehr jovial
Und weil sie hören auch hundertmal
Was ich erzähle den ganzen Tag,
Hab ich stets das, was ich so gern mag.
An meinem Geburtstag da möchte
Ich bloß die Auszeichnung der Rechte,
Zu erzählen meine Geschichten
An sämtliche Tanten und Nichten,
Und daß von Tisch 2 bis Tisch 7,
Der Befehl ergehe, geschrieben:
. Jede Person in jedem Alter
. Hör eine Stunde den Hans Walter.

Viel Glück zum Geburtstag wünschen:

[signatures]

a happy Birthday Congratulation
at KZ. Sachsenhausen 12-14-1944

Birthday poem for Hans Walter

The first letter from my mother, dated 10 July 1944.
The best news it contained was that my sister Isabella had succeeded in escaping from the HG militia in 1942 and reached Palestine

18

Cabaret

OUR WORKSHOP WAS CLOSED ON Saturday afternoons and Sundays. My first Sunday here was like a dream, every prisoner got a clean towel and a piece of soap. Then there was roll call for the unit. The guards searched prisoners for pieces of paper that news of our activities could have been smuggled out on. In the rest of the camp an alarm sounded that meant return to barracks (*Blocksperre*). Only then was the tightly guarded gate of the forgery workshop opened. We were marched five abreast, escorted by our SS guard, along the empty main avenue of the camp to the washrooms. Hot water! Plenty of time for a shower!

In the afternoon everyone occupied himself as he wished. Some sat together chatting and talking of home. Others played cards or chess. We played table tennis. Some read, slept or listened to the radio.

This all seemed to me idyllic, fantastic, just like a Sunday afternoon back in my home town, with my family and friends, and I could not help thinking about the past. I imagined my parents, brothers and sisters, the house where I was born, the little market square with the town hall and the church; I could hear the church bells ringing. Behind the church steeple I could see the majestic silhouette of the high Tatra Mountains in my mind's eye, with their gigantic peaks. What film would be on in the little cinema? Which of my old friends and companions would still be sitting in the local inn, where we used to meet and play cards, listen to the radio and talk passionately about the latest local football game.

Now in the forgery block of KZ Sachsenhausen I began to really appreciate the freedom I had enjoyed and taken for granted. All our hopes were focused on it now. Would I ever experience it again? Would I ever see my native land again?

It may seem paradoxical that we prisoners were allowed to organise 'entertainment evenings'. The inmates of Blocks 18 and19 had many privileges in spite of the fact that we were Jews. Anyone who had relatives was allowed to correspond with them and even receive parcels.

Unlike other prisoners we did not have our heads shaved. We were to be in good health, feel good about ourselves outwardly and inwardly. It was an admission of, and an attempt to counteract, depression among the prisoners. Psychological depression of prisoners could not be allowed to affect the work in hand, which was so important for the German war effort. It was Krüger's clear intention that anyone who was involved in such 'valuable' war effort should be properly looked after.

The entertainments were held from time to time on Saturday evenings. From the very start, our SS guards sat in the front rows. They laughed like the rest of the 'audience' at the cabaret sketches on the improvised stage. The sketches were often spiced with black humour, and each group of prisoners performed their sketches and parodies in their mother tongue. The SS men did not understand the words but they came to the performances and were entertained. They laughed at the mimicry and pantomime. The prisoners often mocked their guards or even reviled them. This created great amusement among the prisoners. The SS men would join in the laughter even though they did not always understand what it was about.

A proper cabaret ensemble developed in our block. Felix Tragholz from Vienna was the first violin, Hans Blass, an excellent café entertainer, played the harmonica. The songs were composed by Levi Groen, a cabaret singer, and his friend Andrias Bosboom, both from Amsterdam. Groen hilariously complemented the ingenious Berliner, Norbert Wilhelm Lewy. Norbert was the most skilful and wittiest of all the prisoners in the unit. He was a photographer. He had a Jewish grandmother and had been sentenced for having a forged birth certificate. A Protestant clergyman had issued the false birth certificate for his grandmother, but with fatal German accuracy had made handwritten notes about the documents he himself had forged. Due to his accuracy dozens of people ended up in court and in concentration camps, including our Norbert.

He was an inexhaustible source of ideas. He compiled the programmes, wrote the songs or improvised, thought up pantomimes, wrote short sketches with convoluted plots and witty dialogues. He was the playwright, director and lead actor or 'actress' in full evening performances. He was such a talented actor that he played all the female roles on our 'stage'. When he played a woman he moved so enchantingly and spoke in such a refined voice that one of the SS men, seeing the cabaret for the first time, asked how a woman had got into Blocks 18 and 19. Norbert said he went to such trouble because he was performing on the richest stage in the world. He was quite right. Instead of ordinary boards the stage was constructed from planks laid on top of the cases full of millions of English banknotes. Of course the stage was valuable – apart from the fact that it was all forged money.

Krüger personally gave the permission to organise these evenings. He provided the musical instruments. Our cabaret was of a good artistic standard, in that comic 'numbers' alternated with more demanding performances. Hans Blass presented a selection from various operas, in particular from *Tiefland*, on the harmonica. Felix often played Dvořák's *Humoresque* and Toselli serenades on the violin. The soloists Victor Kahn and Karel Gottlieb sang Czech folk songs. Some of the most popular numbers were the Dutch street ballads. Bosboom and Groen performed them with such excellent mimicry and wit that they were always called back for an encore. The appreciative audience always sang along with the last line of the chorus, even though they did not understand the words.

SYLVESTERFEIER

Freitag, den 31. Dezember 1943
bei den ‚Moneymakers' von Sachsenhausen

PROGRAMM

Ansager, Zwischentextler und Prologus: MAX BERBO

1. Musikalische Unterhaltung der „Moneymaker-Banden-Kapelle" NOLEVY
2. Zeitbilder aus Vergangenheit und Gegenwart, dargestellt von KNOZEL
3. Die zwei müden Wanderer   OSKAR STEIN und ALFRED PICK
4. Das Ballett von Sachsenhausen, mit den Damen: LI, LO, LU, MA, MO
5. Begrüßung des neuen Jahres durch den „Obermoneymaker" LEO KREBS

PAUSE.

6. Gesangsvorträge   JACKIE PLAPPLA
7. Rezitationen und „komische Verse" zum neuen Jahr   ICKE-ICKE
8. ZIRKUS PIPEL mit seinen Attraktionen und seinem Riesenprogramm, u. a.
    Die 3 Frattelinis, Akrobat Schööön, Pipel als Barbier, EGO, der
    Meisterstemmer, das „JIDDEN-QUARTETT", SEVERIN u. RICO,
    Tanzakt und dann KNOZEL, alias Pipel, in seinen Soloszenen

Wieder daheim!

Ein Spiel in 3 Szenen mit einem Prolog von F. WEISSMANN
PERSONEN:

Der heimgekehrte Schutzhäftling Karl Weiß	Kurt Lewinsky
Seine Gattin Erna	Chaim Zeichner

Die Kinder: Ludwig (Gerhard Nieft), Peter (Perez Zymermann) Franz (Nachim Zakczewski)
Herbert (Severin Tiefenbach) Paul (Sam Wilde) Gustav Tüchtig, Briefträger (Horst Nieft)

Regie: F. Weißmann

Buffett — Schießbuden — Tanz — und andere Belustigungen
Bühnenbilder, Saaldekoration und Ausstattung: JAKOB LAUBER

Beginn 23 Uhr   Ende ???

Programme for New Year Celebration, 31 December 1943

NEW YEAR'S EVE PARTY

Friday 31st January 1943

with the Sachsenhausen Money-Makers

PROGRAMME

Compère and prologue		MAX BERBO
1.	Musical entertainment by the 'Money-makers' band	NOLEVY
2.	Scenes of past and present, presented by	KNOZEL
3.	The two tired hikers	OSKAR STEIN and ALFRED PICK
4.	Sachsenhausen ballet with ladies	LI, LO, LU, MA, MO
5.	Ring in the New Year with the 'Obermoneymaker'	LEO KREBS

INTERVAL

6.	Songs performed by	JACKIE PLAPPLA
7.	Recitations and comic verse for the New Year	ICKE-ICKE
8.	PIPEL CIRCUS with programme of great attractions including	

The 3 Fratellinis, schööön acrobats, Pipel the barber
EGO, super-weightlifter, the 'JIDS QUARTET',
SEVERINI AND RICO, Dance,
Solo act: KNOZEL alias PIPEL

BACK HOME

Play in 3 acts with prologue by F. WEISSMANN

CAST

Released prisoner	KARL WEISS
His wife, Erna	CHAIM ZEICHNER

His children: Ludwig (Gerhard Nieft), Peter (Perez Zimmermann), Franz
(Nachim Zakczewski), Herbert (Severin Tiefenbach), Paul (Saw Wilde), Gustav
Tüchtig, Postman (Horst Nieft)
Director: F. Weissmann

Buffet – Shooting gallery – Dancing – Entertainment

Sets, Decorations, Props   JAKOB LAUBER

Start 11 p.m.   Finish ? ? ?

The Czech folk songs also got great applause. The prisoners wanted to learn the words, so I tried to translate 'Koně vraný' into German and then my German version had its première on the richest stage in the world.

Norbert's appearances with his partner Groen formed the links of the evening. No evening was complete without Pippel, a dwarf from Frankfurt, who had once been a circus clown. He was about 1.4 metres tall and had an extremely large head. His wobbly walk on his short legs was particularly comical. And when he dressed up as a preacher and delivered a bible-thumping sermon full of double entendres and Frankfurt underworld slang, we just fell about laughing. He rewarded the applause with an item from his circus days where he broke plates on his misshapen skull whilst talking and singing.

The engineer Richard Luka always sang his favourite song 'Baruska'. Once he was told to imitate the Führer on Beckmann's orders. Apart from the opening words *'Meine Volkgenossen'* he only knew four or five sentences of a Hitler speech, but his mask and especially his imitation of the voice were so masterful that he was called back for several encores by the SS men. 'You would not get a night like this with such laughs anywhere in the Reich!' roared the SS men sitting in the front row.

Since the SS men did not know French, Czech or Dutch we printed the programme in German for them.

Until now I had only seen death. I suddenly seemed to be transported into another world. Of course I was still a concentration camp prisoner. I knew I would never leave Sachsenhausen alive – but I knew too that I could get used to life here and could laugh at the black humour of it, like the others.

Richard Luka, drawing by Leo Haas

The entertainment evenings were not only held to cheer up the other prisoners and the guards but also to enable us to listen to foreign radio stations during the performances. The SS had the front-row seats not just as guests of honour but also to make it safer for us to try and listen and concentrate fully on the foreign broadcasts. On Saturday evenings there were fewest guards on duty, never more than four. We knew that SS men Heinz Beckmann, Edwin Heizmann, Bruno Psoch and Willi Schmitt were not very strict about rules, not even about the guardroom where the radio was. When they came to our cabaret evenings they did not even lock it.

The performances were held in the sorting room, where a stage and even a curtain had been erected. From there you went through the passage from the entrance into the printing room. Behind that was the guardroom. When all the SS men had taken their reserved seats and the programme highlights were starting was the best time for Oskar Stein to slip away to listen to foreign radio broadcasts.

He first had to switch off the loudspeakers in the workrooms; otherwise he would have given the game away. It was a matter of twisting a few knobs to set the wavelength to London or Moscow or to wherever there were Czech or German broadcasts. He made notes of key points so that he would not miss any important news. He could only do this once every four or six weeks due to the combination of guards on duty, so that we only rarely got true news bulletins but it was enough to know that Germany was near collapse. The joy at this news was tempered by the knowledge that the end of the war would probably be the end of us as well.

Karel Gottlieb from Prague had to keep singing on stage until Oskar Stein came back. Before his arrest Gottlieb had been a member of the 'Club for unknown talent'. He sang his heart out – he had already sung the song twice – but his comrade was still not back. He broke out in a sweat, forgot his lines, and then Stein walked in.

We achieved our aim and found out details of the Allied advance, which was very encouraging. As soon as we found an opportunity we tried to get an objective picture of the situation from the BBC or Moscow. We grasped at any snippet of news, no matter how insignificant. Taking further risks, we found out that in the autumn of 1944 the Red Army had succeeded in driving the German troops and Nazis out of their country.

One Saturday evening Stein solemnly announced the latest news: 'Friends, the Soviets are already in Romania, Bulgaria and Poland . . . the Nazis are being beaten back everywhere.' We tried to calculate how long it would take the front to reach us. But what would the Nazis do? The approaching defeat would rouse the Nazis into a white rage.

Would they not kill us sooner than they had intended? Would they not wish to remove embarrassing witnesses?

The more favourable the news, the more cautious we became. At the beginning of September 1944 we heard about the Slovakian national uprising. 'The Slovaks are fighting. National committees are being set up in villages and towns.' Of course we did not know any details, but the behaviour of the SS men and their nervousness made us think that something decisive was going on.

One SS man shouted in a rage 'That is not a front . . . they are just partisans!' Now partisans were fighting against the Nazi occupation forces.

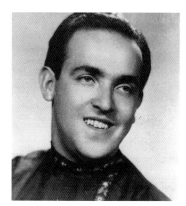

Karel Gottlieb

Leo Haas, drawing by Peter Edel

19

SS – First Doubts of Final Victory

IN THE COMMON ROOM THERE was a big map on which we would mark the points reached by the Wehrmacht on its 'strategic retreat'. In our joy at the Allied advance we scarcely thought about the fateful day when we would no longer be needed and might be mercilessly liquidated.

The map was of the so-called Eastern Front, including the Soviet Union and Poland. The Nazis and their German supporters thought it would be adequate. They never imagined that one day the front would be far further west than the border of Poland and Germany. But finally the big day came. None of us prisoners will ever forget that day.

We were sitting in the common room as usual after work, waiting for the Wehrmacht report. There was an SS lieutenant called Träger sitting in the corner, a Sudeten German who was a native of Karlovy Vary (Karlsbad). He was a personal friend of Krüger's, and Krüger had enlisted him in the special unit to save him from the front. There was still march music coming from the loudspeakers. Then came the voice of the newsreader reading the Wehrmacht report. For the first time he did not use the words 'strategic retreat' but spoke of the evacuation of Warsaw. We would love to have jumped up and hugged each other for joy but did not dare let the SS man see us rejoicing.

After this 'Job's comfort' for the Nazis, the SS man got up and walked around the room. I cautiously spoke to him in Czech, because he was my countryman. First we talked generally, after a while the conversation turned to politics. I told him I had been in Auschwitz and about what I had seen and experienced there. I got so worked up that I forgot I was talking to an SS man. I told him about all the horrors of that hell and how thousands of men, women and children were sent to the gas chambers and how they died a horrible death all cooped up.

The other prisoners who were standing about looked at me shocked. They must have thought I had gone mad to speak to an SS man like that. But he listened to me in silence, incredulous and surprised. When I stopped there was a deadly silence in the room. Then the SS man spoke to me softly and said, 'I am the father of six children and I cannot be indifferent to such inhumanity. I think you know what I mean: I never supported such inhuman practices.'

'A nation that does such inhuman deeds cannot win the war,' I answered.

'We have to win,' he whispered to me and left the room.

Wehrmacht Broadcast of 18 January 1945:
Tschenstochau Fallen to the Enemy, Retreat from Warsaw,
Fall of Zichenau.

(The broadcast consists of reports on the last phase of the war on all fronts.)

Bolshevik advances have been repelled in Hungary, on the northern edge of the Vertes Mountains and in the Pilis range. Budapest is being defended against heavy attack in hand-to-hand street fighting. The enemy was unsuccessful at former flashpoints in the border region of Hungary and Slovakia. Our troops are moving westward between Slovakia and the upper Weichsel. There have been engagements with the enemy advancing on Neusandez.

The battle continues to rage in the Weichsel region. Reserves were brought up to block the enemy offensive at Krakow and Tschenstochau. Soviet tanks have advanced to between Litzmannstadt and Weichsel. Between Kielce and Pilica our units are engaged in heavy fighting against the enemy. A tank division from Lower Saxony shot up eighty-five Soviet tanks in one day. Warsaw was evacuated.

North of the Weichsel, the Bolsheviks managed to advance to the north and west in spite of determined defensive action by our troops. Zichenau fell after heavy fighting.

After a battle lasting five days in the East Prussian border region, our troops successfully resisted the advance of thirty-five Soviet artillery divisions and numerous armoured brigades. In a double battle north of Warsaw, 201 enemy tanks were destroyed yesterday. This brought the number of armoured vehicles destroyed to 903.

…

Waffen-SS mountain troops attacked an American party in the lower Vosges and prevented further advances. The enemy suffered high casualties and lost tanks in fighting around Hatten.

At bridgeheads north of Strasbourg and east of Hagenau several places were taken and a colonel and several hundred Americans taken prisoner. The enemy lost most of its tanks in the attack on Herlissheim. In all fifty-seven enemy tanks came under fire in Alsace.

Bandits in the region of Toplice-Seifenberg suffered heavy losses in an evacuation action by high-ranking SS. There were over 2,300 enemies dead, 1,500 prisoners were taken and large quantities of booty.

Greater London is coming under fire.

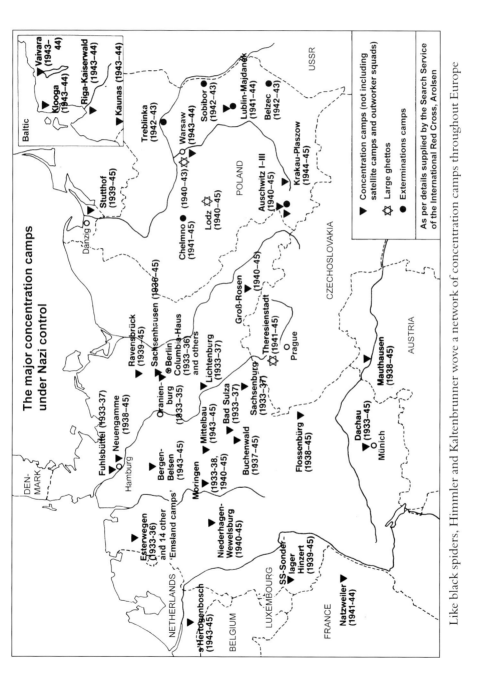

The major concentration camps under Nazi control

Like black spiders, Himmler and Kaltenbrunner wove a network of concentration camps throughout Europe

NETHERLANDS

BELGIUM

LUXEMBOURG

FRANCE

DEN-MARK

POLAND

CZECHOSLOVAKIA

AUSTRIA

USSR

Baltic

's-Hertogenbosch (1943–45)

Esterwegen (1933–36) and 14 other 'Emsland camps'

Niederhagen-Wewelsburg (1940–45)

SS-Sonder-lager Hinzert (1939–45)

Natzweiler (1941–44)

Fuhlsbüttel (1933–37)

Neuengamme (1938–45)

Hamburg

Bergen-Belsen (1943–45)

Moringen (1933–38, 1940–45)

Mittelbau (1943–45)

Buchenwald (1937–45)

Flossenbürg (1938–45)

Dachau (1933–45)

München

Mauthausen (1938–45)

Ravensbrück (1939–45)

Oranien-burg (1933–35)

Sachsenhausen (1936–45)

Berlin Columbia-Haus (1933–36) and others

Lichtenburg (1933–37)

Bad Sulza (1933–37)

Sachsenburg (1933–37)

Groß-Rosen (1940–45)

Theresienstadt (1941–45)

Prague

Danzig

Stutthof (1939–45)

Chelmno (1941–45)

Lodz (1940–45)

Auschwitz I–III (1940–45)

Krakau-Plaszow (1944–45)

Treblinka (1942–43)

Warsaw (1940–43) (1943–44)

Sobibor (1942–43)

Lublin-Majdanek (1941–44)

Belzec (1942–43)

Klooga (1943–44)

Vaivara (1943–44)

Riga-Kaiserwald (1943–44)

Kaunas (1943–44)

▼ Concentration camps (not including satellite camps and outworker squads)

✡ Large ghettos

● Exterminations camps

As per details supplied by the Search Service of the International Red Cross, Arolsen

20

Forgery of Stamps in KZ Sachsenhausen – 'Operation Water Wave'

IN THE MIDDLE OF 1943 stamps turned up in the Ruhrgebiet that were purple imitations of the real 6-pfennig Hitler stamp. However, they did not bear the image of the Führer, but that of RF Heinrich Himmler. The Gestapo discovered the stamps and handed them over to headquarters in Berlin, together with a counter-intelligence report, which stated that the stamps had been found after an air attack by British planes.

As usual we were shown the Himmler stamps as a model. Anyone who thought that Himmler would be delighted to see himself unexpectedly on a stamp was mistaken. On the contrary, he was indignant and felt that he and the National Socialist state were being mocked, and started looking for revenge. Himmler knew who his target was; it stated in his report. He knew exactly how it was to be carried out – he intended to strike back using the same weapon as was used against him, namely stamps.

'Operation Bernhard' was Himmler's domain so it was obvious that he would put Krüger in charge of the stamp forgery project.

Guidelines for forgery of English postage stamps:

1. Current British postage stamps are to be the model. The basic design is to be retained.
2. The basic design and colour tone are to be reproduced as closely as possible to the original.
3. Disparagement of the king is to be avoided at all costs.
4. Bolshevist tendencies, expressing the influence of Moscow on the Western powers, especially on Britain, is to be expressed.
5. Images derived from the events of the war are to be overprinted, with the aim of influencing British national sentiment.
6. The designs for the planned stamps are to be produced in a week to a fortnight.
7. The deadline for the printing of a large issue is six to eight weeks.
8. The stamps are to be dropped over large concentrations of troops and over big cities.

The real Hitler stamp

Forged stamp depicting Himmler

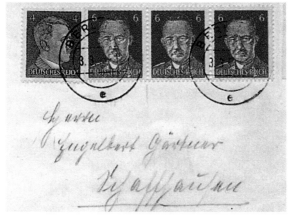

Envelope addressed to Gärtner with three purple stamps

The orders were clear and the final appearance of the stamps was decided. There was enough scope for creativity. Of course it was very difficult to add in propaganda features on the current stamps, given the fact that the king's head was taboo and there was very little room for anything else. But the orders stated that we could overprint. So we started on the forgery of English stamps, following Krüger's orders.

First the stamps were designed; they were photographed and enlarged, then drawn out in large format. The alterations were put in on the drawing. The finer details were not observed because the alterations would ensure that the stamps would look like forgeries.

Three designs were done. The first had the image of the king's head as in the current series of the lowest six denominations. Very few alterations were possible because of the size of the head. The cross on the crown was replaced with the Star of David. The 'D' of the penny was turned into a hammer and sickle. Two other alterations were barely distinguishable on the small format: the rose also became a hammer and sickle and the thistle was enhanced by a Star of David. The Star of David was distinctly recognisable on the crown, and the hammer and sickle on the 1d too. On the other five denominations the alterations to the original were so small that they were hardly noticeable at all on the forgery.

King George VI

Forgery

This design was to be used for six denominations – that is, for six different stamps. The elements to be overprinted were sketched in.

The first stamp to be forged was the rectangular ½d George VI Silver Jubilee issue of 1935. Then it was a matter of the inscriptions. Keeping in mind the wartime slogans 'Jewish' and 'Bolshevik' it was not difficult to think up something. The words 'SILVER JUBILEE' were changed; on the left was the Star of David and then the words 'THIS WAR IS A'. The line ended with a Star of David. On the lower 'HALFPENNY' line was added the hammer and sickle and 'JEWSH WAR'. As if that were not enough, a Star of David was put on the crown on the left and on the right the hammer and sickle and Soviet star replaced the laurel wreath. Lastly the dates were changed. Instead of the jubilee years 1910–1935 the dates of the war were inserted, 1939–1944. A printing error remained: JEWSH instead of JEWISH.

British jubilee stamp

Forged jubilee stamp

The third and last item was the purplish-brown 1½d special coronation issue of 1937. The real stamp showed the king and queen. She was replaced by Josef Stalin. The emblems and inscription 'Postage-Revenue' were replaced by 'SSSR BRITANNIA'. On the lower rim the 1½d was left and the date 12 May 1937 was replaced by the date of the Conference of Teheran 'TEHERAN 28.11.1943.' The eagle on the right edge became the Soviet star with the hammer and sickle in the centre. The central crown was altered on Stalin's side, bisected by the hammer and the star in the curve of the sickle was incorporated. Finally the 'GER' in the centre was replaced by 'SSSR'.

English Coronation stamp   Portrait of the Queen replaced by Stalin

Large editions of these issues were ordered. The printing method was simple offset. Considerable quantities of paper would be needed to print 9 million stamps so it was recommended that we used existing stocks that were no longer needed for their original purpose. In this case it was paper used for German ration stamps. Krüger decided on this paper with its watermark of wavy lines. It was a bit grey and heavy but served the purpose very well. The watermark gave its name to the operation: 'water wave'.

Printing could now start. There were four different series with different overprints. The first series was the bombing series, consisting of six overprints: 'Cathedral of Rouen', 'Castelle Gandolfo', 'Monte Cassino', 'Schaffhausen' (Switzerland), 'San Marino' and 'Cologne Cathedral', and above the overprint was the inscription 'MURDER RUIN' flanked by two bombs.

Overprint series I: 'MURDER RUIN' between two bombs

The two special issues did not need overprints; they looked like propaganda as they were. The second series was entitled 'Nazi propaganda slogans'. The forgeries were simply overprinted with the slogans 'WORLD SLAVERY', 'WORLD CAPITALISM', 'WORLD BOLSHEVISM', flanked by the Soviet star, hammer and sickle. 'WORLD JUDAISM' was flanked by two Stars of David. The fifth stamp referred to the Atlantic Charter, bearing the date 14 March 1941 under the arms. Below the date were wavy lines through the cross; this was supposed to suggest the sea because the agreement had been signed on a ship. The words 'The bluff alliance' were incorporated into the wavy lines.

Overprint series II: 'Nazi propaganda slogans'

The sixth overprint in the series referred to the Conference of Teheran, which was attended by Roosevelt, Churchill and Stalin from 28 November to 1 December 1943. At the top between two crosses were the words 'LIQUIDATION OF EMPIRE', below that was a large Soviet star with the conference dates 28.11.1943 – 1.12.1943 and below that the rest of the sentence 'At Teheran'.

The third overprint series had 'BUT WHO WILL RETURN?', 'BY ORDER OF STALIN', 'ENGLAND BLEEDS ON THE ORDER OF MOSCOW', 'COME ON GERMANY EXPECTS YOU', 'ENGLAND HAS LOST THE WAR', 'A MILITARY ADVENTURE.'

The fourth and fifth series were particularly large, consisting of 14 runs. They were planned to be so. Over each overprint were the words 'Liquidation of Empire' followed by the names of colonies and islands – St. Lucia, Barbados, Grenada, St.Vincent, Jamaica, Trinidad, Bahamas, Bermudas, Sinagpore, Hongkong, Rabaul, Borneo, Bougainville and Rangoon. They were not gummed because the plan was to drop them from planes, which meant that they could be damaged by weather and might stick together.

Overprint series III: layout 'AAA O Invasion'. This series was particularly designed to be dropped over Allied troop concentrations in Normandy

There were further plans. Two types of commemorative leaflets were to be designed. Both bore the British emblem on the left and the Soviet one on the right, on the upper rim. In between was the inscription 'Day 1 of Invasion special issue' in Russian and in English. The six basic forgeries without overprints were stuck on a sheet; on the opposite page were the two propaganda forgeries of the special issue stamps. Because the stamps were not gummed they were stuck on with glue. They were then franked with a stamp forged for the purpose. It read 'London' and the letters 'AAAO 6 June 1944 special-stamp'.

The franking was also forged

The stamp printing was finished. It was the summer of 1944. How were the forged stamps distributed? Germany had a very good network of agents abroad, especially in the few remaining neutral states in Europe: Sweden, Switzerland and Turkey, where the stamps were to be used. So the secret service Section VI F 4 was ordered to send the stamps to these outposts for distribution. The four sections were supplied with the forgeries: Section VI for English-speaking countries; Section VI B for French-speaking countries and Switzerland; and the last, VI C as well as VI E, which covered Scandinavia. The forgeries were sent to agents abroad for distribution.

In fact Himmler succeeded in getting his revenge. The stamps were noticed abroad – in the major Swiss newspapers the international Postal Union discussed them under the heading, 'A new Nazi secret weapon'.

Collectors were after the stamps but only very few managed to get hold of them. We could not understand why the Nazis wanted to use the stamps. So we asked one of the SS men when we caught him in a good mood at the usual Saturday evening entertainment. 'It's quite simple,' he said, 'to arouse hostility towards Jews and Russians. Our agents post the letters with the stamp in England; they are not detected and reach the addressees.' He smiled, proud of what he saw as the Nazis' craftiness and ingenuity.

Actually the forged stamps created a sensation everywhere they turned up. Stamp collectors all over the world tried to buy them. However, the stamps did not achieve the objective of getting a reaction against the anti-Hitler coalition. The British recognised them for what they were: forgeries for crude propaganda purposes.

The George VI 1½d stamp of 1937. Original 34 mm x 29 mm

Forged 1½d stamp

English coronation stamp of 1937. Original 25 mm x 40 mm

The Queen's portrait was replaced by Stalin's
(Michel – Germany special – propaganda forgery number 2b)

British Jubilee stamp. Original 25 mm x 40 mm

Forged British Jubilee stamp. Original 25 mm x 40 mm

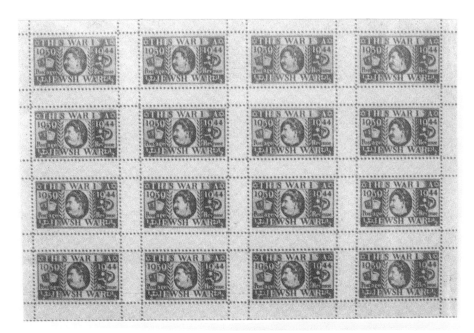

Green stamps. Sheet of forged English 1935 Jubilee stamps

Brownish stamps. Forged 1937 Coronation stamps

Special issue commemorative cover with special stamps dated 6 June 1944, the first day of the Allied invasion

Special issue commemorative cover forged in Sachsenhausen with special stamps dated 6 June 1944

Hammer and sickle — Star of David

POSTAGE REVENUE
smaller and shorter

Hammer and sickle

SSSR BRITANNIA

Star of David right and left

Soviet star with hammer
and sickle

SSSR

Stalin

1½d TEHERAN · 28.11.1943 1½d

TEHERAN 28.11.1943

THIS WAR IS A

Star of David right and left

1939, 1944

Soviet star with hammer
and sickle

Stalin

Hammer and sickle right
and left

Star of David   JEWSH WAR

Alterations on the forged stamps

Anti-British Propaganda in Neutral Countries

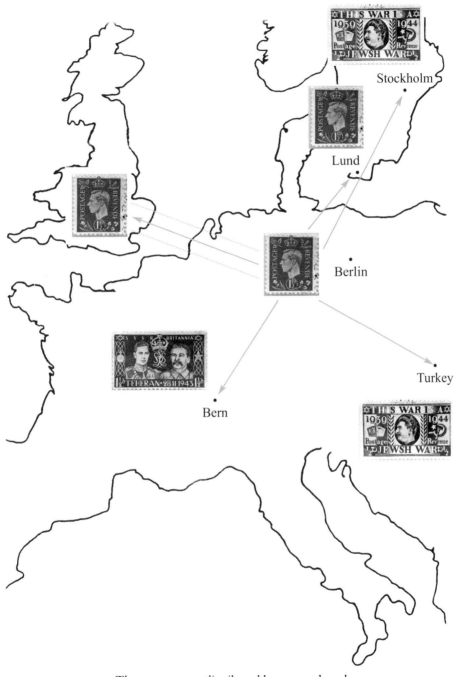

The stamps were distributed by agents abroad

American forgeries, 1944. These forgeries were done in the autumn of 1944 in an American field workshop of the Office of Strategic Services in Rome

Goebbels' Propaganda with Forged Stamps

The secret service published various articles in the occupied countries, in which they blamed others for the forgeries; this was a characteristic Goebbels propaganda ploy.

Special Stamp
Distribution Center
I. kommission för Sverige   Stockholm, 15/9 1944
Postbox 30 11 74
Postgiro 21 12 79

Högt Grade kund!
Vi äro i tillfälle att erbjuda Eder vissa specialmärken, vars försäljning torde bli en god affär for Eder och även ge Eder möjlighet att bidraga till ett allmän nyttigt ändamål. Samma dag som invasionen i väster startade, emitterades vissa specialmärken vilka icke endast avse att tingfästa denna dag utan tillika ge uttryck för den varma vänskapä som räder mellan invasionsfrontens soldater och Röda armén. Genom denna emission av specialmärken dokumenterar den brittiska regeringen den anda, som besjälar dess förbundspolitik med Sovjetunionen.

In komsterna av märkenas försäljning skola ställas till förfogande för ett allmän nyttigt ändamal. Huvuddelen härav skall nämligen utgöga en grundfond avsedd att tjäna utforskandet av den brittiska och den sovjetryska imperialismens gemensamma idé. Vi vore Eder förbundna, om Ni ville översända betalningen för de märkon Ni inköper till vårt Postgiro.

Därest Ni skulle vilja beställa ytterligare märken bedja vi Eder att uppgiva det önskade Entalet till vår postboxadresa.

Prislista bifogas.

Högaktningsfullt
Special Stamp
Distribution Center

Offer from the 'Special Stamp' factory in Sweden

Special Stamp
Distribution Center
I. kommission för Sverige   Stockholm, 15/9 1944
Postbox 30 11 74
Postgiro 21 12 79

Dear Customer!
We are in a position to offer you special issues of stamps, which you may consider useful and may present a business opportunity. On the day of the invasion in the West special commemorative stamps were issued to mark the cordial relationship between the Allied forces and the soldiers of the Red Army. The British government has documented the spirit of the Alliance with the Soviet Union with this special issue.

The profits from the sale of the stamps are intended to serve a common aim. Most of it is to provide a fund for the research and development of British and Soviet imperialist ideals.

We would be grateful if you would deposit the amount you intend to pay for your order in the above Giro account.

Please forward orders to the above postal address.

Please find price list enclosed.

Yours faithfully
Special Stamp
Distribution Center

Translation of the offer from the 'Special Stamp' factory in Sweden

Special Stamp
Distribution Center
I. kommission för Sverige   Stockholm, 23/9/1944
Postbox 30 11 74 Postgiro 21 12 79

Dear Customer!
We are pleased to confirm your order and enclose the special stamps herewith. We would be grateful for recommendations to assist further sales.

Yours faithfully
Special Stamp
Distribution Center

Additional letter from the 'Special Stamp' factory in Sweden

Forged English Stamps in Letterbox of Postmaster General Örnes, Stockholm *Expressen*, 21 September 1944

Criminal Police Investigates

The Royal Mail and serious stamp collectors are currently being plagued by stamp forgers, who flood the market with various forgeries. Yesterday for example, Postmaster General Örnes received a card in an anonymous letter containing perfect reproductions of the English penny stamp with the image of King George. The forgery can only be detected by the quality of the paper and the watermark that show that the stamps must have been produced in Sweden.

Detective Inspector Justus Svensson said in an interview with *Expressen* that this had been going on for a few months. In his opinion there was a series of peculiar circumstances. The forgers do not seem to be interested in economic gain, as they never try to sell these stamps directly to anyone. They simply send the stamps in anonymous letters to postal workers or to collectors. It is of course conceivable that this is a mere prankster, but highly unlikely that anyone would take so much trouble just for a prank. In this connection the police wish to point out that private production of stamps – even without malicious intent – is forbidden. The forgers face serious penalties if they are caught.

There is another peculiarity: the forgers were not only content to forge existing stamps, but also designed their own stamps. A stamp with the image of King George was produced, for example, with the image of Stalin added and the legend 'Teheran 28.11.1942 USSR Britannia'.

Apart from this imitation of the English coronation stamp of 1937, English stamps bearing the overprint 'liquidation of Empire' and the names of some of the colonies lost in the war, e.g. Hong Kong and Singapore, or colonies that were ceded to America – Trinidad, Jamaica. A cover letter from the untraceable firm stated that the stamps had been issued on the day the invasion began in the West, to commemorate the 'warm friendship between the soldiers of the Western Allies and the Red Army'. The commemoration of this friendship by stamps depicting the destruction of the British Empire says plenty about their origin.

A stamp expert, who had already examined the stamps before the police, found that they had a wider perforated rim and were larger than the real stamps. It is clear that they are cleverly forged and printed on stamp paper. Everything points to Germany for whatever reason.

Various stamps are now being examined by the police and measures will be put in place to halt this activity, which has caused the postal service a lot of trouble and given stamp collectors a few more grey hairs.

DU MONDE ENTIER

Alfons VAN VISSCHEL
Kruishofstraat 142 - 30
B - 2020 Antwerpen
Tel. 03 - 8 27 01 05

Propagande postale

Quand les timbres faisaient la guerre

On reconnaît aisément les deux personnages qui figurent sur ce document : le roi George VI et Joseph Staline.

Cette maquette fut réalisée avec d'autres, dans le sinistre camp de concentration d'Oranienburg-Sachsenhausen (pas très loin de Berlin) pour le compte de l'Abteilung VI-F4 de la SIPO (Sicherheitspolizei), la police secrète.

Le but : fabriquer des timbres de propagande pour tourner en dérision les accords passés par Roosevelt, Churchill et Staline lors de la conférence de Téhéran, qui, entre autres, déterminèrent le choix de la France comme lieu de débarquement plutôt que les Balkans (proposés par Churchill).

Ce document, probablement unique, servit bien à réaliser des timbres qui furent diffusés vers 1944. Ils furent imprimés sur du papier de récupération du genre de celui que l'on utilise pour emballer de la nourriture. Les timbres sont cotés environ 600 F en Allemagne...

Mise en vente en même temps que ce document, une autre maquette de la même origine et reproduisant le dossier modifié d'un autre timbre anglais de 1935 (Yvert n° 201).

L'effigie de George VI est remplacée par celle de Staline ; quant aux légendes elles ont été transformées par la mention "THIS WAR IS A JEWSH WAR" (cette guerre est une guerre juive). On note une faute au mot JEWSH, auquel il manque un I pour faire JEWISH.

On raconte que le timbre avec l'inscription corrigée aurait bien été imprimé mais aucun n'a encore été découvert à ce jour.

Ce document, estimé entre 3 000 et 4 000 F par la firme londonienne Sotheby's, sera vendu aux enchères au mois de novembre. Tout en bas, on distingue le timbre anglais authentique (émis en 1937) qui servit de modèle à la réalisation de cette maquette. Outre l'effigie de Staline qui remplace celle de la reine Elisabeth, on remarque que l'inscription "POSTAGE REVENUE" est devenue "SSSR BRITANNIA" soit Soviet Socialist Sionist Britannia *(sic)*.

Article from magazine *Du Monde Entier*
about forgeries of English stamps

English translation of article from *Du Monde Entier*:

Propaganda by Post – the Stamp War

The images on these stamps are readily recognisable as King George VI and Josef Stalin.

This stamp and others were produced in KZ Sachsenhausen (near Berlin) on order from Department VI F4 of Sipo (Sicherheitspolizei).

The aim of propaganda stamps was to ridicule the agreements drawn up between Churchill, Stalin and Roosevelt at the Teheran Conference. The Allied landings on the French coast instead of the Balkan Peninsula was decided upon, as Churchill suggested.

This document, probably a unique specimen, is a good example of the stamps that were circulated in 1944. They were printed on recycled paper, similar to paper used to pack groceries. The stamps are valued at about 600 francs in Germany.

At the same time another stamp was circulated from the same source, which is the altered version of a 1935 English stamp (Yvert No. 201).

The image of George VI is replaced by that of Stalin. The inscription was changed to
'THIS WAR IS A JEWSH WAR', where the 'I' is missing. It should read 'JEWISH'.

It is said that the stamp with the correct inscription was printed, but so far no example has been found.

This document, which has been valued by Sotheby's at 3,000–4,000 francs, will be sold at auction in November. The authentic English stamp pictured below (issued in 1937) is the model for this stamp. Apart from Stalin, instead of the queen, you can see that the legend POSTAGE REVENUE has been replaced by 'SSSR BRITANNIA' or Soviet Socialist Sionist Republic BRITANNIA.

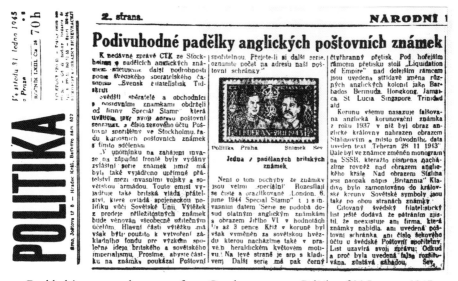

Goebbels' propaganda, extract form Czech newspaper *Politika* of 31 January 1945

English translation of article from *Politika*, 31 January 1945:

Perfect Forgeries of English Stamps

We are pleased to bring you further details from the Swedish philatelists' journal Svens Filatelistik tidskrit *of the news from ČTK, Stockholm, about forged English stamps.*

The firm Special Stamps sent a series of curious English stamps, despatched from its postbox and account number at the GPO Stockholm, to Swedish collectors and dealers with the following information:

'Commemorative stamps were issued on the occasion of the Invasion on the Western front, to celebrate the sincere friendship of the Allied invasion forces and the Soviet army. The British government supported the policy of alliance with the Soviet Union with this special

issue. The revenue from the sale of the commemorative issue is to be used for benevolent purposes and most of it is destined for a fund to promote the common aim of British and Soviet imperialism. Payment for the stamps should be made to our account at the Post Office Savings Bank. If you require further issues, please send your order to our postbox.'

These stamps definitely are 'special'. They are clearly franked London 6 June 1944 – the date of the invasion.

One series is similar to the valid English halfpenny to threepenny stamps with the image of George VI. The cross on the crown has, however, been replaced with a Soviet star, which can also be seen in the centre of the right-hand heraldic flower, while the right-hand flower is covered by the hammer and sickle. A further series is overprinted with a black frame. At the top is printed 'LIQUIDATION OF EMPIRE'; underneath are the names of various English colonies such as Barbados, Bermuda, Hong Kong, Jamaica, St Lucia, Singapore, Trinidad, etc.

But the best one is the 1937 stamp, on which the image of the queen is replaced by Stalin. Instead of the original date, the legend reads 'TEHERAN 28.11.1943'. Furthermore the initials SSSR have been added. The same letters are printed above the king's head, and over the image of Stalin is the word 'BRITANNIA'. The hammer has been worked into the crown, and the Soviet symbols are visible along both sides.

The Swedish journal also reports how further research has proven that both the firm and the account number at the Swedish Savings Bank are non-existent. The journal report ends with the words: 'It remains a mystery who produced these forgeries.'

Evacuation

WE PRISONERS KNEW THAT HITLER had lost the war. Much as we supported the relays of Allied planes with satisfaction, we knew that our days could be numbered. So we hoped all the more that some pilot would just drop a bomb on the concentration camp. At least it seemed to us to be a better way of dying than being shot or gassed. What else could we expect?

Then 13 March 1945 dawned. Heavy artillery fire lasted all day. That day the order arrived from Berlin to cease operations. We did not want to think of what might happen next. Most of us saw ourselves being marched to the gas chambers. There was indescribable tension in the group. We were all gathered in the common room, waiting for further developments. There were more rumours about our fate. This made everyone even more nervous.

The SS men did not leave their guns out of their hands for a moment, and suddenly stopped speaking to us. They were standing by for further orders and did not know what was going to happen next.

The next morning SS-SBF Hansch, Krüger's deputy, stormed into the canteen and roared: 'Dismantle the machinery and prepare for transportation!' We heaved a sigh of relief. This order meant that we were to be evacuated somewhere and that the danger was past for the time being. Our joy was short-lived when another order at 2 p.m. said, 'Stop work.'

It was obvious that Krüger himself did not know what was happening so there was nothing we could do but wait. The following day we were ordered to pack up again. This time we were given thirty-six hours. We thought it was impossible to dismantle, sort, label, pack and load such heavy machines within thirty-six hours. We would never do it! But it was a matter of do or die. We were safe for those thirty-six hours and there was a glimmer of hope too.

We divided into three groups. The first dismantled the machines, the second packed them and the third took them to the station in three vehicles. There was a goods train ready with sixteen sealed wagons. All the equipment for the printing works and workshops was loaded onto them. The banknotes that we had printed were placed in coffin-shaped waterproof cases with flush lids, sealed with twenty long screws apiece. We loaded the equipment for the RSHA secret service espionage laboratories into other wagons. There were also twenty coffin-shaped cases of the same length containing secret service documents from Schloss Friedenthal, which was where Skorzeny's spy school was located.

We managed to finish the job, which had seemed so impossible, in a shorter time than we expected. We had done the dismantling and loading in thirty-four hours flat, which shows what men are capable of when their lives are at stake.

Finally the order came that let us breathe easily: 'Everyone is to take provisions for four days. We leave tomorrow.' So on 16 March 1945 a special train left KZ Sachsenhausen with its strange cargo. The floor in three of the wagons was covered with straw, blankets and a few benches and there was a stove and fuel. It must have been the first time that the Nazis treated concentration camp inmates so well – forty-seven prisoners in heated wagons, guarded by sixteen guards.

A strange feeling came over us. We had become used to imprisonment. Compared to other prisoners we had been well treated in Sachsenhausen and felt relatively safe in our blocks behind the barbed-wire. Now we were sitting side by side in rattling railway wagons, thinking about our fate. Not one of us had ever hoped to get home alive.

Death is the same everywhere. Why were we put on a transport? Could they not have shot us in Sachsenhausen and spared us this arduous, depressing journey? These were the sorts of thoughts going through our heads as the train sped to its unknown destination.

We sat on our seats exhausted. Most of us had eaten our rations and were suffering hunger pangs. We kept trying to find out where we were and what direction we were travelling. Finally the train stopped with a jolt. Gottlieb, a native of Prague, looked through the ventilation grille. Suddenly he shouted hoarsely with tears in his eyes, his voice breaking: 'Boys, we are in Prague.'

We Czechs and Slovaks all jumped up as everyone pushed up to the little window to get a look at the city's hundred spires, even for a minute. We had so often talked about Prague and wished we could be there again. In the distance we could see the outline of Hradčany Castle.

The train was standing in a siding in Vršovice. We kept looking over at the golden city and could not tear ourselves away from the familiar sights. A red-and-white tram was moving along through the streets as if nothing had happened. We saw workers on their way to work.

'Do you see that house in Kluboučnicka Street? That's where I live. What about my wife and three-year-old son? I wonder where they are. It is more than two years since I last saw them. Imagine, being so close to home and to the family and yet so terribly far away!'

Gottlieb stood lost in thought; staring at his home for the two hours that the train was stopped. We could imagine his feelings and did not want to disturb him. Escape was impossible.

The workers who passed the train certainly did not know what sort of transport it was. They noticed by looking through the grilles on the windows that it contained prisoners. But no one was allowed to approach the train. Nevertheless, for the first time in three years I could detect sympathy in people's eyes.

A woman threw us a piece of bread. It did not reach us but fell on the ground outside our wagon. That did not bother us. The mere thought that there were sympathetic people out there meant an awful lot to us. We Czechs and Slovaks were proud that this first gesture of sympathy was made in our own homeland.

Towards 7 p.m. the train moved off slowly again. We looked through the grille as the city disappeared. There was not a dry eye among us. The other prisoners understood. They knew how they would have felt if we had passed through Warsaw, Belgrade, Paris or Antwerp. We sat down again in silence, one after the other.

It was late on the 20 March when the train ground to a halt. This time it was Smolianoff who got up to see where we were. Suddenly his face twisted into a horrified smile. 'And I thought I would never see it again. Lads, we are in Mauthausen.'

Steps sounded alongside the wagon, and after a few minutes two SS men opened the door. Down below stood SBF Hansch. 'Everybody out . . . Get out!' he ordered in a deep voice. Hansch had taken over command of our special unit before leaving; Krüger had stayed in Berlin. Hansch was known as a murderer from his time in Warsaw, where he had been responsible for the deaths of many Poles. We were not the only ones afraid of him – even his own SS men who were escorting the transport feared him.

We climbed out of the wagons. The mountain could be seen faintly in the distance. A cold wind was blowing in our faces. The sixteen SS men escorted us through the deserted streets of Mauthausen. We dragged ourselves weakly uphill. What would the next day bring? We had heard plenty about this notorious camp. It was known as 'Mordhausen' among us prisoners. The SS had killed thousands of prisoners in forced labour in the quarries.

There was not much time for reflection. We reached the camp. The high stone wall with its towering watchtowers loomed shadowy in the pitch darkness. It was my fourth concentration camp.

Part III

KZ Mauthausen – KZ 'Schlier' – Redl-Zipf – KZ Ebensee – Toplitzsee

KZ Mauthausen

• 1 •

MAUTHAUSEN WAS LIKE A FORTRESS. The commander was SS-Standartenführer Franz Ziereis: a very brutal man, who had lampshades and other objects made out of the skin of tattooed victims.

After a while two high-ranking SS officers, camp leaders Bachmayer and Ziereis, appeared. They wanted to take over our column, but Werner said they were not authorised. We were high-security SD prisoners. So the two officers had to open the gates to us. We were led through the camp to Block 20, which was isolated from the camp by a wall, barbed-wire and three watchtowers.

We were re-registered in the office, we were issued new prisoner numbers and new file cards were filled out. I had been number 64401 in Auschwitz, number 79161 in Sachsenhausen and now I became number 138409. The next morning we marched six kilometres to the station to unload the machines and the cases. First the waterproof cases were transported to a store. The machines were put in a shed at the station for the time being.

When we moved into Block 20, we had no idea what crimes had been perpetrated there, or why the block was so hermetically sealed off. I only found out long after the war what had happened there. Soviet POWs, officers and men had been held there. They had decided to escape. Their sick comrades had given them their clothes and stayed behind although they knew it meant death for them. So on 3 February 1945 they opened the windows and jumped into the yard in a hail of bullets, they threw paving stones and wooden clogs at their captors, sprayed them in the face with fire extinguishers and tried to attack them. Then they caused a short in the electric fence by throwing wet blankets and clothes onto it. So they got through the perimeter fence, leaving their dead comrades behind in the yard.

Then the sirens sounded and the hunt was on – Ziereis and Bachmayer called it 'hare-coursing'. The Wehrmacht joined in too, it was not a fair fight. Most of the POWs were recaptured and led back into the camp. They were most brutally tortured to death. But the revolt of the Soviet prisoners gave thousands of prisoners in Mauthausen renewed courage and a belief in victory over the Nazis.

One group, under Colonel Grigori Sabolotnjak is supposed to have got away as far as the Danube. They had attacked and overcome an anti-aircraft unit with their bare hands and hijacked a lorry to transport their wounded, but only a few succeeded in evading all pursuit and getting away to freedom.

We were led along this street to the concentration camp

Watchtowers in KZ Mauthausen

Nazi leaders inspecting KZ Mauthausen – Himmler,
Kaltenbrunner, Ziereis and Bachmeyer

Mauthausen quarry – camp director Bachmayer on his inspection rounds

After a full day's work in the quarry, prisoners had to carry heavy stone blocks
up 186 steps to the camp

• 2 •

KZ 'Schlier' – Redl-Zipf

On 4 April 1945 we suddenly got orders to pack up and load everything again. So we had to load up all the things that we had unloaded. The SS men were raging, they cursed and swore and beat the prisoners they thought were not working fast enough. It was the first time they had behaved so brutally towards us in the special *Kommando*. The worse they treated us, the more we noticed that they feared for their lives, and that gave us some satisfaction.

Some time in the afternoon the train set off to an unknown destination. German transport was by now so disorganised that they had only open carriages for us prisoners, which confirmed our impression that we were fleeing the enemy.

After a five-hour journey the train reached Redl-Zipf in Upper Austria, which was a sub-camp of Mauthausen.

It was a small camp, consisting of only six or eight wooden huts, surrounded by ordinary barbed-wire. It lay in a valley with wooded slopes on either side. Because the aeronautic factory in Wiener-Neustadt had been heavily bombed on 13 August and again on 1 and 26 October 1943, they had begun to build KZ 'Schlier' – Redl-Zipf – in order to continue the rocket-building programme and as a protection against air raids. Schlier was the cover name. The prisoners had already started working on the conversion of the cellars of the brewery in September 1943. Standing in water and using only picks and shovels, they worked in two twelve-hour shifts. That is how the sub-camp was built.

Most of the prisoners held here were republicans or volunteers from the International Brigades, who had defended democracy in the Spanish Civil War. Our *Kommando* was allocated two separate huts, which we had to fence off ourselves with barbed-wire. We arrived in the late afternoon and before we had finished it was dark. Sounds of singing and guitar music drifted over from the nearby huts, where the Spanish prisoners were. The words were strange, but we understood the longing in the melodies. Although we were dead tired, we lay awake on our bunks, listening to the Spanish songs.

The next morning a surprise awaited us. The mountains we had seen the day before were hung with camouflage nets, behind which there were secret entrances leading to deep underground tunnels. The existence of this camp was to be kept secret. That is why it had a cover name, even though there was nowhere called Schlier in the neighbouring area. The prisoners were registered in the main camp in Mauthausen: on their file cards was written 'transferred to Schlier'.

The first job we had was to carry the 'coffins' filled with banknotes into the underground mine shafts. Just inside the entrance were heavy lorries in which we travelled way down to spacious storage halls. There were more than twenty huge halls, each one about 13 metres wide, over 30 metres long and about 7 metres high with barrel-vaulted roofs. There was a crane in each hall – in short, an entire factory for the production of the secret V1 weapon. The truck tracks had been assembled so that wagons could go down to the entrances of the halls. From there, material was transported on a narrow gauge track into each hall.

After storing the banknotes, we started to set up the forgery workshop in two blocks. We made concrete bases for the printing machines and set up each section, as if the war was going to last another few years. Production of dollar notes was due to start on 1 May.

3

End of 'Operation Bernhard'

IT MUST HAVE BEEN 24 April 1945. The door of our workshop opened and Krüger came in, smiling broadly. We had not seen him since we left Sachsenhausen. He strode round the room, greeting us in a friendly fashion and said: 'Well, lads, you have done a great job. But I've come in today to save you. The Americans are not far away and we cannot stay here any longer. A new printing works has been set up in the Alpine fortress, and you will continue the work there.' He passed round cigarettes and left.

Outside Hansch was patrolling the block and we heard him saying to Krüger: 'So, see you in three weeks as arranged?' There was great excitement in the workshop. Most of us did not believe Krüger's words, thinking it was just another bluff. Towards evening, Werner, who had succeeded Hansch in command since the afternoon they told all the prisoners to line up, appeared. More excitement: what was Werner going to tell us? We were dying with curiosity, impatiently we rushed out into the yard.

This time no one checked that the lines were straight. Werner appeared with two officers, stood up on a small box and addressed us in a serious voice: 'The Americans and the English are a few miles from the camp. I am expecting you to follow all orders and to show good discipline. Do not let yourselves be led astray by a changing situation. In a few days we will destroy the remains of the American, English and Soviet armies and embark on a victorious offensive on all fronts.

'Keep calm. I have orders to shoot on sight anyone who tries to escape. Tomorrow morning we will set off for the Alpine fortress. We cannot take the machines with us, so they will have to be destroyed, so that they do not fall into enemy hands. There are other machines available in the Alps. We will continue the work there. Now dismiss!'

They woke us at 6 a.m. on 1 May and the work started at 7 a.m. It promised to be a glorious spring day. Suddenly we noticed that the camp flag with the swastika was flying at half-mast. As usual on these occasions, there were plenty of opinions and rumours circulating, until at midday a black-rimmed notice was put up in the camp, announcing the death of Hitler. Then the speculation ceased.

Führerhauptquartier, 1. Mai
Unser Führer Adolf Hitler ist heute nachmittag in seinem Befehlsstand in der Reichskanzlie, bis zum letzten Atemzug gegen den Bolschewismus kämpfend, für Deutschland gefallen.

Am 30. April hat der Fürher den Großadmiral Dönitz zu seinem Nachfolger bestimmt.

Führer's headquarters, 1 May
Today, in the Reichs Chancellery, our Führer, Adolf Hitler, fell, fighting Bolshevism with his last breath, and died for Germany.[1]

On 30 April the Führer nominated Great Admiral Dönitz as his successor.

We were very excited. We had waited for this moment and now our wish had come true. We could not let our joy be noticed, and speculated about how this event would affect our future. We had to be more careful than ever now. We all knew that the fight for our lives had begun.

Even though the dollar notes would pass as excellent forgeries, after many months of painstaking work the SS was no longer in a position to begin actual production. The situation at the front had deteriorated so catastrophically for Nazi Germany that the RSHA considered it more important to get the entire enterprise out of the danger zone, which amounted to liquidation, rather than printing dollars.

The trial samples had been presented to Himmler for approval, but the planned production of dollars on a large scale never took place. Jacobson's sabotage had worked, so that not a single forged dollar note went into circulation.

On the evening of 28 April forty waterproof cases and the secret archive of Section VI F4 RSHA were loaded on to two lorries and we never saw them again.

---

1 *Author's note: that too is a lie, he did not fight but committed suicide.*

Murder of Karl Sussmann

THE SS MEN GREW INCREASINGLY uncertain and confused. During that time Karl Sussmann, prisoner number 75245, an artist from Vienna, took ill. As his condition deteriorated OSF Willi Schmitt took him away. Everyone knew what was going to happen. Werner had him killed by injection.

This was not the first killing of this sort. We had experienced all sorts of brutality. But this time it was more tragic because it was a few hours before liberation. If he had been taken ill a few days later, he would have been saved.

His comrades made a coffin for him. It must have been the first time in the history of Nazi concentration camps that prisoners got permission to hold a proper burial. It was also a reflection of the Nazis' fear at the time. The funeral made a deep impression on all of us. We wondered privately whether he was to be the last victim or whether we would be next. The uncertainty was the worst.

Karl Sussmann – murdered a few days before liberation

KZ Ebensee

ON 3 MAY 1945, THE order came from the main camp in Mauthausen to evacuate KZ Schlier! At this point there were 150 Spaniards, 80 prisoners of various other nationalities as well as the 135 prisoners of our special *Kommando*.

The next day Werner commandeered two lorries with difficulty, then the SS men shouted, 'Line up.' Werner ordered us to 'Sit down' – 115 prisoners and six SS men were packed in. Everyone wanted to be last, hoping that there would not be enough room. Whoever stayed behind had the chance of being liberated, before being deported. Werner lost his temper and began hitting us with the butt of his pistol.

'Idiots!' he roared. 'We only have a few minutes. Understand?' We understood only too well. We had to sit down under a hail of blows from the SS men working with him. The block-warden went with the first group, which I was in. Werner, ten guards and twenty prisoners stayed behind. He ordered the driver to go and come straight back. The driver tore along the mountain road. He had to go back for the second group before the Allies arrived.

It started to snow. We looked at the beautiful mountain scenery, all white and sparkling. It made a great impression on me. My thoughts flew back to my youth and to my skiing days in the high Tatra, in similar scenery. Was this to be the last time I would see it? Everyone wondered, would we turn right or left at the next junction? On the left lay the mountains, on the right Mauthausen and death in the gas chamber. Everyone's nerves were on edge as we approached the fateful crossroads.

No one spoke. The lorry was travelling very fast; it was getting nearer and nearer. Only 500 metres . . . 300 . . . 200. We held our breath. Right or left turn? It turned left. We heaved a sigh of relief. We had escaped death once more.

We arrived at another camp, which was our last stop – KZ Ebensee, the very last camp to be liberated. Whilst all other prisoners had been freed, we were entering a Nazi hellhole. On a hill overlooking the concentration camp was a small SS camp. We were not allowed to come into contact with other prisoners, so we were accommodated in an empty wooden hut in the SS camp. Everyone got a piece of bread. Then the SS locked us in.

Through the window we saw two SS officers with machine guns directed at the hut. Below us lay the camp, where lights came on one by one. It grew dark. There was so little space, that we had to stand pressed against each other. It was pitch dark in the hut and depressing. Time passed very slowly, we were very tense. The night seemed endless. We thought the sun would never rise. No one spoke in those terrible, long hours.

Finally day dawned. When it was light we could make out the road, winding through the valley and saw a dreadful sight. A long column of thousands of human skeletons was making its way towards the camp. It was prisoners on a death march, a gruesome sight.

We heard Gauleiter Eigruber's appeal not to resist the advancing Americans or to blow up bridges, but to give them free passage. There was wild confusion in the SS camp. It was 5 May and the SS were fleeing. These were the last hours of the 'Thousand-Year Reich'.

6

Liberation

SUDDENLY ONE OF THE MEN standing at the window called out: 'They have raised a white flag down in the camp. They are surrendering.' We thought the Americans had liberated the camp. Everyone pushed over to the window to see the flag of surrender that might save us too. The loud voice of SS man Schmidt shouting 'Line up!' jolted us out of our amazement.

So it was a trap! Outside were five SS officers with machine guns trained on us to mow us down when we went out. No one moved. 'Did you not hear my order? Am I to shoot you?' The SS man had a revolver in his right hand, his face was red, his finger on the trigger. He would have shot at anyone who spoke out of turn. We saw that he meant it, and surged out of the hut. Would they shoot or not? They did not shoot.

'Line up in threes. Keep in step – March!' The tidy column marched off. Our situation was still very serious. Six sentries armed with machine guns walked alongside our column. We were still afraid that we would not reach our goal – the white flag in the middle of the concentration camp. Would they open fire on us at the last minute?

We drew nearer to the camp. How we longed to get inside that barbed-wire fence – what an irony that it meant freedom and hope. We finally reached the gate. There were no SS guards any more – just Josef Poltrum, a Wehrmacht officer with a Red Cross armband and an armed political prisoner. When the SS fled, the prisoners had taken over the camp administration.

Jansen stood to attention, saluted the officer and formally handed over 115 prisoners. The officer looked at us incredulously. What sort of prisoners were these, well dressed, well fed, with normal haircuts? What was this about?

'Who are you and what were you doing there?' asked the surprised officer.

'My orders are to hand these prisoners over to you. That's all I know.'

'In that case, I cannot accept them.'

We were nearly in despair. The armed prisoner looked us up and down, wondering what sort of prisoners we were. One of our group dashed over to the armed prisoner, showed him the number tattooed on his forearm and said we were members of a special *Kommando*. 'For God's sake, let us into the camp,' he begged. The prisoner was amazed, looked at us again, then nodded to the officer and he opened the gate. We rushed in as if we were being chased. Anything to get away from those six SS guards. They could still change their minds and open fire.

We ran to the far side of the camp.

Saved!

It was 11 a.m. on 5 May 1945 – we felt newborn.

It was a miracle. We had escaped out of hell. We finally felt free, safe behind the barbed-wire. Before us was the way home, to our country, families and friends.

Our joy was marred by concern for our comrades, Karel Gottlieb, Alfred Pick and the others who had been left behind in Redl-Zipf.

Only then did we learn that the Americans had arrived earlier than expected. The evacuation by the SS was not supposed to have been so hasty. We waited all day, doing nothing, waiting contentedly for the arrival of the Allies. When would they finally get here?

We waited impatiently and towards evening the last group of prisoners from the forgery unit arrived from Ebensee. We hugged each other, deeply moved, happy to have escaped death. They told us how they had got to Ebensee.

Gate of KZ Ebensee, the gateway to freedom for the prisoners of the forgery unit

Entrance to the mine shaft where all the Ebensee prisoners and the members of the forgery unit were to have been killed

7

The Last March

AFTER WE HAD BEEN TAKEN away in the two lorries on 4 May, the rest of the prisoners waited for them to come back for them. Meanwhile the SS were packing up. A one-armed SS man, OSF Willi Schmitt, lived in a villa at the edge of the forest outside the camp. He picked Norbert Leonard, Eduard Bier and Hans Kurzweil to help him carry his luggage to the camp. They went along with him to his house and when they got there the SS man said: 'Sit on that bench and wait while I pack my things.'

Then he went in to pack, forgetting that the garden fence bordered the edge of the forest. Leonard and Bier had noticed this and took their opportunity, climbing over the fence and disappearing into the woods. Kurzweil was not quick enough off the mark and got left behind.

When the SS man came out he asked where the other two had gone. Hans said they had gone into the woods. The SS man rushed after them but could not catch up so he fired a few shots in the direction of the forest. When they got back to the camp he told Werner that he could not give chase because he was on his own and that the prisoners had fired at him from different directions. Werner believed him and conducted a search for weapons among the prisoners in Redl-Zipf. Of course none were found.

So the afternoon dragged on and the lorry that was to transport the second group of prisoners had not turned up. Werner organised distribution of food. Each prisoner got cigarettes as well. Werner did not want to hang on waiting for the lorry – another sign that the end was near. Finally he ordered the prisoners to march out. The column that set off was a strange sight. At the head of it was a group of Spaniards, who had been stationed in the vicinity, then came a horse-drawn carriage, carrying the provisions and luggage for the SS men, then eighteen prisoners from the special *Kommando*, guarded by SS men. No one knew where they were going but they felt there was some hope, since they were high-security prisoners.

The Spaniards had found out who the prisoners were and they helped by marching very slowly. It was important for the prisoners to play for time. They marched on and reached the village of Gampern. The column came to a halt at a fork in the road, not quite sure which way to go. One path led upwards through a wood, and was shorter; the other one was a new road that led round the wood, but was longer. The Spaniards decided on the shorter route and in the end Werner followed with his prisoners. It was bad luck for him, because just after they disappeared into the wood, the lorry drove back along the new road – too late for Werner, but advantageous for the prisoners.

They walked right through the village of Gampern, past Seewalchen and marched slowly along the bank of the beautiful Attersee. The Spaniards, who were setting the pace, stopped for a rest every few minutes, which irritated Werner and his SS men. In the evening the column reached Weissenbach, in lovely spring weather. The prisoners' rations were all finished so the Spaniards shared out what they had.

The next morning, 5 May, the Spanish unit left the column and the special *Kommando* was left behind with its escort, but shortly after that set off in the direction of Ebensee. Werner commandeered a horse and cart on the way. He let anyone with sore feet sit on it; there were five of them. Werner got up in front and they stopped in Mitterweissenbach to wait for the column. While they were waiting, the prisoners tried to talk Werner into letting them all go. But he insisted on following his orders.

Soon the marchers caught up with them and they learnt from the five prisoners who were travelling with Werner that their destination was Ebensee, as he had disclosed it. Everyone was very disappointed to hear this because KZ Ebensee had a very bad reputation and they wondered why they were being taken there.

There was terrible confusion on the road to Ebensee – four prisoners took advantage of the situation and made their escape. The remaining prisoners saw them escaping and succeeded in distracting the SS guards. When Werner noticed that there were four missing, he started to rant and rage and threatened to shoot them all. The four escapees were captured by a Luftwaffe unit and brought back. By this time Werner's anger had cooled. He gave them an awful dressing down but nothing more.

The group sat on the roadside for hours. Werner could not make up his mind whether to go on or not. He kept trying to get through to Ebensee camp on the phone from Mitterweissenbach Post Office. Finally he came back, saying that the Wehrmacht had taken over the camp administration and that it was no longer in SS hands. SS men coming from Ebensee confirmed this news. The prisoners were now beginning to believe that liberation was near and they would survive. Werner succeeded in stopping a military lorry, which brought them all to the guardhouse at the gate of the SS camp. He could hardly believe his eyes: the camp was empty. He went over to the concentration camp with his prisoners. The Wehrmacht officer was standing at the gate wearing a Red Cross armband and beside him was an armed political prisoner.

Werner asked the officer whether he had seen his men and the 115 prisoners, or knew where they were. 'Yes, your men handed over the 115 prisoners at 10.30. Now there are 16,000 here.'

The Wehrmacht officer explained that it was unlikely he would be able to pick out the 115 from all the others. Furthermore he pointed out that the camp administration was now in the hands of political prisoners and that he had better disappear before it was too late. There was nothing Werner could do but hand over the eighteen prisoners and withdraw angrily. Thus the last prisoners in the forgery unit were liberated.

We sat around all night and celebrated our liberation. It was only then that we realised how lucky we were to get out of the clutches of the SS. We talked about all we had experienced and suffered during the past three years. Images of the thousands who had been driven to the gas chambers haunted us, of other unfortunates who had been buried alive, burnt or otherwise killed, and the thousands of half-starved human skeletons we had seen on their death march to Ebensee. We were resolved, to a man, to do all in our power to prevent such things ever happening again.

No one in the world could ever list all those who lost their lives in Hitler's concentration camps. The nameless dead need no statistics, no roll of honour or record of the tortured. They don't even demand revenge. The only sound coming from these unmarked graves is the warning, 'Never again.'

Never again!

Even today, so many years later, it is difficult to find words to express the thoughts and feelings that went through our heads then. Was it really true? We were free. We were so immersed in our thoughts, memories and happy conversations, that we did not even notice day breaking. We had sat up all night, yet still felt happy and fresh! The next day we heard the muffled sound of American tanks and soldiers on the way to Ebensee.

We are in charge, we are alive. The SS have fled. We are free! But right beside us were more than two or three hundred dead comrades. We needed diggers instead of gravediggers to bury them. Some had closed eyes, others had their hands joined, but most of them lay just the way death had taken them.

Where is the clergyman to recite the prayers for the dead and to bless them? So many graves have to be dug . . . we walked past them, we who were alive and free.

The sound of the tanks grew louder. It was the Americans, the soldiers of the 3rd Cavalry Battalion under the command of Major Timothy C. Brennan. An officer opened the gate of the concentration camp. Soldiers jumped out of the tanks. They were tired and dirty, but they were the people who confirmed our newfound freedom. The half-starved creatures tried to clamber up on the tanks. They were human beings but looked like laughing skeletons.

What a throng! The soldiers were speechless. It was their first experience of a German concentration camp. They covered their faces. They had seen action in heavy battles and had faced death thousands of times and were hardened, but not to this sight. So this was National Socialism!

Joy and horror went hand in hand; the joy of the survivors with the revulsion of the liberators, ordinary soldiers and officers. They could not understand how rational human beings could think up such cruelty and inhumanity.

Straight after liberation an international police force was formed, made up of former political prisoners, who arrested members of the Gestapo, SA and SS and took them into custody.

Our way home was now clear and safe. We, who have survived this hell, can and will never forget this darkest period in European history. Neither will we forget the millions of innocent victims.

Due to the advance of the Americans into Austria, the SS could not carry out their orders to liquidate all members of the forgery unit. This picture shows two of the group immediately after liberation on 6 May 1945 (Adolf Burger on right)

Confirmation:

This is to certify that the int. policeman BURGER adolf handed
over the former SA man Weinzierl Karl after his arrest to the
Liberation committee at Ebensee.
Ebensee on 14.5.45   American Occupation Authority
                                                ila
                                        Liberation committee

Freed political prisoners helped the American occupying forces
to arrest SS and Gestapo personnel

KZ Ebensee – thousands of prisoners who were close to starvation were liberated

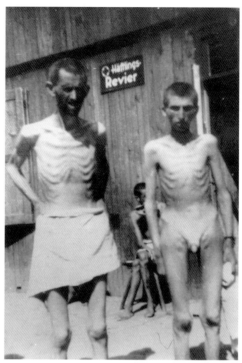

Thousands of prisoners at KZ Ebensee looked like this at liberation

Crematorium of KZ Ebensee, set amid beautiful Alpine scenery

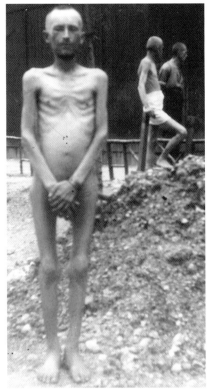

Starvation – a former university professor

After liberation the American army looked after the surviving prisoners

The forgery *Kommando* after liberation: left to right: Meyer Levi Groen from Holland,
Ernst Gottlieb from Austria; second from end: Salamon Smolianoff;
second row, right: Adolf Burger

Prisoner 64401 with his liberators – KZ Ebensee, 8 May 1945.
Left to right: Marz Catherine Beggs, Davis, Burger, Ada Timmer

No Home to Go To

ON 20 MAY 1945 I arrived in Prague. My first thought was to get home. But there would be no trains from Prague to Poprad for six weeks. So I had to wait again. I was hoping to find my mother and stepfather at home. I had received only one letter from my mother in October 1944 in KZ Sachsenhausen.

I can remember the journey clearly. I was making plans for the future . . . I was hopeful. I walked along the familiar road from the station to my home. I opened the door . . . and it could not have been more of a disappointment: an empty apartment, completely empty, no furniture at all. I stood in the doorway leaning against the jamb. I was in despair and cold hardly take it in. It was a while before I noticed someone standing behind me. I turned round – it was our neighbour. 'Is it you? You are really here?' She looked at me incredulously. I learnt from her what had happened. My mother had been deported to KZ Ravensbrück and my father to Sachsenhausen, only four months before the end of the war. I never saw them again.

Standing in the doorway of the empty flat, I could only think, 'I cannot live here any more.' I turned round and went back to the station and back to Prague, resolved to bear witness to everything I had experienced and survived.

In October 1945 the book *Number 64401 Speaks* was published in Prague.
It was an account of everything I had to suffer during three years in the concentration camp in order to survive. Drawing: Leo Haas

Nazis Flee

AFTER THE WAR, TWO GROUPS were formed to organise the widespread network of Nazi connections, ODESSA and SPINNE. They helped Nazi war criminals, the leaders of SD and SS and high-ranking party officials, the so-called 'golden pheasants', to escape abroad. They had contacts in Spain, South America, Portugal, Argentina, Chile and some Arab countries. They organised thousands of forged passports using the supply prepared by the forgery unit. With the active help of South American regimes and contacts, including Vatican diplomats such as Bishop Hudal, quite a few Nazis got away to these countries, including Peru and Brazil. The names of Nazi war criminals such as Eichmann, Dr Mengele, Barbie, Rauff, Stangl and Cukurs became well known.

Subsequent to the Nuremberg Trials, guilty industrialists, judges, civil servants. doctors and generals faced charges in twelve other trials held by American military tribunals. The most important was 'Trial 11', the Wilhelmstrasse trial, in which four government ministers, seven departmental secretaries and a series of higher civil servants were charged. The American legal staff prepared 55,000 files. Walter Schellenberg, head of the foreign service of the RSHA, Graf Schwerin von Krosigk, finance minister of the Reich and Emil Puhl, president of the Deutsche Reichsbank of many years' standing, sat together in the dock.

Spectators who had hoped for revelations following the statements about the vanished millions and that Schellenberg would be held accountable for the extraordinary forgery and related crimes left the court disappointed. Schellenberg was sentenced to six years' penal servitude, Emil Puhl, the silent keeper of the Nazi hoard, got a five-year custodial sentence. A procession of defence witnesses, who usually stood self-condemned, trailed through courts and tribunals. People of high social standing appeared quite soon in elegant clothes and even in formal wear, later again in ironed uniforms.

Some of them were university professors or lecturers, engineers, doctors of law, medicine and philosophy, generals and high-ranking officers. They had been participants in mass murder, had either killed people themselves or, by fraud, theft and forgery, helped to carry out crimes that had no parallel in history.

But what happened to the Nazi criminals?

OSF Dr Wilhelm Höttl, a close friend of Eichmann and Mengele, confidant of Kaltenbrunner, had been involved in the forgery operation and led a carefree existence after the war. His benefactors ensured that he was not handed over to the Hungarian government, who had a warrant out for his arrest. He founded a private school in the former 'Alpine fortress' and in 1955 wrote a book called *Operation Bernhard* under the pseudonym Walter Hagen, in which he slandered the prisoners who worked in the forgery *Kommando*. In 1956, and again in 1960, prisoner Hans Kurzweil from Vienna sued him.

SS-SBF Fritz Schwend, the currency dealer with the worldwide contacts spent only one day as a prisoner of the Americans. The Italians had a warrant out for his arrest and in Bolzano he was sentenced *in absentia* after a trial by jury in 1964 to twenty-one years' imprisonment. Likewise, on 8 June 1979, in a court in Munich he received a suspended sentence of two years. Since 1945 he has not spent a day in prison.

The head of the distribution network, George Spencer Spitz, was never caught either. Otto Skorzeny went to live in Spain. He was charged with a series of war crimes. Bernhard Krüger disappeared in May 1945. He was pursued by Major George McNelly, Washington's counter-forgery expert. Scotland Yard was also involved in the hunt for Krüger. In 1952 McNelly recorded in a report that: 'Nothing had been heard of the master forger, in spite of extensive efforts by police in several countries to find him.' Interpol circulated Krüger's description around the world, in vain.

Gerald Reitlinger, the British contemporary historian who had researched the facts of Krüger's enterprise at Scotland Yard, wrote that he had never been traced. There were other versions; it was claimed that Krüger had fled to Italy via Switzerland after the war. Others claimed he was living and working as a banker in Buenos Aires. Other 'inside' sources claimed he had died destitute in Baghdad. It was even claimed that he had hanged himself in a British prison. It was a web of false trails and conflicting stories. The elusive Krüger, key figure in the forgery operation, had vanished into thin air. But had he?

In fact he had been interned by the Americans for four months from 4 May 1945. Then he had fled. On 26 November 1946 he was arrested by the secret service and held until May 1949. Then he took refuge in the Hahnemühle paper mill in Dassel. The managing director, Robert Bartsch, his former paper supplier, sheltered him. He remained incognito and knew that charges in the money forgery operation would be statute-barred in 1955. He waited for ten long years.

Then on 23 August 1956 Krüger made a sworn statement: 'In my capacity as technical director in Section VI of the foreign service, I carried out a forgery operation on the orders of Reichsführer H. Himmler, under the cover name "Operation Bernhard", which was intended as an economic measure against England.'

How modest of him!

Krüger, born on 26 November 1904, Nazi Party member number 528,739, SS number 15,249, claims to have been only a technical adviser and director of a technical department in Section VI of the RSHA. This statement was taken at face value, and he was not prosecuted for membership of two criminal organisations. He should have been prosecuted under German law for the money forgery. The fact that he had been a party member since 1931 was no longer of any consequence and not a punishable offence.

Krüger, as commander of the forgery workshop in Sachsenhausen, was responsible for the execution of the sick prisoner Isaak Sukienik from USSR, Karl Sussmann from Vienna, Georg Jilovský from Prague, Abraham Kleinfeld from Austria, Ernst Stiasny from Brünn, Abraham Fingerhut and Hermann Gütig. All had been murdered. He had also ordered the execution of the remaining prisoners in the forgery unit, which was only prevented by liberation in May 1945.

He never spoke about his victims, claiming that he was only the technical director of operations:

> My orders were to carry out the operation using Jewish prisoners, so I first selected thirty-nine prisoners from KZ Sachsenhausen, and a further hundred from Auschwitz.
>
> I must emphasise that none of these prisoners were criminals, or professional forgers, except for one.
>
> It is relevant that many had been imprisoned because of their racial origin, and were classified as political. This is supported by the fact that they wore a red badge to indicate this category on their prison clothes.
>
> The prisoners had nothing to do with the manufacture of the printing blocks, which were made by SS contract labour in Schloss Friedenthal, about 3 kilometres from Sachsenhausen.

Head of forgery, SBF Krüger, engineer.
Photo from 1942

Krüger lived in Hamburg after the war.
Photo from 1984

Bernhard Krüger
DASSEL Kr.Einbeck
(20b) Maschweg 369 =

den 23. August 1956

Ich, Bernhard K r ü g e r , wohnhaft in D a s s e l Krs.
E i n b e c k , Bundesrepublik Deutschland, erkläre mich
bereit, nachstehende eidesstattliche Erklärung für Herrn
Hans K u r z w e i l , wohnhaft in W i e n , Burggasse 60,
hinsichtlich seiner Beleidigungsklage gegen H a g e n ,
abzugeben.
Ich erkläre außerdem, daß ich mir der Bedeutung der Abgabe
einer derartigen Erklärung vollkommen bewußt bin.

Eidesstattliche Erklärung

In der Eigenschaft als techn.Referent und Leiter eines
technischen Referates innerhalb des Amtes VI, Auslands-
nachrichtendienst, führte ich auf Befehl des Reichsführers
SS, H.Himmler , die Falschgeldproduktion mit der
Docknamenbezeichnung "Unternehmen Bernhard," die sich als
wirtschaftsstratbgische Maßnahme gegen E n g l a n d rich-
tete, durch.

Entsprechend dem Befehl hatte ich die Aufgabe mit Häft-
lingen jüdischer Abstammung durchzuführen. Aus diesem
Grunde suchte ich zunächst 39 Häftlinge aus, die dem KL-
Sachsenhausen zugehörig. Weitere, über 100 Häftlinge,
übernahm ich vom KL-Auschwitz.

Ich betone ausdrücklich, daß es sich bei diesen Häft-
lingen, von einer Ausnahme abgesehen, um keine kriminellen
Elemente, bzw. berufsmäßige Fälscher und Zuchthäusler ge-
handelt hat.

Zutreffend ist, daß sämtliche Häftlinge wegen ihrer
rassemäßigen Zugehörigkeit in das Konzentrationslager
verbracht worden waren und als politische Gefangene klassi-
fiziert worden sind. Diese Tatsache wird dadurch noch be-
kräftigt, weil alle diese Häftlinge das rote Stoffkennzei-
chen an ihrer Gefangenenkleidung trugen, welches nach außen
hin den Haftgrund anzeigte.

Mit der Herstellung der Druckstöcke hatten die Häftlinge nichts zu tun. Die Druckstöcke wurden in Friedenthal, ca.2 bis 3 km von Sachsenhausen gelegen, durch SS-
Leute, bzw. Vertragsangestellte hergestellt.

B. Krüger

Die vorstehende Unter-Schrift do.1
Bernhard Krüger
wird hiermit amtlich beglaubigt
Dassel, den 23. August 1956
Stadt Dassel
J.A. Niebe

Sworn statement of Bernhard Krüger, 23 August 1956

23 August 1956

I, Bernhard Krüger, resident in Dassel, FRG, do make the following sworn statement in support of Hans Kurzweil, of Vienna, Burggasse 60, in the matter of an action for defamation against HAGEN.

Sworn Statement

As Technical Adviser, Head of Section VI, under orders of H. Himmler, I was in charge of the money forgery operation, known by the cover name of 'Operation Bernhard', which was designed to be an economic measure against England.

My orders were to carry out the operation, using Jewish prisoners so I first selected 39 prisoners from KZ Sachsenhausen, and a further 100 from Auschwitz.

I must emphasise that none of these prisoners were criminals, or professional forgers, except for one.

It is relevant that many had been imprisoned because of their racial origin, were classified as political. This is supported by the fact that they wore a red badge to indicate this category on their prison clothes.

The prisoners had nothing to do with the manufacture of the printing blocks, which were made by SS contract labour in Schloss Friedenthal, about 3 km from Sachsenhausen.

The translation of the previous statement

In 1957 Krüger submitted an application for a job in the Bundeskriminalamt (Federal Criminal Investigation Bureau). The master forger was unsuccessful, but apart from that nothing else happened.

It is understandable that he only became concerned when he realised that his crimes were not statute-barred, that someone was on his tracks and that his employers and crimes were not forgotten in Germany. First he disappeared from 63, Maschweg in Dassel and withdrew to an isolated house in Sievershäuserstrasse. Then he left Dassel and spread the word that he was going to live abroad. In fact he moved to Stuttgart to the suburb of Krontal, where he rented a room from Dr Peter Fritz in 29, Martin-Luther-Strasse.

Proceedings were issued against him twice: on 2 December 1955 by the state prosecutor of Stuttgart, and in 1964 by the Berlin Senate (government). On 7 May 1965 the charges were dropped and Krüger lived out his life in Hamburg, without ever being sentenced.

Memories of an Eyewitness

Hans Hoffinger remembers the production of handmade paper for the forged sterling banknotes and the end of the secret operation in 1945.

Hans Hoffinger

The commercial college I attended was closed in the autumn of 1944 on Hitler's order for 'total war', so that all workers were called up in the push for 'final victory'. I was a schoolboy and was assigned to war service in the nearby Hahnemühle paper mill in Dassel, Einbeck district.

It was between Christmas and New Year 1944 when I was put to work cleaning the sieve and pulping machine. The drying drums had been cooled down, the machines stopped and the usual tight security was relaxed to allow the cleaning and maintenance work to proceed. I crawled in to clean the drying pads and found a sheet of paper, covered in complicated watermarks and divided into eight sections, that had slipped down. I could read through the transparent watermark on each of the eight sections: 'BANK OF ENGLAND TWENTY' and '20'. I wondered about it and came to the conclusion that I had hit on the top-secret operation being carried out here under high security. All the workers employed here were sworn to secrecy under threat of the death penalty. So none of the other workers knew anything about it.

Just as I was folding the amazing find to put it in my pocket, the machine operator snatched it from me.

He took the sheet of paper to the manager, without giving my name or the circumstances of the find, because he was a colleague of my father's, whose job was to dry the handmade paper in the machine on the other twelve-hour shift.

My father, who was one of the secret workforce, begged me not to speak to anyone about it for fear of our lives. By that time we knew about the severe, inhuman methods of the Gestapo and SS.

The paper mill operated from 1942 until the beginning of April 1945, including the production of the secret banknote paper, when the approaching Allied armies forced it to shut down. During the last days of the war I came into contact with the 'special' paper, when we were able to watch all the banknote paper being burnt in the boiler house. The big secret was out.

After the war, when normal paper production had started up again, we showed English officers round the mill and told them about the secret operation and they could scarcely believe it. Four years later, in 1949, I finished my apprenticeship and was employed as a bookkeeper, when a new colleague was introduced to our department. He was none other than the former head of Section VI F 4 of the Security Department of the Reich, Bernhard Krüger, organiser of the entire forgery operation from 1941 to 1945. Hitler's ingenious forger had ended up with us.[1]

Krüger's family had been living in Dassel near the paper mill for the last years of the war to escape the bombing. This meant that the two expert forgers Robert Bartsch (paper manufacturer) and Bernhard Krüger (organiser and forger) were with us. From then till 1956 Krüger shared a desk with me. I learnt many details of the story of 'Operation Bernhard'. He told me how he had 'cracked' the complicated numbering code of the banknotes.

---

1 *Author's note: there is evidence that Krüger was wanted by Interpol for murder and forgery. Robert Bartsch was aware of it too but nevertheless provided a bolthole for him for seven years in the Hahnemühle paper mill. Krüger knew that Bartsch would not betray him. He also worked as an accountant for seven years which made up a total of ten since 1945. He knew that his criminal activity was statute-barred after ten years. After that he could no longer be punished. There was no evidence of his murder of the seven sick prisoners. There were no written orders. The sick prisoners were shot by his subordinate, SS-OSF Edwin Heizmann, 'without orders'.*

10

Toplitzsee

View of Toplitzsee

WHAT DID ACTUALLY HAPPEN TO the cases after SBF Hansch took them away from Redl-Zipf on 1st May?

After the war I found out where the forged banknotes had been hidden – not only the cases, but also many secret documents, lists and reports that were proof of numerous Nazi crimes.

Toplitzsee is located in the Salzkammergut, a few kilometres from the famous resort of Bad Aussee. It is approached by a narrow track, which ends at the lake. It is surrounded on three sides by craggy slopes and is only open at the southern end. It is very inaccessible. The Nazis had chosen the lake to bury their secret treasure. They intended to hide the proof of their crimes. According to eyewitnesses they had a large quantity of metal cases, weighing between 30 and 100 kilogrammes, transported to the lake. The cases were full of currency, gold and other valuables brought from the concentration camps of Buchenwald, Auschwitz and Sachsenhausen. The cases also contained records from Potsdam Prison, the criminal investigations bureau in Düsseldorf and from the Reichstag building. All the cases were loaded onto a boat and taken far up the lake and sunk. The boats came back carrying only the guards. There was no sign of the prisoners who had loaded the boat.

OSF Otto Skorzeny had transported twenty-two cases, each one weighing 48 kilogrammes, containing twenty gold bars. These were also supposed to have been sunk in Toplitzsee at the beginning of May 1945. At the end of April 1945 Krüger and Schwend between them held banknotes to the value of £20 million, in addition to considerable quantities of foreign currency and gold bullion, as well as the most important forgery equipment, such as printing plates and the instruction book. A lot of money and the supplies of unprinted paper had been burned; a few cases of forged money ended up in the Enns, other cases containing money and documents were sunk in Toplitzsee.

General Fabiunke brought his war booty, consisting of twenty cases of stamped gold and foreign currency worth RM5 million, and a further amount of RM4.3 million, to Bad Aussee. Adolf Eichmann turned up at the beginning of 1945 at the so-called Rauchfang on the Blue Alp at Aussee with twenty-two heavy cases of confiscated valuables. The estimated value was about $8 million, which at the time was worth RM24 million.

Eichmann was born in Solingen and grew up in Linz. A friend of Ernst Kaltenbrunner, he joined the Austrian Nazi Party (NSDAP) and the SS in 1932. In 1934 he was stationed in the secret service headquarters in Berlin where he dealt with 'Jewish affairs'. In 1938, he built up a central office for Jewish emigration in Vienna, then in Prague and finally in Berlin. After the war began and all immigration was stopped, Eichmann assumed charge of Section IV B 4 of the RSHA (to which he had belonged since 1939) and the direction of the

Adolf Eichmann, organiser of the mass liquidation of 6 million Jews.
He was sentenced to death by an Israeli court and executed on 1 June 1962

'Final Solution'. He carried out the decisions taken at the Wannsee conference (15 September 1942).

Eichmann was picked up by an American patrol in May 1945. He gave his name as 'USF Otto Eckmann'. Before his identity could be discovered he managed to escape from an American internment camp early in 1946. Then he laid low in West Germany, and in 1950 he fled to Argentina with help from the Vatican.

The Israeli secret service tracked him down and captured him in 1960. He was brought before a court in Jerusalem. He was sentenced to death in December 1961, after a sensational trial with worldwide publicity, and executed on 1 June 1962.

The SS chief in Hungary, Kurt Becher, arrived in the Aussee area with several wagons of Jewish property. Among his personal belongings were cases full of gold. Gauleiter Eigruber was also thinking of his future. He sank a steel safe in Toplitzsee, reputed to have contained a rubber bag full of diamonds.

Dr Helmut von Hummel could not bear to be separated from a coin collection in two heavy cases. They had been stolen from the monastery in Kremsmünster and he hid them, of course, in the 'Alpine fortress'.

It was not only patriotic sentiment that inspired Ferenc Szalasi, leader of the Hungarian Pfeilkreuzler troop, to bury the stolen chest containing the relics of St Stephen and some of the Hungarian crown jewels.

It would have seemed strange if Kaltenbrunner had been the most modest of them all. He brought five cases full of diamonds and precious stones, 50 kilogrammes of pure gold bars from the vaults of the Deutsche Reichsbank, fifty

SS-SF Kurt Becher stole Jewish property in Hungary, 1944–5. He was declared a war criminal

Former SS officer Kurt Becher (left) became one of the richest men in West Germany

cases of gold objects, 2 million Swiss francs and a collection of rare stamps worth 5 million gold marks at the time.

In comparison, according to a special list drawn up by the Americans, Hitler, Goering, Goebbels, Ley, Himmler and Ribbentrop alone possessed foreign bonds worth a total of $14,883,162, £465,000 and shares to a value of £600,000. Goebbels had deposited $1,850,000 under the name 'Deutsch' in Buenos Aires. Himmmler had also thought of his old age and had assets worth about $2 million in cash and share certificates on deposit.

The Nazis were not going to live on gold, diamonds and foreign currency alone. There were also priceless art treasures in the Alpine fortress. They were stashed away in the disused shafts of a salt mine near Aussee. They had been stolen from France, Belgium, Holland, Poland, Czechoslovakia and Hungary. In the dark passages underground were also collections from Germany and Austria: 6,500 world-famous paintings, 15,000 precious manuscripts, illuminated texts, medieval tapestries, sculptures, woodcarvings, church treasures studded with gems and hundreds of unique wall hangings. These included the Ghent Altarpiece, original works by Michelangelo, dozens of Dürer engravings, the Rothschild collection from Vienna, jewels from the galleries in Naples, and, from the monastery of Monte Cassino, paintings by Vermeer, Titian and others. All these works of art were to have been destroyed – it was not due to lack of destructive urge that Hitler's order was not carried out.

The last arsenal of weapons and weapon research station was located near Toplitzsee. What could have been gained by the Nazis holding out? What sort of weapons could the expiring Nazi regime have mustered?

The research department of the navy was located near Toplitzsee, where mostly technicians and weapons designers worked. They had all sworn loyalty to Hitler to the death and had promised that their 'wonder weapon' would place Hitler at the helm again. Faith is sometimes blind! These blind fanatics were working on four projects. They were developing special missiles for firing at concrete targets, self-destructing torpedoes, miniature submarines of all sorts and rockets to be fired from submarines.

The 'T5' torpedo was developed here, for example. It was called the 'Wren' because it was fitted with an hydro-acoustic gadget, which meant it could find targets by the sound of the ship's propellers and direct itself to them.

The Anglo-American landings were to be destroyed by miniature submarines of the type 'Shark', 'Dolphin', 'Beaver', 'Salamander' and others. The torpedoes developed for war at sea were increasingly sophisticated: for example, the famous fish series – 'Turbot', 'Goldfish' and 'Rockfish'. Hitler was most interested in rockets with which he wanted to bombard New York and other cities along the coast of America from submarines. What would happen if several missiles landed in Manhattan? The Nazis took advantage of the spreading panic.

The attitude of the last of the Nibelungen was: 'We may lose this war, but our day will come.' For that reason the plans of the wonder weapons had to be kept well hidden – where better than in the depths of Toplitzsee?

There was a special group who, in March–May 1945, brought the secret plans and the research documentation to the Aussee district. Some were sunk in the lake in waterproof casings. A special naval unit marked the spot on maps of the lakebed. Wooden blocks were attached with wire to the packages, which were then visible about 5 to 7 metres below the surface. There were even plans for sophisticated defences against enemy attack. The group sank detonators, cases of explosives, trial bombs, V1-type missiles and a V2 ballistic missile in the lake.

In April 1945 Gauleiter Eigruber (third from left) directed the sinking of all technical and documentary materials from the research station 'Marine'

Reinhard Gehlen, colonel in the Wehrmacht secret service, later head of the Federal Intelligence Service, had set up his base in the vicinity of Toplitzsee

The massive treasure lying on the bed of the lake meant that some people did not sleep easy in their beds. During the post-war years, many divers went down in relays to try to salvage some of the gold. The results were often tragic. Many died in the attempt; some threw themselves from the surrounding cliffs for unknown reasons. Some went down and never came up. It is surmised that there were a few murders. There is no proof.

Wolfgang Löhde, a reporter with *Stern*, who was in the navy until the end of the war, is supposed to have followed the trail of a group of coin-forgers who were members of the secret service, for three years. For months he chased witnesses – in South America, especially in Peru, in Spain, Austria, Italy, Yugoslavia and in Switzerland. He claimed to have questioned a hundred people, and to have gathered 3,600 pages of evidence. Many pointed to Toplitzsee as the place where all trails went cold in the last days of the Third Reich.

In July 1959 a team sponsored by *Stern* magazine, after discussion with the Federal Ministry of Forestry in Vienna, acquired a permit from the government of the state of Steiermark to search in the lake for buried valuables and to undertake the salvage of all types of objects (except munitions). Ten days after the start of the 'fishing', the first seven cases were located. Two weeks later the first case was brought up. It contained forged banknotes from 'Operation Bernhard'. The sterling forgeries were not of any interest to the expedition: they were not considered valuable. The *Stern* report was entitled 'Heaps of Money'.

Later a case labelled 'B9' was hauled up. It contained the records of the RSHA. The next issue of *Stern* carried the lead story: 'Toplitzsee the Centre of World Attention'. For weeks the salvage operation was covered by *Stern* reporters. The first case of forged sterling banknotes, which were to enable the Nazis to win the war, was brought up from a depth of 80 metres, where it had been intended the treasure would remain hidden forever. This provided the evidence for the forgery story.

The tracks of this forgery operation could not be covered up. There are piles of money in the depths of Toplitzsee and in the coffers of the Austrian police. Then the biggest haul was brought up – the secret records of the forgery operation by the SS, listing details of agents, forgers and dealers, who had all hoped to disperse and go underground in 1945.

'We thought they would contain money, lots of sterling notes,' said Löhde on the phone. 'We thought there would be more money in there, when we hauled the big case onto the raft. Detective inspector Rolf von Plottegg from the security department in Graz and I took off the rotten lid and found files. There were exact details of instructions for SS agents in Dutch, Norwegian, English and German – specifications of acts of sabotage such as bombing of enemy ships, airfields and other targets. There were identity documents, logs of the production of forged money – hundreds of secret files.'

This news unleashed a political storm: there was widespread fear and anxiety just as there had been back in 1945 when the Nazi treasure had to be buried. Too

Frogmen searching for sunken Nazi treasures in Toplitzsee

Forged sterling notes: the 'catch' from the Toplitzsee. Diver Herwig Hunger from Kiel

Wolfgang Löhde with the files of the RSHA

many careers and firms had been founded on stolen gold and forged money. That was it for Buccerius, publisher of *Stern*. The editorial board terminated the salvage operation fourteen days early, even though it had already cost DM30,000. Löhde was recalled by telegram: 'Your continued presence at Toplitzsee is incompatible with the terms of your employment!' As the search ended, the location of an additional fifteen to twenty objects had been identified on the bed of the lake.

75206	Ajdels, Beri					
75240	Aron, Samu					
102445	Bialer, David					
79163	Bier, Eduard	1				
75221	Blass, Hans	'				
61113	Blaustein, Max	:				
46855	Bober, Max	:				
75213	Bosboom, Andries	1				
75202	Burday, Josef	-				
79101	Burger, Adolf	:-'				
14898	Cytrin, Felix	1				
75248	Sinankiewicz, Wolf					

The list of prisoners in the forgery *Kommando* was in one of the files salvaged by *Stern*
and the Austrians. The author's name is third from the end

Salvage Report

This is a record of the consignment of forged sterling notes, files and cases of printing equipment salvaged by members of the editorial team of the weekly *Stern*, recorded on 10.8.1959.

Attendance: ORR. Dr Peternell, Section II regional government of Steiermark,
ORR. Dr Uray, Chief of Police, Exp. os. Bad-Aussee,
Wolfgang Löhde, editor representing *Der Stern*, Vienna, holder of salvage permit,
Dr Brauner, editorial board of *Stern*, Vienna,
Rev. Insp. Wolff Plottegg, Erh. Abtg. d. Lgk. Steiermark No. Sidion. P. Steiermark, Graz.

The following salvaged items were handed over to the authorities:

Case B 32: Contents approx. 55,000 English £50 notes
Case B 12: Contents approx. 55,000 £5 & £10 notes
Case A 105: Contents approx. 55,000 £10 & £20 notes
Case B (not numbered): Contents approx. 55,000 £50 & other notes

The contents of Case B 32 was repacked into Cases 1–9 provided by the authorities.
The contents of Case B 12 was repacked into Cases 10–16.
Case A 105 and the unnumbered B was repacked into Cases 17–29.
The contents of 2 other cases was repacked into Cases 30 & 31, which were then sealed.

1 original case contained the files and printing equipment, such as moulds as recorded on 10.8.1959.

Various cases were handed over to Rev. Insp. Rodlauer of GP. Bad Aussee for removal to secure storage in Graz.

Licensee: Authority:

Translation of salvage report of 11 August 1959. Austrian police

Statement of a Contemporary Witness

Forty years after the salvage of the forged money, diver Herwig Hunger
and the head of development of IBAK, Erich Gülck (right)

Salvage of forged currency, 1959
Money hoard found by IBAK TV underwater camera

Wolfgang Löhde, a reporter for *Stern* magazine had been researching reports of
alleged forgery operations during the Hitler regime for two years and had come
across reports that the remainder of the forged money, printing blocks and gold
bars had been sunk in Toplitzsee at the end of the war. Löhde succeeded in
tracking down a retired lieutenant commander, D. Determann, who was the
former commander of the naval research station at Lake Toplitz, who confirmed
the rumour.

In the early summer of 1959, Löhde was now sure he had a story and wrote
up his findings in a serial 'Geld wie Heu' for *Stern* magazine. He engaged a
firm called IBAK, the only German manufacturer of underwater TV cameras,
to investigate Toplitzsee in this worthwhile project. (Divers could not be used
because the lake was more than 80 metres deep, cold, and visibility was very
poor. Compressed air becomes toxic at 60 metres. Furthermore, attempts
by English and American divers straight after the end of the war had been
unsuccessful.)

The head of IBAK, Helmut Hunger, his seventeen-year-old son Herwig
Hunger, who was on his school holidays, and the director of development at
IBAK, Erich Gülck, went down to Toplitzsee at the beginning of July 1959 with
underwater TV equipment. They were accompanied by the team from *Stern*. A
raft was made using empty oil drums as floats. There was a hut on it for shelter
from the rain and for the sound equipment and TV cameras. Three lines were

connected to the shore so that the raft could be moved in circles, searching the most probable area for the packages. The TV camera in its pressurised container was lowered perpendicularly from the edge of the raft. The camera cable was lowered by hand until the bed of the lake was visible, illuminated by underwater searchlights. Day after day the bed of the lake was scanned in circular movements, but no cases were found.

Just as they were about to give up, on 20–21 July the team saw four wooden packing cases on the monitor, so they laid marker buoys. In order to find out more they tied a grappling hook to a rope and tried to lift the lid of one of the cases at a depth of 78 metres. After two hours of patient effort, they succeeded in pulling up the hook, which caught, lifting the lid as it rose. Several paper notes floated up on the current, as if from a ghostly hand. A £5 note was clearly visible on camera. Then the hook slipped off and the lid closed again, sucking the banknote back into the case.

In the excitement no one took a photo of the screen, but it would probably not have been clear enough to serve as evidence. Löhde and the IBAK experts discussed how to organise a salvage operation. IBAK's contract was extended by three weeks with the approval of the editor in Hamburg. IBAK was to attempt to salvage the cases as well as to examine the bed of the lake. Gülck and Hunger got a local mechanic in Bad Aussee to build a metal cage of slightly larger dimensions than the cases. He had it ready by 25 July. Löhde contacted the world's press.

On the Sunday they spent twelve hours in vain attempts to lower the cage onto the packing case within the narrow range of the camera, lit by the underwater searchlights. It was like operating a puppet on 78-metre-long strings. Bavarian TV was there to cover it but the crew left in the evening. There was no question of stopping now. Löhde urged them to keep trying with the 'cage puppet'. Then, just before midnight, it caught the case and held as it was winched up by the homemade rig on another raft. It was winched by a retired lieutenant commander slowly and carefully metre by metre, till it was two metres below the surface. The underside of the case was gone and they were afraid that the bundles of notes could have slipped out and that there would be nothing for the media to see in the morning. Löhde dived in and came up jubilant, clutching a bundle of notes. Herwig Hunger, an amateur diver, rowed back to the shore and put on his wetsuit. He brought up more bundles of notes and secured the case with a rope. Then the crew collapsed into bed at their lakeside campsite, whilst Löhde could hardly sleep for excitement.

The following day, Monday, reporters and TV crews arrived and filmed and photographed the finds from every angle. The raft was brought near the shore and Herwig Hunger dived into action bringing up bundle after bundle of forged banknotes.

Austrian crime investigation officials supervised the complete removal of the banknotes, in spite of large crowds of onlookers and teams of pressmen. For the next few weeks the police maintained a constant presence during the salvage operation. The members of the salvage team managed to keep a few notes as souvenirs (they really were souvenirs because English banknotes had changed completely since then). Löhde issued a press release that evening about his findings and the salvage operation, which contained some exaggeration.

At that point the holidays were over for seventeen-year-old Herwig and for the second *Stern* reporter, Harald Kosel. The head of the firm, Helmut Hunger went back to Kiel, to work. Two other IBAK employees and Herr Gülck continued the search for a further two weeks. In all, nineteen cases full of notes were found by the IBAK underwater cameras and raised to the surface. Apart from documents, printed copies and forged notes to the value of approximately RM30 million, no gold was found.

Meanwhile Löhde flew to London and presented some dried-out forged notes to the Bank of England. After close examination it was established that the forgeries could not be distinguished from real notes. These out-of-date white notes, printed only on one side, would even have been exchanged for valid notes if the corresponding serial numbers had not been presented and if their provenance had been plausible.

For the participants there remained the memory of an exciting holiday, now forty years ago, when a sensational find was reported all over the world. These memories were recalled at a gathering in Kiel at the end of 1998, when Adolf Burger, former concentration camp inmate, gave a talk on his part in the forgery operation.

Herwig Hunger

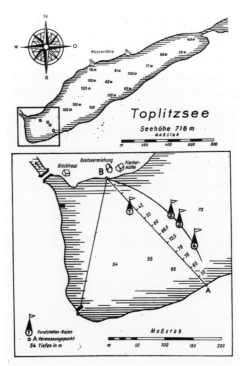

Toplitzsee – Himmler's underwater treasury.
More than forty cases full of forged money and secret files were hidden in its depths

After 16 August 1959, all was quiet again in Toplitzsee.

There was a flurry of activity in certain quarters and in some businesses. On 8 October 1963, there was a further attempt to salvage the material. Alfred Egner, a nineteen-year-old amateur diver from Munich put on his diving gear for the last time: he vanished in the depths of the lake. There was a suspicion of murder, as his lifeline had been cut. This time the involvement of West German secret agents could not be concealed. The Austrian police had to set up an inquiry. Who would be charged in the case?

Certain people were identified: Georg Freiberger, Dr Karl Heinz Schmidt and his close associate Gottfried Oswald, a mechanical engineer from Augsburg. Freiberger had directed the salvage operation. He was the comfortable owner of a printing works, nondescript founder of a right-wing political party, long-time secret service agent, and associate of Reinhard Gehlen, who had been head of espionage for Hitler and later founder and director of the Federal Intelligence Service (BND). Schmidt had received a sentence for forgery in Bonn. It would have been remarkable if Freiberger and co. had tried to salvage the treasure themselves. They were not that brave and had employed young Egner to do the job. But he did not survive to enjoy his reward.

Then it was announced that the lake would be cleared by the Austrian authorities. So in the second half of October 1963 the lake was sealed off by 300 police officers armed with rapid-fire weapons, helicopters circled overhead and seventy foreign journalists arrived. It was a significant operation that looked promising. But there was a hint of involvement by the German federal services, suggesting disapproval. There were warning headlines: 'Divers risk lives in search for gold', 'No luck for divers in Toplitzsee', 'Search costs 6,500 marks a day'. There was talk of booby-trap bombs, threats, anonymous letters and wanted posters.

The salvage operation by the Austria authorities lasted from 23 October to 7 December 1963 and cost roughly 600,000 schilling. It was not totally in vain, but only 16 per cent of the lakebed was examined. The underwater TV cameras and electronic sounding equipment were used separately, even though it is well know that they are only effective in combination.

As far as the cases are concerned, eighteen were brought to the surface, all containing forged sterling notes and the thirty-four printing plates and the list of prisoners from Blocks 18 and 19 in Sachsenhausen. The wet treasure was opened but was not completely salvaged.

Special artillery missile for penetrating concrete.
Calibre: 15–20 cm, length 222 cm (from Toplitzsee)

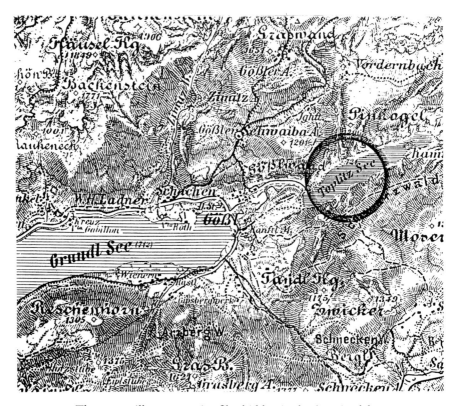

There are still secret service files hidden in the Austrian lake

11

US TV Channel CBS Search with 'Oceaneering' Diving Team – WASP Salvages Wooden Cases Full of Sterling Notes

Toplitzsee: a diver in his 'space suit' searches for valuable relics of the Nazi era

At the age of eighty-three, I was taken back in time to Toplitzsee by the American TV
station CBS during the course of the salvage operation in July 2000

After Fifty-Five Years, History Caught Up With Me Again

The raft on which I stood on 5 July 2000 swayed gently to and fro, rocking to the
rhythm of the waves on the lake. It was a beautiful, sunny, calm day. It was much
too calm for me. My insides were surging like a stormy sea. For me this day on
the lake was a journey back to a painful and tortured past. This upper Austrian
Alpine lake in Salzkammergut, Styria is cursed and its secrets give me no peace.

On the bottom lies evidence of forgery that I was forced to carry out against my will in the year 1944.

American CBS TV cameras were trained on me; the team of reporters awaited my explanation of the events of the spring of 1945. Was my past catching up on me after fifty-five years? I stared out over the almost 2-kilometre-long and 400-metre-wide Toplitzsee, lost in thought. I knew that in its muddy depths, around 65 metres down, lay forty waterproof cases containing material from the secret archives of the RSHA, which I had packed in February 1945. Among this material were thousands of pounds' worth of sterling notes, which had been produced in Blocks 18 and 19 of KZ Sachsenhausen.

The raft 'Oceaneering', equipped with the newest technology

The diver's image appears on the monitor at a depth of 65 metres, pointing to a board and asking if this could be the lid of one of the cases that had burst open. The faint letters 'No. A.B' are recognisable. I asked Mr Owens to ask the diver to search deeper in the mud with the metal grab where the open cases were supposed to be. And in fact in a few minutes an encrusted package turned up.

I recognised the packing. There were 500 English banknotes in each one. Several bundles were found; they were all put in a wire basket and brought to the surface. Suddenly one of the bundles burst open and 500 English notes were floating in the water.

The secret archive and the code numbers of the millions of sterling notes thought to be in Swiss banks were never found. Maybe the paper on which the codes were written had been destroyed in the water.

I watch the diver working on the monitor

'Search and Find'

Neue Kronen Zeitung Independent

Tuesday 4 July 2000/No. 14.420, S9

First Haul of Diving Robot
Countless Forged Sterling Banknotes

On Wednesday at 14.30 the mini-submarine 'Wasp' struck lucky. A cage full of soaked, forged banknotes was salvaged from the secret depths of the lake. Then a wooden case was hauled up.

Fifty-five years after his liberation from KZ Sachsenhausen, the past caught up with eighty-three-year-old Adolf Burger from Prague. Together with other prisoners he had forged millions of British pound notes in a secret mission for the Nazis. He had put the notes in bundles of 500 and packed them in the cases.

On Wednesday at 14.30 the first salvage cage containing these very notes was brought to the surface. Half an hour later, the US 'Oceaneering' team announced another success: a wooden case 80 x 30 x 30 cm was brought up. It too was one of an estimated forty 'Burger cases' containing mostly completely destroyed forged money!

The place where the team is searching is supposed to be where the container with the explosive documents may be hidden.

Werner Kopacka

English translation of article from *Neue Kronen Zietung*, 4 July 2000

"Gesuchtes ist Gefunden"

Neue Kronen Zeitung

UNABHÄNGIG

Dienstag, 4. Juli 2000 / Nr. 14.420, S 9

A First for 'Oceaneering' team: 'Wasp' succeeds in salvaging sterling banknotes

Erste Beute des Tauchroboters: Unzählige falsche Pfund-Noten!

Mittwoch um 14.30 Uhr wurde Mini-U-Boot „Wasp" in 65 Metern Tiefe im Toplitzsee zum ersten Mal fündig. Aus dem Geheimnis umwitterten See konnten zunächst ein Bergekorb voll mit perfekt gefälschten und völlig durchweichten Pfundnoten geborgen werden. Dann kam auch noch eine Holzkiste zu Tage.

55 Jahre nach seiner Befreiung aus dem Konzentrationslager Sachsenhausen holte den 83-jährigen Adolf Burger aus Prag am Mittwoch beim Toplitzsee die Vergangenheit wieder ein. Er war es nämlich, der mit anderen Mitgefangenen in streng geheimer Mission für die Nazis Millionen von britischen Pfund fälschen musste. Er war es auch, der damals die Banknoten gebündelt – zu 500 Stück – in Kisten verpackt hatte.

Am Mittwoch um 14.30 Uhr wurde der erste Bergekorb mit eben diesen Pfundnoten an die Oberfläche gebracht. Eine halbe Stunde später konnte das US-„Oceaneering"-Team den nächsten Erfolg verbuchen: Eine Holzkiste (80 x 30 x 30 Zentimeter) wurde empor gezogen. Ebenfalls eine von vermuteten 40 „Burger-Kisten" – der Inhalt: Zum Teil nur völlig zerstörtes Falschgeld!

Der Ort, wo das Team derzeit im Einsatz ist, dürfte auch jene Stelle sein, an welcher der Behälter mit den hoch brisanten Dokumenten vermutet wird.

Werner Kopacka

CBS getting ready for the lifting of forged pounds from the lake

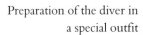

Preparation of the diver in a special outfit

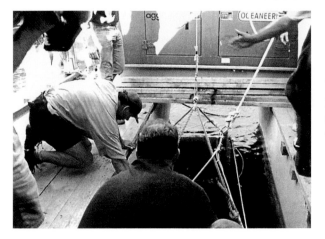

The box full of British pounds sees light again after almost sixty long years

A forged sterling note had lain 65 metres down in the lake for fifty-five years.
The print is still perfect

Albrecht Syen, warden of the fisherman's hut at Toplitzsee, is known as the historian of
the 'Treasure of Toplitzsee'

Toplitzsee contains many secrets

'If we can't find it, no one can,' says Bill Owens at the
American salvage operation at Toplitzsee

'Oceaneering' diving team

PART IV

APPENDICES

Summary of Numbers Interned and Killed in Concentration Camps

Nazi concentration camps		
	Passed through	*Perished*
Auschwitz	1,250,000	1,150,000
Belźec	600,000	600,000
Bergen-Belsen	75,000	48,000
Buchenwald	238,000	60,000
Chelmno	300,000	300,000
Dachau	106,000	67,000
Dora-Mittelbau	32,000	10,364
Flossenbürg	111,000	73,296
Gross-Rosen	120,000	40,000
Majdanek	300,000	235,000
Mauthausen	194,464	102,796
Natzweiler	70,000	25,000
Neuengamme	106,000	82,000
Ravensbrück	132,000	92,000
Sachsenhausen	204,000	100,000
Sobibor	500,000	500,000
Stutthof	120,000	85,000
Svatobořice	3,500	30
Ghetto Terezín	150,000	33,430
Treblinka	900,000	900,000
Prisons and penitentiaries		
Small fortress Terezín	32,000	2,500
Kounic dormitories	35,000	750
Mirošov	765	64

List of Prisoners in the Forgery Kommando in KZ Sachsenhausen

Prisoner number	Surname and first name	Date of birth	Occupation	Country of birth
73099	Hoffgard, Sven	08.09.1895	bank clerk	Denmark
61127	Nachtstern, Moritz	11.11.1908	audio-typist	Norway
75238	Stolowitz, Harry	10.11.1916	lorry driver	Belgium
75220	Drechsler, Georg	08.04.1913	accountant	Yugoslavia
75206	Burday, Josef	21.12.1904	tailor	France
75204	Landau, Paul	05.08.1922	cabinet-maker	"
79166	Weill, Roger	23.09.1908	photographer	"
	Braschewitzki, Leon	15.06.1923	optician	"
75200	Jacobson, Abraham	08.09.1905	industrialist	Holland
75213	Bosboom, Andries	26.06.1913	lithographer	"
75217	Groen, Meyer Levi	23.01.1918	projectionist	"
75224	Knoek, Samuel	16.01.1901		"
79164	Van Prag, Mozes	03.05.1910		"
46676	Gottlieb, Ernst	??.08.1907	decorator	Austria
46853	Kurzweil, Hans	01.07.1908	bookbinder	"
48854	Steiner, Karl Viktor	13.08.1907	bookbinder	"
51110	Tragholz, Felix	01.12.1908	stove fitter	"
51316	Springer, Arthur	04. 03.1888	salesman	"
75245	Sussmann, Karl	21. 06.1898	draughtsman	"
	Kleinfeld, Abraham			"
47140	Gecht, Josef	01. 09.1918		USSR
47148	Zessarskij, Matwej	08.12.1914	elec. mainten. mechanic	"
67175	Zahrzewski, Nachum	19.01.1926	printer	"
67867	Kosa Mojsche	02.09.1904	typesetter	"
67869	Zyberski, Leib	03.07.1898	engraver	"
67870	Kosak, Hirsch	12.12.1897	machine operator	"
67874	Plac, Chiell	02.03.1885	typesetter	"
93594	Smolianoff, Salamon	26.03.1887	painter	"
	Sukienik, Isaak			"

Prisoner number	Surname and first name	Date of birth	Occupation	Country of birth
102430	Weiss, Bela	29.11.1891	printer	Hungary
102431	Rubinstein, Ladislav	23.02.1909	printer	"
102432	Rubinstein, Zoltan	28.03.1913	printer	"
102433	Rubinstein, Alexander	03.09.1914	bookbinder	"
102434	Rusznak, Henrik	07.02.1890	printer	"
102437	Nyul, Erno	25.05.1908	textile printer	"
102438	Salman, Reszo	10.01.1904		"
102439	Frenkel, David	20.10.1903	collotype printer	"
102440	Weisz, Henrik	07.01.1905	printer	"
102442	Sugár, Izso	05.09.1885	printer	"
102443	Sonnenfeld, Andreas	18.11.1886	printer	"
102444	Somas, Stefan	11.01.1911	lithographer	"
102446	Sonnenfeld, Stefan	23.12.1924	printer	"
102435	Lancz, Jenö	17.06.1900	printer	"
	Sonnenfeld, Gustav	12.12.1905	painter	"
	Jilovský, Georg	15. 03.1884	painter	Czechoslovakia
46837	Luka, Richard	30.10. 1913	mining engineer	"
46848	Tuppler, Artur	10.06. 1890		"
46678	Pick, Alfred	12.10. 1906	dental technician	"
46680	Kaufmann, Jaroslav	19.01.1901	dentist	"
47832	Stein, Oskar	05.08.1902	engineer	"
75207	Stein, Max	22.08.1899	weaver	"
75193	Hahn, Viktor	21.08.1909	bank clerk	"
75195	Klein, Artur	25.04.1907		"
75197	Gottlieb, Karel	l2.05.1917	carpenter	"
79161	Burger, Adolf	12.08.1917	printer	"
138429	Haas, Leopold	15.04.1901	graphic artist	"
	Stiastní Ernst			"
	Lenthal, Hans	18.12.1914	painter	Germany
43811	Speier, Walter	27.04.1893	electrical mechanic	"
46674	Plappler, Isaak	11.11.1919	painter	"
46675	Kohn, Georg	03.02.1901		"
46681	Krebs, Leo	17.11.1910	printer	"
46834	Lewin, Artur	31.07.1888	printer	"
46840	Lauber, Jakob	01.09.1906	painter	"
46850	Lewinsky, Kurt	17.03.1908	illuminator	"
46855	Bober, Max Hermann	05.01.1896	typesetter	"
68061	Nieft, Horst	23.03.1906	decorator	"
68064	Nieft, Gerhard	07.7.1917	shop assistant	"
61113	Blaustein, Max	05.02.1904	printer	"

Prisoner number	Surname and first name	Date of birth	Occupation	Country of birth
61120	Schnapper, Fritz	10.12.1893	printer	Germany
73351	Lawy, Norbert Wilhelm (Levy, Leonard)	30.03.1913	printer	"
75192	Hirschweh, H.P.	12.07.1912	painter	"
75199	Walter, Hans	14.12.1921	labourer	"
75210	Kühnauer, Rudolf Leopold	04.04.1906	lithographer	"
75221	Blass, Hans	12.01.1907	factory hand	"
75246	Spenadl, Herbert	04.11.1920	barber	"
75247	Obler, Walter	02.02.1906	master mechanic	"
14898	Cytrin, Felix	05.06.1894	toolmaker	Poland
23768	Wilde, Samuel	16.01.1919	typesetter	"
46852	Ehrlich, Leib	28.04.1905	printer	"
61129	Epsztein, Lejba	05.04.1919	printer	"
61117	Zymermann, Perez	18.06.1908	writer	"
61136	Libermann, Josef	20.10.1914	printer	"
61138	Schurek, Chajim	11.03.1915		"
67865	Tiefenbach, Severin	22.03.1919	engraver	"
67866	Italiener, Laib	27.07.1913	engraver	"
67868	Jahlicznik, Noah	18.10.1901	printer	"
67871	Rapaport, Towie	12.11.1903	printer	"
67873	Edelsburg, Nachim	14.04.1907	printer	"
75191	Rozenzwajg, Jakob	22.12.1898	clerk	"
75192	Fajerman, Symcha	20.01.1915	mechanical engineer	"
75194	Holander, Fajwel	19.08.1906	carpenter	"
75196	Werdyger, Szyja	04.03.1908		"
75198	Fajman, Icik	02.03.1919	tailor	"
75200	Weiskop, Max	18.01.1909		"
75206	Ajdels, Bernhard	26.12.1911	clerk	"
75208	Markus, Mordke	11.05.1909	labourer	"
75211	Krakowský, Abraham	09.09.1918	clerk	"
75212	Iwanowicz, Rojnen	25.11.1901	bookkeeper	"
75214	Salamon, Bernhard	05.02.1903	bookkeeper	"
75215	Goldglas, Jakob	22.01.1911	carpenter	"
75216	Fajerman, Heinrich	29.03.1905	mechanical technician	"
75217	Löwi, Mendel	16.09.1908		"
75220	Heitler, Chili (Chiel)	06.05.1911	bookbinder	"
75222	Zylberberg, Chajim	26.09.1900	labourer	"
75223	Perkal, Chajim	10.03.1912	printer	"

Prisoner number	Surname and first name	Date of birth	Occupation	Country of birth
75225	Lewkowicz, Szlarna	19.03.1917	bookkeeper	Poland
75226	Lehrhaft, Leon	06.08.1903	bookbinder	"
75227	Holänder, Chaim	20.04.1908	painter	"
75228	Rejzen, Baruch	03.04.1907		"
75229	Marjanka, David	20.10.1907	wood specialist	"
75231	Tuchmajer, Mordka	14.05.1914	printer	"
75232	Lehrhaft, Leonard	23.10.1924	bookbinder	"
75233	Rais, Josef	27.11.1915	painter	"
75234	Laskier, Jakob	07.08.1900	clerk	"
75236	Rajzner, Rafail	15.01.1904	typesetter	"
75239	Zaubermann, Fajwel	29.06.1917		"
75241	Leibsohn, Karl Chaim	06.08.1919		"
75242	Lewkowicz, Simon	19.01.1917		"
75243	Doinankiewicz, Wolf	20.01.1906	carpenter	"
75244	Krzepický, Mojzesz	26.10.1919		"
75248	Stammer, Samuel	05.07.1907	watchmaker	"
75249	Jura, Wolf	12.01.1905	bookbinder	"
75250	Rozenberg, Mendel	17.05.1905	bookbinder	"
79100	Salzer, Herman	16.11.1912		"
79158	Schipper, Ascher	09.01.1915	printer	"
79159	Gafne, Leib	06.01.1915	printer	"
79165	Lubetzki, David	15.03.1905	printer	"
102441	Fried, Leib	24.12.1902	engraver	"
102445	Bialer, David	01.01.1908	engraver	"
138493	Rudoler, Joachim	28.02.1912	printer	"
	Nejman, Max	25.02.1922	draughtsman	"
46842	Weissmann, Friedrich	11.05.1901	typesetter	stateless
46845	Goldberg, Aron	08.01.1909	printer	"
	Fingerhut, Abraham			"
	Gütig, Hermann			"
61125	Glanzer, Isaak	22.08.1899	printer	"
75234	Wulfowicz, Max	20.09.1899	mechanic	"
75235	Milikowski, Herman Philip	08.01.1909	teacher	"
75240	Aron, Samuel	28.06.1902	technician	"
76677	Zeichner, Chaim	08.01.1896	carpenter	"
79163	Bier, Eduard	10.06.1910	chemical engineer	"

Occupations of 141 Political Prisoners and 1 Criminal Prisoner from Blocks 18 and 19 in KZ Sachsenhausen

Labourer	3	Machine technician	1
Bank clerk	2	Stove fitter	1
Civil servant/clerk	4	Optician	1
Bookbinder	8	Reprographic photographer	1
Printer	30	Mechanic	2
Bookkeeper	3	Tailor	2
Chemical engineer	1	Carpenter	5
Decorator	2	Typesetter	6
Electrician	2	Writer	1
Cabinet Maker	1	Illuminator	1
Industrialist	1	Lithographer	3
Film projectionist	1	Audio-typist	1
Photographer	1	Textile printer	1
Barber	1	Technician	1
Engraver	5	Mining engineer	1
Wood specialist	1	Watchmaker	1
Salesman	1	Shop assistant	1
Lorry driver	1	Weaver	1
Teacher	1	Factory hand	1
Collotype printer	1	Toolmaker	1
Artist/painter	10	Draughtsman	2
Machine operator	1	Dentist	1
Master mechanic	1	Dental technician	1
Mechanical engineer	1	No occupation	22

Total: 142

Nationalities of 141 Political Prisoners and 1 Criminal Prisoner from Blocks 18 and 19 in KZ Sachsenhausen

Belgian	1
Danish	1
German	20
French	4
Yugoslavian	1
Dutch	5
Norwegian	1
Austrian	7
Polish	55
Czechoslovakian	13
USSR	9
Hungarian	15
Stateless	10
Total	142

Prisoners from Blocks 18 and 19 who were murdered:

Fingerhut, Abraham – stateless
Gütig, Herman – stateless
Jilovský, Georg – Prague/Czech
Kleinfeld, Abraham – Austria
Stiasny, Ernst – Brünn/Czech
Sukienik, Isaak – USSR
Sussmann, Karl – Vienna/Austria

133 prisoners of the 142 in the forgery *Kommando* were liberated by the Americans in KZ Ebensee on 6 May 1945.

Two prisoners escaped to Ebensee on 4 May 1945 before the final march.

Seven prisoners who had fallen ill were shot by SS-HSF Edwin Heizmann on the orders of Bernhard Krüger.

Members of RHSA who Directed or Guarded the Forgery Operation

Heinz BECKMANN, SS-HSF, from Chemnitz. He came to Sachsenhausen at the end of 1943.

BERNARD, lieutenant colonel of secret police, forgery expert

BOBETH, SS-HSF, born 1912, originally on Heydrich's staff in Prague

Heinz BUCKELMANN, SS-OSF, born 1912, from Güstrow (Gussdorf) in Mecklenburg

DÖRNER, SS-OF, first director of production line 'A'

Heinz GEBHARD, SS-SF, from Leipzig, born 1913. He was involved in production of 'A'.

GEPPNER, SS-RF

HAAS, SS-SF, worked in the special unit of RSHA

HANSCH, SS-SF, Krüger's deputy

Fritz HEIDER, SS-USF, born 1922, from Cologne-Deutz

Edwin HEIZMANN, born 1912, from Kaiserslautern

Robert HOFFMAN, SS-OSF, born 1916, from Berlin

HOFFMANN, SS-HSF, born 1914, from Berlin. He was on Heydrich's staff in Prague.

Hans JANSEN, SS-OSF, born 1912, from Cologne

Alfred KRAMER, SS-USF, born 1919, from Oldenburg

Bernhard KRÜGER, SS-SF, director of special *Kommando* of RSHA, from Chemnitz, born 1904, Nazi Party member number 528,739, SS member number 15,249

LASSIG, SS-SF, RSHA official

MAROCK, SS-SF

Herbert PAUL, civilian, artist or typesetter, born 1902, employed in the Friedenthal workshop, from Berlin

August PETRICK, former owner of a printing works in Berlin, born 1897, Nazi Party member, technical adviser to the special unit

Bruno PSOCH, SS-USF, born 1920

RAU, civilian, artist, born 1904, resident and employed in Friedenthal

Willi SCHMITT, SS-OSF from Petrovagrad in Banat

THIELE, SS-USF, official in RSHA

TRÄGER, SS-SF from Tachau, Eger district, former manager of the hospital in Tachau

TRAUTNER, SS-RF, from Bayreuth

Heinz WEBER, SS-OSF, from Nordhausen

Kurt WERNER, SS-HSF, from Effeldernplatendorf

Willi WILDFANG, SS-OSF, from Ludwigslust

Frau ZEITEK, Krüger's secretary in RSHA, born 1912, from Berlin

Comparative Table of Military Ranks

Wehrmacht rank	SS rank	Translation of SS rank	American rank	British rank
Oberste Führer (Adolf Hitler)	Der oberste Führer der Schutzstaffel. Der Führer Adolf Hitler	Supreme Leader of the protection squad. The Leader Adolf Hitler	President	Monarch
None	Reichsführer-SS	Empire leader of the SS	None	None
General-Feldmarschall	None	None	General of the Army	Field Marshall
Generaloberst	SS-Oberstgruppen-Führer	SS-Supreme Group Leader	General	General
General der Infanterie, der Artillerie etc.	SS-Obergruppenführer	SS-Senior Group Leader	Lieutenant General	Lieutenant General
Generalleutnant	SS-Gruppenführer	SS-Group Leader	Major General	Major General
Generalmajor	SS-Brigadeführer	SS-Brigade Leader	Brigadier General	Brigadier
None	SS-Oberführer	SS-Senior Leader	None	None
Oberst	SS-Standartenführer	SS-Standard Leader	Colonel	Colonel
Oberstleutnant	SS-Obersturmbann-führer	SS-Senior Storm Leader	Lieutenant Colonel	Lieutenant Colonel
Major	SS-Sturmbannführer	SS-Storm Command Leader	Major	Major
Hauptmann	SS-Hauptsturmführer	SS-Head Storm Leader	Captain	Captain
Oberleutnant	SS-Obersturmführer	SS-Senior Storm Leader	1st Lieutenant	Lieutenant
Leutnant	SS-Untersturmführer	SS-Under Storm Leader	2nd Lieutenant	2nd Lieutenant
Stabsfeldwebel	SS-Sturmscharführer	SS-Storm Company Leader	Sergeant Major	Regimental Sergeant Major

Wehrmacht rank	SS rank	Translation of SS rank	American rank	British rank
Oberfähnrich	SS-Standarten-Oberjunker	SS-Standard Senior Officer Cadet	None	None
Oberfeldwebel	SS-Hauptscharführer	SS-Head Company Leader	Master Sergeant	Battalion Sergeant Major
Feldwebel	SS-Oberscharführer	SS-Senior Company Leader	Sergeant 1st class	Company Sergeant Major
Fähnrich	SS-Standartenjunker	SS-Standard Office Cadet	None	None
Unterfeldwebel	SS-Scharführer	SS-Company Leader	Staff Sergeant	Platoon Sergeant Major
Unteroffizier	SS-Unterscharführer	SS-Under Company Leader	Sergeant	Sergeant
Obergefreiter	SS-Rottenführer	SS-Band Leader	Corporal	Corporal
Gefreiter	SS-Sturmmann	SS-Storm Man	None	Lance Corporal
Oberschutze	SS-Oberschütze	SS-Head Private	Private 1st Class	None
Schütze	SS-Schütze	SS-Private	Private	Private

Select Bibliography

Lucie Adelsberger, *Auschwitz – Ein Tatsachenbericht*, Lettner Verlag, Berlin, 1956

Peter Edel, *Wenn es ans Leben geht – Zweiter Teil*, Verlag der Nationen, Berlin, 1979

Gedenkbuch – Die Sinti und Roma im Konzentrationslager Auschwitz–Birkenau, Publisher Staatliches Museum Auschwitz-Birkenau, 1993

Julius Mader, *Poklad banditu – Nakladelstvi Nase vojsko*, Prague, 1967

Filip Müller, *Sonderbehandlung*, Publisher Steinhausen, Munich, 1979

Reinhard Rürup, *Topographie des Terrors*, Publisher Willmuth Arenhövel, Berlin, 1989

Tragödie der Slowakischen Juden, *Dokumente und Fotografien*, Publisher Neubert and Söhne, Bratislava, March 1949

Information and reports from foreign and local publications for the period 1959–63, covering the search for the Nazi hoard in Toplitzsee.

Drawings: Salamon Smolianoff, Leo Haas, Peter Edel

Photos: SPB Archive Prague; author's personal archive; Wolfgang Pratsch Archive, Lund Sweden; DPA

In spite of intensive efforts, it has not been possible to find the addresses of persons cited, or of their heirs. We would ask them to contact the publisher.

Abbreviations

AVNOJ	Anti-Fascist Council of National Liberation of Yugoslavia
BF	Brigadeführer
BND	Bundesnachrichtendienst
DAW	Deutsche Ausrustungs-Werke
Gestapo	Geheime Staatspolizei
GF	Gruppenführer
HG	Hlinka-Garde
HSF	Hauptsturmführer
KL	Konzentrationslager (concentration camp – an abbreviation used in official documents)
KK	Kriminalkommisar
KZ	Konzentrationslager (concentration camp)
NKWD	Sowjetischer Sicherheitsdienst (Soviet secret service)
NN	Nacht und Nebel (under cover of darkness)
NSDAP	Nationalsozialistische Deutsche Arbeiterpartei (Nazi Party)
OGF	Obergruppenführer
OSF	Obersturmbannführer
RM	Reichsmark
RSHA	Reichssicherheitshauptamt (Reich Security Ministry)
SA	Sturmabteilung
SBF	Sturmbannführer
SD	Sicherheitsdienst
SF	Scharführer
Sipo	Sicherheitspolizei
SS	Schutz-Staffel
USF	Unterscharführer

Index of Names